A CORNUCOPIA OF PACKᴜ

First Edition
First published in 2010 by

Woodfield Publishing Ltd
Bognor Regis ~ West Sussex ~ England ~ PO21 5EL
www.woodfieldpublishing.co.uk

ISBN 1-84683-104-0

Last updated 27 November 2010

A Cornucopia
of Packs

An informal history of the Pack family

RESEARCHED AND WRITTEN BY
JEFFREY PACK

Woodfield

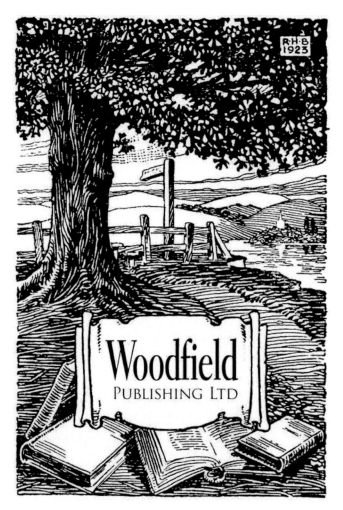

Woodfield Publishing Ltd

Bognor Regis ~ West Sussex ~ England ~ PO21 5EL
tel 01243 821234 ~ **e/m** info@woodfieldpublishing.co.uk

Interesting and informative books on a variety of subjects

For full details of all our published titles, visit our website at

www.woodfieldpublishing.co.uk

*This book is dedicated to **my** Pack family*
Jacky, Arabella and Joe

~ CONTENTS ~

Preface

Genealogy can be just a list of names and dates, of passing interest to members of that family but not to anyone else. But it can also be a way of following the history of the times though a family, or a name, and, if you are lucky, it can reveal some very interesting personal stories.

This book traces the Pack family, or name, for obvious reasons, over 500 years or more, in England, the USA and beyond and describes Packs in the highest levels of government and in the workhouse and in many intermediate places.

An early working title for the book was *"On the origin of the Pack species, the one that Darwin missed, an account of the curious genus called Pack in all its mutations over many centuries and in many continents"*. This was, however, rather cumbersome for the front page but it does sum up what I have tried to do in this book.

Not all of the Packs described herein are definitely related to each but there are some interesting linkages as well as some fascinating personal stories.

Jeff Pack
October 2010

Chapter 1 - Introduction

It was the conjunction of a number of things that led me to research the Pack family history; a history I thought when I started would be confined entirely to Egerton, a small village in Kent. The first was Thomas Pack. Previously unknown to me his death necessitated researching a branch of the family for probate reasons. This story is fully told in the book. Then it was my wife's discovery of my baptism certificate. My godparents were Mr and Mrs Hubert Pack. This reminded me that my father had always said that there were a lot of Packs in Egerton but that there were two separate unrelated families and that Hubert Pack was one of the "other lot". In the back of my mind it had always seemed unlikely that in a small village like Egerton an uncommon name like Pack could naturally arise twice. I decided to get to the bottom of this.

The research bug had already bitten as I had produced my father's war story, published as "Love is in the air". These reasons were more than enough inspiration to do the research but, had I needed more, it arrived when I had nearly finished the book with the discovery by my cousin of a notebook kept by my grandfather, Jeffrey, a page of which is pictured below. An edited transcript of the diary is contained in an appendix and extracts are included at relevant points in the story. I used the word inspiration above because I had never realised that my father had written as much as he did which had led to "Love is in the air" and now I found that my grandfather had also been a writer and observer as well and so completing this book almost felt like a family obligation.

Jeffrey's diary.

In fact I only managed to get back to the 18th century for my own certain family. This story starts with a George Pack who married in Egerton, Kent in July 1788. He died in March 1824, aged 57, and so was born in 1766/7 almost certainly (see later) the son of Lucy Pack of nearby Pluckley. This story is fully told in the book. But along the way I also accumulated a number of other Packs up to 300 years before George. Many of these are highly distinguished families, which is not surprising, since it tends to be the distinguished families for whom records survive. Naturally I tried to link them all up with my family but I cannot claim total success in this. As we shall see below the name Pack is not a common one, which gives one some hope that all these families are related, but this is the same as saying that we are all related because we are all descended from Adam and Eve or a Tanzanian monkey and is scientifically unhelpful.

The following analysis gives an idea of Pack numbers. In 1901 the population of England and Wales (and for most of this period England included Ireland) was 15.7 million and there were 1,709 Packs. On the crude assumption that the Packs were the same percentage of the total population in earlier years then the following table charts the numbers. There is also an assumption that family sizes were an average of 8 members, 2 parents and 6 children. The further assumption is that the average family had parents in their late thirties and that each family had 10 children, 5 sons and 5 daughters, but that 1 daughter would already have left home to marry and change her name and 3 children were yet to be born thus giving the assumed 8.

Year	Population of England and Wales	Pack individuals	Pack families
1901	15.7 million	1709	214
1801	8.3	903	112
1700	6.5	707	88
1603	5.8	631	79
1570	4.8	522	65
1348	3.75	408	51
1215	2.5	272	34
1066	1.1	120	15

It must immediately be acknowledged that the above is not very scientific but does give an idea of the relatively small number of Pack families there must have been in much earlier years. One qualification to this must be mentioned. In earlier centuries the name was not spread nationally but was heavily concentrated in a few areas – especially Kent, Norfolk and Huntingdonshire, and later London. Thus when George was born in 1766/7 there would have been about 800 Packs in the country in 100 families. This leads naturally to the question of the origin of the name.

The study of names is called onomastics or onomatology, from the Greek word for name, onoma, proving, as we all know, that there is an "ology" for everything. The need for names, as the human race expanded is obvious. But, in England, until the Norman Conquest people only had one name, a personal name or a nickname. After 1066 the Norman Barons introduced surnames and they were probably necessary as the population increased. This will have been compounded by a limited number of personal names. In the 13th century it is estimated that a third of the male population had a given name of either William, Richard or John. By 1400 most English families had hereditary surnames. There are broadly 5 sources of surnames. The first is surnames derived from given names. Thus William, the son of John, became William Johnson. Then there are occupational surnames – Smith, Clark, Wright etc – once adopted the name wasn't changed even if the occupation was. Next there are locational or topographic names. Richard, from the Woods, became Richard Woods. Surnames often derived from nicknames – White, Young and Long for instance, even if subsequent generations were not. And finally migration brought in many new names – Moore from Morocco and Lubbock from Lubeck in Germany for instance.

There is no certainty where the name Pack came from however. It may well be an English name to do with packhorses. It may also be a derivative of the old English personal name of Pacca. The Dutch word for a driver of pack animals is Pak and, for what it is worth, the French for Easter is Paques. There is also a theory that the name derives from a peak, John who lives on the peak of the hill, and peak led to Pack. There are many theories but no certainty. But one thing is certain; all the families called Wood because their ancestors lived near woods are not necessarily related just because they share the same name and the same of course applies to Packs.

One interesting and very recent branch of genealogy is DNA profiling. DNA, or Deoxyribonucleic acid, is a nucleic acid that contains the genetic instructions used in the development and functioning of all known living organisms. Genes are made from the long DNA molecule, which is copied and inherited across generations. The search for the structure of DNA had occupied the scientific world for 100 years until it was finally defined by Francis Crick and James Watson (and others) in April 1953. DNA has many applications especially in police work. It has also been extensively used in sociology and genealogy.

It is possible to have your DNA measured and then compared against a data base of readings from all over the world and thus to have your ancestry defined. This was used in a recent TV programme in the UK that attempted to find how many of the population were descended from Vikings, from Normans and from Celts.

J. Ron Thompson introduced me to this branch of genealogy, as well as telling me of the possible Peak origin of Pack, above. This sort of research is, of course, *real* genealogy because it is tracing family groups not mere surnames. Imagine 1 family 2000 years ago that bred and spread and by the time surnames came along, a thousand years later, one was living near a hill and became Hill, another was by a peak and became Pack, another was short etc. They are all family but the names are different.

Ron reports that there are Pack DNA links all over the UK and also in Germany and Scandinavia. But, which Packs or Peaks or Paks are these and are they related to me and the Packs that follow in this book? Interestingly Ron reports also that there is a branch of Packs in the US that appears to have no genetic similarities to any European races. This implies that the native Americans adopted the surname independently of any Europeans.

This I fear is as far as I can take this highly specialised subject but anyone wishing to know more or with more to contribute can post a message to the web site mentioned below. I have not tried to trace every single descendant of every Pack, whether related or not. I have also tried to make sure this is not just a list of names and dates. The main purpose of the book is to look for stories and to try and set them against the history of the times. Shortly after the publication of this book a web site will be launched called www.Packhistory.com. The web site will give the opportunity for corrections and additions to be made and for a comprehensive account to emerge. Because my interest is mainly in the stories of the Pack families, and in the interests of readability, I have not littered the story with source references but if any reader is interested in them queries can be sent to the above web site.

Genealogy is a curious science. The genes or traits of my great great great great grandfather George, who is my certain ancestor, will be highly diluted in me and will be much less than the contribution of a more recent non-Pack, my mother, and yet most genealogical studies tend to exclude the female lines and concentrate on where the surname goes, not least because it is easier even if unscientific. But it is nonetheless interesting to try to trace a story of related folk, and some unrelated ones, and see what happened. But first a few words about the process of gathering the information might be of interest.

Censuses have been used by governments for a long time; initially to raise taxes to fight wars, latterly to assess social trends to influence policy. The first known census was taken by the Babylonians in 3800BC. Italian city-states regularly held censuses in the Middle Ages to establish tax records. In 1086 the Doomsday book was compiled, the most famous census in Europe, so William the Conqueror could assess the territory he had won at the Battle of Hastings in 1066. The first US census was undertaken in 1790 (the population was 3.9million, today it is 300million+) in order to establish representation in Congress (the Senate comprises 2 senators per state irrespective of the sizes of the states, the House of Representatives comprises 435 members elected by districts that are redrawn every 10 years to be consistent with population changes) and this continues to this day.

The first modern UK census was in 1831 but contained only headcount numbers with no personal information. The 1841 census was the first to contain the names of everyone and censuses then continued every 10 years (except 1941) progressively seeking more and more information. Under freedom of information legislation the 100-year rule means that UK census results are not made public for 100 years. Thus census information is available from 1841 until 1901. The 1911 census would normally have been made public in 2011 but in fact for technical reasons the records were released in 2009. In the U.S.A. the first useful modern census was in 1850 and they have a 75-year rule meaning that census information is available up to 1930. The only exception is the 1890 census, which was largely lost when a government building in Washington burnt to the ground.

Census information is particularly valuable to a study such as this as all the members of a family can be found in one go. For families before 1841 or after 1901, recently 1911, each family member has to be discovered individually which can be painstaking and sometimes impossible. Thus 1841 to 1901 was the easiest part of the research for this book. Post 1901 I was helped considerably by three sources a) living descendants b) the remarkable amount of research done by others and available on the internet and c) by the publication by the Egerton local history group of three books – Pictorial Egerton, A history of Egerton 1900 – 2000 and Egerton People Past and Present (details are shown in the appendix).

Pre 1841 is and remains the hardest part. Of course people born from 1780 or so onwards still figured in the censuses from 1841 but before this one is reliant on Parish records of Births, Marriages and Deaths but you have to know a name to search for first and you have to know which parish to look in. In Kent alone there are 102 parishes.

And so we start our expedition through nearly 500 years of Pack history, the last 250 years being a certain story from George Pack onwards leading eventually to yours truly, and the 250 years before that being a story of some illustrious Packs some of whom may or may not be related to George. This will be a journey that will take in significant events in British and World history; Waterloo and battlefields all over the world, including WW2; that will take us to the heart of UK government in the 17th century, Ireland, the United States of America, Montevideo, Zanzibar and also to the bucolic delights of a small Kentish village called Egerton.

Chapter 2 - Early Pack History

In the previous chapter we saw the haphazard way in which surnames developed. Thus a John in Kent, who lived near a wood, might become John Wood. But he would not necessarily be related to a Richard who also lived near a wood in Yorkshire and became Richard Wood. The same, of course, applies to Packs. I have come across references, but little detail, to a number of early Packs who may or may not be related to each other and may or may not be related to George Pack, my ancestor.

The earliest reference was given to me by Sylvia Pack who reports that her husband's Packs go back to Cambridge in 1275 and she believes they are descended from German immigrants who settled in East Anglia and Cambridge.

Then there is a reference to a Nicholas Pack whose will was proved in August 1428 but there is no further information. He must have been someone substantial to have had a will in the 15th Century.

The earliest certain Pack was Christopher Pack, born in 1560. Christopher almost certainly had a relative called Thomas, probably a brother or cousin, born in 1564. Christopher was resident in England but Thomas was resident in Ireland at Ballynakill in Queens County. The reason for my confidence that these two are related is that 150 years later descendants of Christopher would make their way to Ballynakill, as we shall see later.

Ballinakill, sometimes Ballynakill, is a fairly common place name in Ireland and this one is about 18 miles north of Kilkenny. There are some substantial houses but nothing very large or old. A lot of Protestant properties were destroyed after Home Rule was granted to Ireland. A lot of the Pack history of the next few chapters, and that of families into which they married such as the Cliftons, the Beresfords, the Reynells and others, lived around Ballynakill but today there is no trace. Ballynakill means place of the church in Gaelic.

Thomas had 1 son, again Thomas, born in 1585 and resident now in England. This Thomas would have 1 son, Denis, born in 1620 and resident in England, and Denis would then have a son, Christopher. They may all have had larger families but I have been unable to trace others. As will become clear this Pack family were an Anglo Irish family not afraid of the Irish Sea and regularly crossing it in both directions. Whether they were Irish originally and came to England or the reverse is not known for certain but they were clearly prosperous and occupied important positions and were Protestant so it is almost certain that they were of English origin.

At this point and before getting into too much family detail a very short history of the British Isles may help the reader. For a thousand years or more after Christ the British Isles were a seething cauldron of competing tribes, clans and families and it only began to settle down about 1000 years ago. The Kingdom of England came into being in about 871 when Alfred, King of Wessex, finally overcame his rivals. Having established itself as a kingdom, although there would be plenty of squabbles later over who should be the monarch, and even a brief period without one, in which a Pack would play a significant role, England then set about colonising its neighbours; Scotland, Wales, Ireland and France and later even further afield. The histories of England and Wales have been intertwined over many years and this was formalised finally in 1535 with Wales' merger into England. Scotland was a Kingdom from 843 under Kenneth 1st and remained so until 1707 when the Act of Union brought it into the United Kingdom. Henry 2nd of England invaded Ireland in 1155 and from then on Kings of England were also the Lords of Ireland. In 1541 Henry 8th changed this title to King of Ireland and there was a later further integration into the United Kingdom in 1801. Ireland became independent in 1927.

There were two important historical events that are part of the history of one Pack family. The first is the Dissolution of the Monasteries. In 1534 Henry 8th passed the Act of Supremacy which made him the Supreme head of the Church of England and from 1538 to 1541 he dissolved and confiscated the property of the Roman Catholic monasteries. A key accomplice in this was Thomas Cromwell, Vice Gerent, vicar general and Henry's chief minister. As we shall see below, about 100 years later another Cromwell, Oliver, Thomas' great great grandnephew, was also prominent on the national stage and a close friend of his was the Christopher Pack noted above. It is possible that the Pack and the Cromwell families knew each other over a long time.

The background to the dissolution of the monasteries was the Pope's intransigence to what Henry wanted to do in his personal life as well as dissatisfaction with a seemingly self satisfied Roman Catholic church, a State within a State. Henry took the only way out he knew, he created a new church which would do his bidding; he also set about suppressing Roman Catholicism in the British Isles and this was carried further by his daughter Queen Elizabeth 1st. Whilst Ireland had been nominally controlled by England since 1155 it had been on a fairly loose rein. By 1607 England finally won full control and started to consolidate its power especially by suppressing the Catholics who were denied many of the liberties that the Protestants had; they were barred from public office, military service and from entering the professions. One effect of this was that England had to provide many of the administrators, officials, Protestant ministers and professionals since the local Roman Catholics could not hold these positions. This gave rise to the "Anglo Irish".

"Anglo Irish" is a term used to describe a privileged social class in Ireland whose members were the descendants and successors of the Protestant Ascendancy, which started in the 17th century. They mostly belonged to the Anglican Church of Ireland. There were many famous Anglo Irishmen including Bram Stoker, Oscar Wilde, W.B. Yeats, Cecil Day Lewis and Bernard Shaw. Brendan Behan, a staunch Irish Republican, defined an Anglo Irishman as "a Protestant with a horse". In today's language that doesn't sound as bitter as it was meant to be. But in Behan's times anyone on a horse was either in the police or the military. In fact, in the 1790s, an Irish Catholic seen riding a horse worth more than £5 was obliged to surrender it to any Protestant who challenged him. For many of the Protestant Anglo Irish, and as we shall see for many of the Packs, Trinity College Dublin was their Alma Mater having been established exclusively for them and only taking Catholics in relatively recent years. 12 Packs attended Trinity between 1725 and 1848 and they are mentioned as they arise herein.

The second important event occurred in the middle of the 17th century when severe strains were occurring between Parliament and the King. Charles 1st believed in the divine right of Kings, "a sovereign power above the laws and statutes of this kingdom" and there developed a struggle for power between him and Parliament, which disapproved of his marriage to a Catholic princess, Henrietta Maria of France. The "Long Parliament" was called by Charles 1st,who desperately needed money to finance his foreign wars, but which didn't satisfy him and which he refused to dissolve until they did and so the Parliament ran from 1629 to 1640 undissolved. Eventually this would lead to the English Civil wars from 1642 – 51 between Parliamentarians and Royalists, which led to the trial and execution of Charles 1st and the replacement of the monarchy with the Protectorate under

Oliver Cromwell. The Monarchy was restored in 1660, following Cromwell's death, under Charles 2nd who had gone into exile when his father was executed.

Back then to Christopher Pack who was born in 1560 and married Mary Catherine Jones from Wales sometime between 1585 and 1590. He is noted as a merchant of London but originally from Northamptonshire. They had a son, again Christopher, born in 1599 in Grafton, Northamptonshire, who would become Sir Christopher Pack and then Lord Pack, and would have a rather interesting history, which is the subject of the next chapter. The family so far are shown below with dotted lines where the connection is not certain and straight lines where it is certain. Note that there will have been 5 or 6 generations between Nicholas and then Thomas and Christopher. In the historical records the individuals below are variously shown as Pack or Packe. The reasons for this are explained in the next chapter. Pack only became Packe during Christopher's lifetime (1599 – 1682), the subject of the next chapter, but there has been some rewriting of history by his ancestors also being described as Packe.

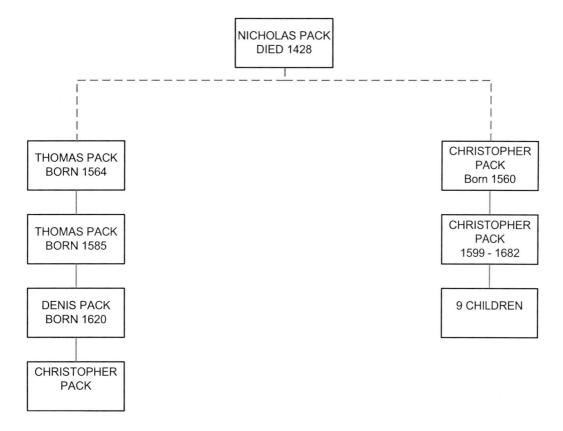

Chapter 3 - Sir Christopher Packe (1599-1682)
Lord Mayor of London and Friend of Oliver Cromwell

Christopher Packe was born in 1599 in Grafton, Northamptonshire. He began his career as a bound apprentice in the Drapers Company of London. This implies a middling level of family wealth and influence. The landed gentry did not go in for apprenticeships or trades and the poor would not have had the influence to gain access to London apprenticeships 150 miles away. After gaining his freedom from his apprenticeship in 1633 he was admitted to the Livery in 1639 and for more than 30 years he served on its governing body and was twice it's Master. He had been bound to John Kendrick, a merchant adventurer, who died in 1624 leaving Christopher £100 and a £300 loan to set up in business in the woollen trade, which he then proceeded to do with considerable success. He acquired substantial wealth trading in cloth in English and European markets and investing in the Company of Merchant Adventurers and the East India Company. He lived in Basinghall Street, immediately adjoining Blackwell Hall, the headquarters of the woollen trade and near to the Guildhall and also had a suburban house in Mortlake.

He had 3 wives; Jane Newman, the granddaughter of his master in the Draper's Company (she died in 1638); Anne Edmonds, eldest daughter of Simon Edmonds, Alderman and Lord Mayor of London, with whom he had all his children (she died in 1658); and Elizabeth, widow of Alderman Herring, another prosperous London merchant. But his main claim to fame was his political career.

We have seen in an earlier chapter the political tensions in the middle of the 17th century between Parliament and the King and, from the early 1640s, his fortune having been made, Christopher Packe became more involved in politics especially in Parliamentary matters; initially advising committees, becoming a ward assessor, then councillor and then serving on numerous committees. He was a Presbyterian but above all appears to have been a consummate politician. He was elected MP for Cripplegate in London in 1647 and was one of fifteen aldermen who attended the formal proclamation of the abolition of the monarchy on May 30th 1649. At the beginning of 1649 he had bought the Huntingdonshire manor of Buckden and the Leicestershire manors of Prestwold (occupied by Packes for the next 350 years) and Cotes (around 1700 Cotes Park House burned down and Prestwold became the family seat and is pictured below as it is today. Cotes was a fortified manor house, smaller than Prestwold, and apparently burnt down as a result of a careless and inebriated butler; it was never rebuilt and all that remains is a kitchen garden).

Prestwold today

The history of Prestwold is interesting. Prestwold and the surrounding villages have Saxon origins ("Wolds" meaning woods easily cleared for settlement). Settlement in the area is noted in the Doomsday Survey of 1086 AD. The owner before Sir Christopher was the grandson of Sir Henry Skipwith who supported the Royalist cause in the Civil War. After fines and sequestration by Cromwell, the estate was sold to Sir Christopher in 1653. This may well have been a forced sale. The Skipwiths then emigrated to America and, it is said, created a new Prestwold in Virginia, even larger than the English one, although I have not been able to find it. St Andrews Parish Church is within the grounds of Prestwold House and is, in effect, the family church. The family have taken great care in maintaining the Church which is in pristine condition and still operational. There are 19 Packes buried in the church with memorials many of which are shown below and in the next chapter.

Although unsuccessful in the City elections of July 1654 for the first protectorate parliament, Packe was shortly afterwards elected Lord Mayor of London and he worked closely with Oliver Cromwell as they purged opponents from City offices. Following his mayoralty Christopher Packe was knighted by a grateful Cromwell. He was returned again as a City MP in the 1656 elections to the second protectorate parliament and was very active particularly in affairs of trade, religion and the City. He became governor of the Company of Merchant Adventurers in 1656 and he joined the governing body of the East India Company in 1657 and later that year proposed to Parliament a new constitution that would provide for a second chamber to Parliament and would open the way for the possibility of Cromwell becoming King. Cromwell rejected the Kingship in 1657. Unsurprisingly, on 10th December 1657 Sir Christopher was called to the new second chamber as Lord Packe. Lord Packe was by then a very wealthy man; in 1658 he lent the State £4000 to pay the wages of the fleet, lately returned to port (in today's values this would be about half a million pounds).

Sir Christopher's portrait hangs at Prestwold and is pictured below.

Sir Christopher Packe

With the end of the Protectorate however his fortunes changed. At the Restoration of the monarchy in 1660 Packe attended the proclamation of the new King and pledged obedience to the Crown and received a royal pardon. He was then removed from all his public positions and excluded from office for life. After his 3rd marriage in 1669 he retired to his manor at Cotes where he died on 27th May 1682. He is buried in the parish church of St Andrews at Prestwold where his son, Christopher, erected a fine monument to him and the church and the monument are pictured below.

St Andrews outside   *and inside*

Sir Christopher's memorial

Sir Christopher is shown in the robes of the Lord Mayor of London and with the memorial shields of his 3 wives; Jane, Anne and Elizabeth behind him.

His memorial, written in Latin, is shown below.

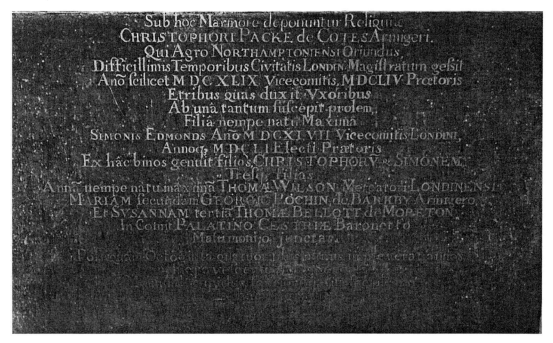

Prestwold has remained a family seat to the present day although through intermarriage the lineage is now Packe-Drury-Lowe. The house is also available for weddings, corporate events and motorised activities and full details are can be accessed at www.prestwold-hall.com Simon Packe-Drury-Lowe and his charming wife, Rita, kindly showed the author and his wife, Jacky, around Prestwold and St Andrews church allowing the pictures in this chapter and the next to be taken. Many other descendants are buried or commemorated at St Andrews church and some are pictured in the next chapter.

As we have seen Sir Christopher's career was closely intertwined with that of Oliver Cromwell. Cromwell was born in Huntingdon and Packe was born in Grafton, Northamptonshire. These places are not far apart and the 2 men were the same age, both born in 1599, so it is quite possible that they had known each other most of their lives. Cromwell remains a controversial figure to this day. To some he was a regicidal dictator who developed the trappings of the monarchy he had overthrown. To others he was a hero of liberty and laid the foundations of parliamentary democracy. He was buried in Westminster Abbey in 1658 but when the Royalists returned to power in 1660 his corpse was dug up, hung in chains and beheaded. The English civil wars were curious as civil wars go. They were very bloody. In England the losses were 4% of the population, in Scotland 6% and in Ireland 40%! But 10 years later the Monarchy was restored and the Monarch, the loser in the civil wars, was pardoning the victors. England was a deeply conservative country that did not favour revolutionary excess. Cromwell was subsequently honoured by a statue standing outside the Houses of Parliament erected in 1899 to commemorate the 300th anniversary of his birth (pictured below). It was donated by a private benefactor, almost certainly Lord Rosebery, the Prime Minister at the time, and an admirer of Cromwell. The statue was controversial and was opposed by Irish MPs. To avoid a public scene it was unveiled at 7.30 am and there was no ceremony. Cromwell is shown head bowed in thought and one view is that this is to avoid the accusing gaze of King Charles whose bust is on the wall of St Margaret's church opposite.

Oliver Cromwell

King Charles 2nd

Prior to his death Sir Christopher had already settled much of his estate on his family. His final will, made on 10th November 1681 and proved on 26th June 1682, was essentially a tidying up exercise and in it he left the rest of his estate to his 5 children, most of it to his eldest son, Christopher, and the rest divided equally among his "three surviving daughters", Mary, Anne and Sarah (probably Susannah) and Simon, his youngest son, together with a number of charitable bequests including £100 for ejected godly ministers and their widows.

Like the prudent man he was Sir Christopher made more than one will during his lifetime. An earlier, undated version makes interesting reading. In this will he names 4 children who are not mentioned in his final will and Simon is not mentioned at all implying this earlier will was prepared before Simon was born in 1654. The 4 children in the earlier will are Elizabeth, Edmond, Richard and John. Elizabeth married William Nunn and in the early will there is extensive wording to provide that William Nunn should not benefit from anything left to Elizabeth. It may be that in the final version the family disagreement had escalated to the point that he just took Elizabeth out. It may also be that she had died given his reference to "surviving daughters". Then there are the three sons; Edmond, Richard and John, provided for in the early will but not in his last will. It can only be assumed that they had died before their father made his final will.

Anne Packe, per the records, married Thomas Wilson who was born in 1570 and thus, if the records are correct (which they surely can't be), was more than 70 years older than her. Mary married George Pochin and Susannah (Sarah?) married Sir Thomas Bellot, 2nd Baronet, producing John who would become 3rd Baronet, but he produced no male issue and the baronetcy became extinct.

The family tree, as it is believed to be, is shown below.

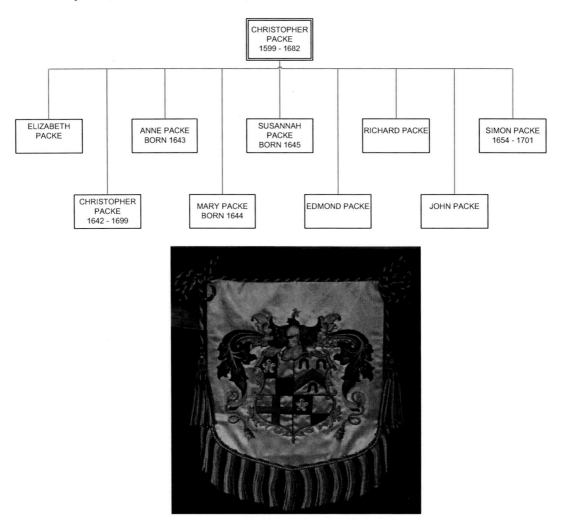

Sir Christopher's coat of arms

As has become apparent there are 2 spellings of the surname; one with a trailing "e" and the other without and there are a number of theories, but no certainty, as to how this came about. Whilst there is no certainty about who Sir Christopher's parents were, none of the candidates had an "e" and Sir Christopher appears to have been a Pack in his early career but adopted an extra "e" later in life perhaps to aggrandise his name in view of the exalted status he achieved. The stories of Sir Christopher's two sons, Christopher and Simon, are told in the next 2 chapters. Christopher inherited Prestwold and established the English line of the family all of whom, it is believed, continued with this spelling. But the descendants of Sir Christopher's other son, Simon, who are the Irish line of the family, soon dropped the "e" perhaps because it was too anglicised for their circumstances. Because Sir Christopher died a Packe historians appear to have assumed that his ancestors were also Packes, which is certainly not true. Interestingly, but probably accidentally, about 100 years after Sir Christopher died, my certain ancestor, George Pack and his wife were registering the birth of their 3rd daughter and the parents were noted in the Egerton parish records as Geo and Elizabeth Pack<u>e</u>.

We turn now in the next chapter to Sir Christopher's first son, Christopher, and then later, in chapter 7, to his other son, Simon.

Chapter 4 - Christopher Packe (1642-1699)
The English Line of Sir Christopher's Family

Sir Christopher will have bequeathed substantial wealth on his sons as well as a legacy of contacts in Parliament, the City, the East India Company, the Company of Merchant Adventurers and overseas and a mercantilist spirit of adventure. He may also have bequeathed a difficult situation for them given that he had been in semi-disgrace in 1660, banned from holding any public office. The traditional career paths for the sons of a wealthy and privileged family like this would have been the church, the army or government. Christopher, the eldest son, aged 18 when his father was disgraced, inherited the family estate in the Midlands and became a barrister. Simon, the youngest son, 12 years younger than Christopher, departed for the Army and Ireland and later descendants would spread even more widely. Christopher's descendants will be taken as far as possible in this chapter and Simon's descendants in later chapters. Although Christopher did not join the army many of his descendants did, and although Simon chose the army many of his descendants then chose the church.

Christopher succeeded his father and inherited Prestwold, the family home, and was a justice of the peace there, but appears to have also worked in London as a barrister. In 1666 his father, Sir Christopher, had attempted to procure a baronetcy for him but this mysteriously failed after it had been agreed.

Christopher Packe's portrait hangs at Prestwold and is pictured below together with his wife Jane Clifton.

Christopher Packe married Jane Clifton in 1665, her father was Sir Gervase Clifton, and they had at least 7 children as below. The Cliftons are a very old family being originally descended from Alvared, one of William the Conqueror's knights. They took the name Clifton from the village where they settled in 1272. The Clifton family were Royalists during the civil war, on the opposite side to the Packes. Christopher married Jane 5 years after the Restoration of the Monarchy. Christopher junior would appear to have inherited the pragmatic nature of his father in accepting the changed circumstances and adapting to them and this may well have saved the family from far worse consequences than Sir

Christopher simply being banned from public office. The Cliftons were also large landowners in Ballinakill in Ireland. Christopher's memorial at St Andrews church in Prestwold is shown below.

Christopher's family tree is shown below.

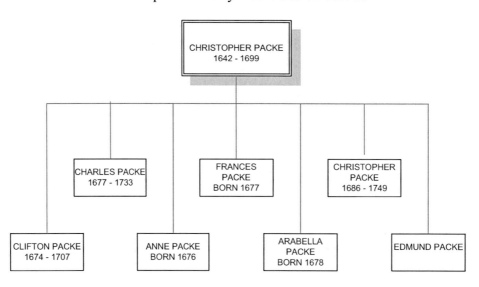

Clifton Packe is the only child about whom much is known. Charles Packe married Penelope Jenkinson and their memorial at St Andrews is shown below. Frances married Sir Robert Clifton who was presumably a cousin but nothing more is known of her or anything of Anne, Arabella, Christopher or Edmund.

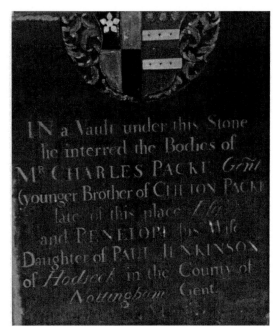

Clifton Packe (1674 – 1707)

He is pictured below from a portrait at Prestwold. He was only 33 when he died but produced some remarkable descendants. It is interesting that they gave Clifton his mother's maiden name as a Christian name and this was, apparently, quite common at the time for the landed classes. He succeeded his father and inherited Prestwold and married Penelope Bate in 1698 and he was High Sheriff of Leicestershire.

Clifton's family tree, as far as I have been able to trace it, is shown below.

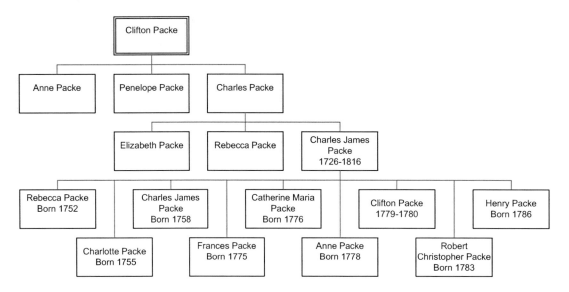

Clifton and Penelope had 3 children; Anne married Francis Stratford; Penelope married Richard Verney who would become 13th Baron Willoughby de Broke and Charles (1701 – 1735) married Rebecca Harvey and succeeded, in due course, his father and they had 3 children; Elizabeth, Rebecca and a son, Charles James (1726 – 1816) who would later follow his father as High Sheriff of Leicestershire. Charles James' portrait hangs at Prestwold and he is commemorated in the church at St Andrews, pictured below.

Charles James Packe

Charles James the Elder married twice and between them they produced 9 children. His first marriage was to Charlotte Pochin and this produced Rebecca, Charlotte and Charles James the Younger (1758 – 1837). Charlotte's portrait hangs at Prestwold and is pictured below.

His second marriage was to Catherine Clifton (leading to Frances, Anne, Clifton [Catherine Clifton was related to Charles James' great grandmother Jane Clifton and the maiden name is used again as a first name)] Catherine Maria, Henry and Robert

Christopher (1783 – 1815). Frances has a memorial at St Andrews (pictured below) but otherwise nothing is known of the 5 daughters or of Clifton.

Henry, as we shall see later, also joined the army but little else is known. The 2 sons of whom more is known are Charles James the Younger and Robert Christopher.

The first-born son was **Charles James** the Younger (1758 – 1837). He succeeded his father, Charles James the Elder when he died in 1816 and assumed Prestwold. He was a lieutenant- colonel in the Leicestershire militia and married Penelope Dugdale and they had 5 children; Charles William (born 1792), George Hussey (born 1796), Edmund (1799), James (1801) and Augustus (1805).

Charles William would become Member of Parliament for Leicestershire and is pictured below from a portrait at Prestwold (the dog is a Prestwold terrier).

George Hussey fought at Waterloo as a Cornet in the 13th Light Dragoons and was wounded. He would later inherit the Prestwold estate when his older brother died. Charles James' memorial at St James' church is shown below.

SACRED TO THE MEMORY OF
CHARLES JAMES PACKE, ESQ.RE. OF PRESTWOLD;
WHO DEPARTED THIS LIFE ON THE 1ST OF MARCH, 1837,
IN THE 80TH YEAR OF HIS AGE.
HE MARRIED PENELOPE, ELDEST DAUGHTER OF RICHARD DUGDALE, ESQ.
OF BLYTH, AND MEREVALE, IN THE COUNTY OF WARWICK;
AND BY HER HAD ISSUE, CHARLES WILLIAM, GEORGE HUSSEY,
EDMUND, JAMES, AND AUGUSTUS; ALSO A DAUGHTER WHO DIED YOUNG.
HIS ELDEST SON HAS CAUSED THIS MONUMENT TO BE ERECTED
TO RECORD THE BEREAVEMENT TO HIS WIDOW
OF AN AFFECTIONATE HUSBAND,
TO HIS CHILDREN OF A KIND PARENT,
AND THE LOSS TO SOCIETY OF A WARM AND SINCERE FRIEND.
ALSO OF REBECCA PACKE, SISTER OF THE ABOVE,
WHO DIED AT HER HOUSE, IN WIMPOLE STREET, LONDON, UNMARRIED,
ON THE 26TH FEBRUARY, 1837, IN THE 86TH YEAR OF HER AGE
AFTER A LONG LIFE OF MUTUAL ATTACHMENT.
THEIR MORTAL REMAINS WERE INTERRED BY ONE RITE OF BURIAL
IN THE FAMILY VAULT UNDER THIS CHANCEL.
AND OF PENELOPE, WIDOW OF THE ABOVE CHARLES JAMES PACKE, ESQ.RE,
WHO DIED JUNE 17TH 1841, IN THE 74TH YEAR OF HER AGE; DAUGHTER OF
RICHARD GEAST, ESQ. WHO AFTER HER MARRIAGE ASSUMED THE NAME AND ARMS OF
HIS MOTHER, THE HEIRESS AND REPRESENTATIVE OF THE FAMILY OF DUGDALE.

George Hussey Packe's memorial at St Andrew's church, Prestwold is shown below, as is that of his only daughter, Marianne Penelope Catherine Packe, and his elder son Charles Hussey Packe, who died aged 15, and whose memorial is shown below.

George Hussey Packe   *Marianne Penelope Catherine Packe*

21

Charles Hussey Packe

The inscription on the memorial reads;

"IT PLEASED AN ALL WISE PROVIDENCE TO CUT HIS LIFE SHORT BY A MALIGNENT FEVER AT THE EARLY AGE OF FIFTEEN YEARS WHILE AT SCHOOL AT ETON ON THE 28TH OCTOBER 1842.

AND TO HIS INSCRUTABLE WILL HIS AFFLICTED PARENTS AFTER HAVING PAINFULLY WATCHED HIS DISEASE TO ITS FATAL TERMINATION, BOWED WITH PIOUS RESIGNATION IN FIRM RELIANCE THAT THEIR AFFECTIONATE, EXCELLENT AND PROMISING CHILD HAD EXCHANGED THE CARES OF THIS WORLD FOR ETERNAL BLISS IN HEAVEN".

Charles James' penultimate son was **Robert Christopher Packe** and he was an army major and was killed leading a cavalry charge at Waterloo. After Eton he joined the Royal Horse Guards Blue in 1800 as a Cornet rising to Lieutenant. By 1812 he was involved in the Peninsula war and by 1813 he was a Major. In a letter home from Spain he wrote "This is not cavalry country…I met up with Henry (his younger brother Lt-Col Henry Packe of the Grenadier Guards) at Salvatierra on 25th June 1813 after the fight of the brigade" and in a later letter from Windsor barracks he wrote "Wellington and York are coming to see the regiment and give us dinner….I am sending 2 hogsheads of wine from Bordeaux for father".

Robert Christopher Packe

At the battle of Waterloo Robert was killed when charging French curassiers. He was buried on the battlefield. The officers of the regiment he had served for over 15 years erected a memorial in the north choir aisle of St George's Chapel, Windsor, " in testimony of their high veneration of his distinguished military merit and regret for the loss of a companion endeared to them by his amiable manner and virtue". His parents also erected a monument at the church in Prestwold and both are pictured below.

The Prestwold Memorial

The inscription on the memorial reads as follows;

TO THE MEMORY OF ROBERT CHRISTOPHER PACKE
MAJOR OF THE ROYAL REGIMENT OF HORSE GUARDS BLUE
WHO WAS KILLED AT THE BATTLE OF WATERLOO, JUNE 18TH, 1815,
AGED 32 YEARS;
HIS REMAINS LIE BURIED ON THE FIELD; AND HIS PARENTS
HAVE RAISED THIS COMMEMORATIVE MARBLE

THO' MANLY VIRTUE, WITHER'D IN THE BLOOM,
HAS SUNK FOR EVER TO AN EARLY TOMB,
WE WILL NOT MOURN FOR HIM, THAT RAISED HIS HAND
TO GUARD THE BLESSINGS OF HIS NATIVE LAND;
AND SEAL'D, OBSERVANT OF HIS COUNTRY'S CLAIM,
A LIFE OF HONOR WITH A DEATH OF FAME.

PRIDE OF THY PARENTS, GALLANT SPIRIT, REST;
IN LIFE BELOVED, AND IN THINE END HOW BLEST;
WHEN WILD AMBITION WAVED HIS BANNER HIGH,
FEARLESS AND FOREMOST THOU HAST DARED TO DIE;
AND NOBLY WON, ON ENGLAND'S BRIGHTEST DAY,
A VICTOR-WREATH THAT SHALL NOT FADE AWAY.

The memorial at St George's chapel, Windsor

The inscription on the memorial reads;

To the Memory of Robert Christopher Packe, Esquire
Second son of Charles James Packe, Esquire of Prestwold, Leicestershire
And Major in the Royal Regiment of Horse Guards Blue
Who was killed at the head of his squadron
When charging the French Cuirassiers, at the ever
Memorable Battle of Waterloo, on the 18th of June 1815
In the 33rd year of his age

This monument is erected by the officers of the regiment
In which he had served more than fifteen years
In testimony of their high veneration for
His distinguished military merit
And of their sincere regret for the loss of a companion
So long endeared to their affections, by his
Amiable manners and private virtues.

The Royal regiment of Horse Guards Blue, in which Robert Christopher Packe served, was a cavalry regiment founded in 1650. It's regimental uniform was blue and the regiment became known as "the Blues". The regiment was amalgamated with the Royal Dragoons in 1969 to form "the Blues and Royals".

This chapter has traced some of the descendants of Christopher Packe, eldest son of Sir Christopher Packe, and the English line of his family. The chapter started with Christopher's birth in 1642 and ended with the death of Charles Hussey Packe in 1842. 200 years in 11 pages can only give a superficial account and perhaps over time others may wish to expand the story through www.Packhistory.com In Chapter 7 we turn to Sir Christopher's youngest son, Simon, born in 1654 and the starter of the Irish line of the family, although, as we shall see, there are historical doubts about this Irish lineage.

In researching these stories the Dictionary of National Biography was invaluable. It also threw up some other, unrelated Packs and, since this is a Cornucopia of Packs I will include them chronologically. The Christopher Packe of this chapter lived from 1642 to 1699. I wonder if he knew either of the following Packs, or those in the next 2 chapters or even perhaps were they related?

Richardson Pack (1682 – 1728) was an Army officer and writer and the son of John Pack (1652 – 1723) of London. He qualified as a lawyer and was called to the bar but preferred an active life and joined the army. He served in Spain from about 1709 to 1714 and then returned to Ipswich only to be recalled as a major at the time of the Jacobite rebellion. He married Mary Campbell and they moved to Bury St Edmonds in Suffolk where he acquired the ruins of the great abbey. It was during his last years that he began writing poetry and being published. In 1722 he bought Northgate House in Bury St Edmonds and was then recalled as a major in Colonel Montague's regiment of the Devonshires, the 11th foot, and he died naturally in service in Scotland. He left most of his estate not to his wife but to his son, John, then 10 years old, who would go on to Pembroke College, Cambridge and become ordained, serving as rector of Little Whelnetham until he died in 1752.

George Pack (late 17th century to early 18th) was an actor and singer; he is said to have had a voice that bordered on the contralto and often took the female part in sung dialogues. In 1701 he and others were brought to trial for "using indecent expressions in some late plays" They were acquitted. He performed at Drury Lane, in Southwark and in Lincolns Inn Fields. According to a history of the stage Pack was unmarried but an otherwise unknown Mrs Pack was awarded a benefit at Lincolns Inn Fields on 28th May 1719 and she may have been his wife. But where he came from no one knows.

Before we revert to Sir Christopher's family and his youngest son, Simon and the Irish lineage, we will look in slightly more detail in the next two chapters at 2 more Pack(e)s who lived at approximately the same time. Neither is certainly related to Sir Christopher's Prestwold Packes, both have interesting stories.

Chapter 5 - Yet Another Christopher Packe
and Nearly a Genealogical Bloomer

This (or these) Christopher Packe(s) were discovered in the Dictionary of National Biography but there is no known link between them and the preceding Packes, although for a long time I thought there was.

Christopher Packe's dates are given in the DNB as 1686 to 1749 precisely the same dates as those of the Christopher Packe in the previous chapter, the grandson of Sir Christopher. This is almost certainly a historical mistranscription. This Christopher was born in St Albans, Hertfordshire, the son of another Christopher whose probable dates are 1657 – 1708. For a long time I thought these Christophers were part of the Prestwold story. The redoubtable Peggy Dolan corrected me. Whilst the dates are broadly contemporaneous (although probably wrong) and the spelling (with the trailing "e") is the same, the careers of these Packes are not what one would expect of the landed Gentry.

The DNB notes this Christopher Packe as a physician and cartographer. In their description I believe they have mixed up the 2 Christopher Packes; the father, whose probable dates are 1657 – 1708, and the son whose dates are circa 1686 – 1749. Despite all these discrepancies there is enough detail to believe that these Christopher Packes did exist.

Christopher Packe (this must have been the father) set up a laboratory in 1670 at the sign of the Globe and Chemical Furnaces in Little Moorfields, London, and styled himself a professor of chemical medicine. He supposedly practised as a quack under powerful patronage, including that of Robert Boyle and the King's physician, Edmund Dickinson.

In 1689 he brought out in a folio his translation of the writings of Johann Rudolph Glauber, which he published as the "Works of the Highly Experienced and Famous Chymist, Johann Rudolph Glauber", accompanied by the original copperplates, which he had purchased in Amsterdam. This task occupied him for three years, and he secured a large number of subscribers. His other publications were chiefly designed to promote the sale of his book. They include "One Hundred and Fifty Three Chymical Aphorisms" (1688); "Mineralogia, or, An account of the preparation, manifold vertues, and uses of a mineral salt, both in physick and chirurgery" (1693); and "Medela chymica, or, An account of the vertues and uses of a select number of chymical medicines" (1708), at the end of which is a catalogue of his medicines, with their prices.

Christopher Packe (the son) was born in 1686 and appears to have carried on with his father's business at the Golden Head in Southampton Street, Covent Garden, calling himself 'M.D. and chemist'. He was educated at Merchant Taylors' School, London and later graduated as a doctor of medicine at Cambridge in 1717 and then joined the Royal College of Physicians in 1723. In 1726 he married Mary Randolph of the precincts, Canterbury, in Canterbury Cathedral and from about that date settled with her in Canterbury, where he practised medicine until his death.

Shortly after marrying he became embroiled in a heated controversy and pamphlet war with Dr John Gray of Canterbury. The dispute concerned the treatment of one Robert Worger of Hinxhill, Kent, who died of 'concussion of the brain' after falling from his horse. Worger had at first been treated by Packe, but his relatives, not satisfied with

Packe's methods, called in Gray and two surgeons, who, Packe argued, caused Worger's death by excessive bleeding and trepanning.

He published an edition of his father's Mineralogia and "An answer to Dr Turner's letter to Dr Jurin on the subject of Mr Ward's drop and pill, wherein his ignorance of chymical pharmacy is fairly exposed" (1735). As well as writing a number of philosophical treatises, he also published two cartographical works: A dissertation upon the surface of the earth, as delineated in a specimen of a philosophical-chorographical chart of East Kent (1737) and Ankographia (1743, by subscription), an expanded version of the former. Cartography occupied his thoughts during 'many otherwise tedious journeys' around his Kentish medical practice and both works endeavoured to describe and explain the topography around Canterbury by using charts, which Packe had made by taking bearings from the tower of Canterbury Cathedral. They also indicate that Packe considered the structure of the human body to be a microcosm of the natural world, for when writing of the River Stour he claimed that its "minute divisions and the graphic portrait of the vallies and their waters ... differ[s] but little, if at all, from the anatomical descriptions of the several systems of the arteries, veins, or nerves, that are with such exquisite art distributed all through our bodies".

Christopher Packe died 15th November 1749 and was buried at St Mary Magdalene, Canterbury. He left a son, another Christopher, who also became a physician (graduating bachelor of medicine from Peterhouse, Cambridge, in 1751); who also practised in Canterbury; and who, after his death on 21st October 1800, aged seventy-two, was buried in St Mary Magdalene, alongside his father.

Before returning to Sir Christopher's family and his youngest son, Simon, we will undertake another diversion to another apparently unrelated Pack, Thomas Pack, for whom there are a number of interesting parallels.

Chapter 6 - Thomas Pack, Bellfounder (17??-1781)

Thomas Pack was associated with the Whitechapel Bell Foundry in London. The Whitechapel Bell Foundry was started by Robert Chamberlain in 1420 in Aldgate and later moved just up the road to Whitechapel. In 1570 it was at Essex Street, Whitechapel and its early managers were Joseph Carter from 1606 to 1619, Thomas Bartlet from 1619 to 1647, Anthony Bartlet 1647 to 1676 and James Bartlet 1676 to 1701. In 1701 Richard Phelps entered the Foundry and later bequeathed the business to Thomas Lester, his partner for several years who moved it to its present site in Whitechapel Road (see below) in 1738. The present buildings date from 1670 and were originally a coaching inn called The Artichoke. The firm then became Lester & Pack in 1752, Lester, Pack and Chapman in 1769 and Pack and Chapman from 1770 until 1781 when it became Chapman & Mears and then further partnerships follow which do not involve Packs. Thomas Pack was thus involved in running the business for 29 years and working there for even longer since he had previously been a foreman.

The picture above just shows the frontage of the foundry. In fact it extends considerably back behind this as shown below. The foundry is still operational to this day

Thomas died in 1781. He became a partner at Whitechapel in 1752 (Lester and Pack) and was a partner when he died (Pack and Chapman). It would seem likely that bell founding is sufficiently specialised that workers there must have started as apprentices. Thus I went to check the Apprenticeship books. There was no trace of Thomas in the Apprenticeship books leading to the conclusion that he did not have to work his way up but came in at a high level presumably by patronage. Since I spent days and days going through the Apprenticeship books at the National Archives at Kew looking for Thomas, and others, I will use the material to digress slightly to explain those books.

The statute of Apprentices was passed in 1563 and forbad anyone entering a trade who has not served an apprenticeship. This remained on the statute book until 1814. In 1710 Queen Anne made stamp duty payable on indentures of apprenticeship.

From 1710 until 1811 the Commissioner of Stamps kept a register of the stamp duty received and there are 79 Apprenticeship books in the National Archives at Kew. Duty was payable by the master at the rate of 6d for every £1 under £50 received for taking on the apprentice, and 1s for every £1 above that sum. The deadline for payment was 1 year after the expiry of the indenture. Apprentices were often as young as 7 when they started and were frequently abused. Some parents paid to have their children accepted. If the child survived the apprenticeship for 40 days then they became settled in their new parish as a resident. This was important because it meant that the parish would have to take responsibility if they became destitute. In many areas the statute was not enforced and many new trades, such as weaving, were excluded. A lot of apprentices were taken on by masters at the expense of the parish or a public charity and these were exempt from stamp duty and thus not included. The Apprentice books were, of course, a record of taxes collected and survive to this day. An extract of a page is shown below. In fact this page got me quite excited because about half way down in the last column appears to be Geo Pack, an apprentice Cordwainer (shoemaker). I also separately discovered that in the papers of Penley, Milward & Bayley of Dursley, Gloucs, there is a record of "compensation for Henry Evans, Cordwainer of Horsley, having been embezzled by his apprentice George Pick, 1787. Sadly upon closer inspection of the Apprentice book it is Pick not Pack.

30

So Thomas Pack, Bellfounder had not been an apprentice but had been with the company for a considerable time. When his partner Thomas Lester died he posted the following announcement in the Middlesex Journal or Chronicle of Liberty on 6th July 1769. The same announcement had also appeared a week earlier in The Gazetteer and New Daily Advertiser. I am grateful to Chris Ridley, Librarian of the Society of College Youths (which exists to this day) for finding the advertisements for me. In 1769 Thomas had been at Whitechapel for 27 years and it is believed that when he died in 1781 he was still at Whitechapel so his career spanned 39 years.

To the P U B L I C.

THE surviving Partner of the late THOMAS LESTER, Bell-Founder, deceafed, intends to continue on the faid bufinefs, on the premifes, in Whitechapel, London, as ufual, having been with him 27 years, and hopes for the continuance of the favours of his and the faid Thomas Lefter's friends in particular; and the public in general, who pleafe to honour him with their commands, may depend on being ferved to their fatisfaction, and on the lowest terms, by their humble fervant,
White hapel, June 30.   THOMAS PACK.

Thomas Pack's will, available from the Probate office, starts "I Thomas Pack of the parish of Saint Mary, Whitechapel, bell founder, being of sound mind…" Thomas left a considerable estate. The total of the direct bequests is approximately £3.7 million in today's values but having made these there is then provision for what is left to go to Sarah Patrick and Elizabeth Patrick and since the will makes no mention of property this residue could be considerable. There are generous bequests to 5 servants (averaging £20000 each in today's money) then bequests to his sisters Elizabeth Sharman and Sarah Croon and their children, his nieces and nephews (about £140000 each to his sisters and amounts varying between half this and twice this to his nieces and nephews), but then he left £1.5 million (in today's money) to Elizabeth Patrick, all his household goods to Sarah Patrick, and the residue of the estate to the 2 sisters.

Sarah Oliver, the granddaughter of Thomas Lester, Thomas Pack's partner, married Robert Patrick, a cheesemonger in Whitechapel. The Sarah and Elizabeth above are their daughters. Why did Thomas Pack leave his considerable wealth mostly to other than his family? In the will there is no mention of a wife or children of his own. There is however a record of a marriage on 26th January 1754 between a Thomas Pack and Elizabeth Oliver, presumably another granddaughter of Thomas Lester, in Bethnal Green. Bethnal Green today carries connotations of poverty and council estates. In the 18th century it was a small leafy hamlet where the rich merchants lived who worked in the City of London. It would seem therefore that Thomas' wife died sometime before his will was made and Thomas then settled substantial sums on the daughters of his wife's sister. Perhaps they became his family living in East London as they did compared to his own sisters who lived in Suffolk. Robert Patrick, who started out as a cheesemonger, started up a rival bell foundry business in Whitechapel and it may have been that Thomas was trying to encourage this venture.

The Whitechapel bell foundry is probably the most famous bell foundry in the world. It manufactures large bells for change ringing in church towers as well as hand bells and all the accessories that go with them. It is said that under "Lester's management it was not successful and the fortunes of the foundry were at a low ebb until 1752 when he took into partnership Thomas Pack, previously his foreman". This made the business more prosperous and Pack introduced, among other things, rhyming couplets inscribed on the bells. The treble at Ingatestone, Essex, for instance, records:

"The Founder he has play'd his part,
which shews him master of his art,
So hang me well and ring me true,
and I will sing your praises due"

Pack and Chapman also installed new bells at St James' church in Egerton in 1759. St James' has six bells. Two were installed in 1602 (the third and the tenor, by Joseph Hatch), one in 1717 (the fifth by Robert Hope and Thomas Wildish) and then three in 1759 the second, fourth and treble, which was recast in 1927 by Alfred Bowell of Ipswich). The last three bells are from the Whitechapel bell foundry in London and one of them has the inscription "Peace and Good Neighbourhood". The Foundry was certainly busy in the area as one bell was recast for Dartford church in 1773 and 5 bells were installed in Boughton under Blean by Pack and Chapman in 1775, both of these are close to Egerton.

Amongst the bells made at Whitechapel were a set sent to St Petersburg, Russia, in 1747, the Liberty bell for Philadelphia in 1752 (which famously cracked the first time it was rung - note that Thomas Pack became a partner of the firm in 1752; was he promoted to help clear up the mess surrounding the Liberty bell?), a set to Christ Church, Philadelphia in 1754 and Big Ben at the Palace of Westminster in 1858, at 13.5 tons the biggest bell ever cast there.

Big Ben, whose real name is "The hour bell of the Great Clock at Westminster" was so large that it took 20 minutes for the molten metal to be poured into the bell mould and 20 days for it to cool. It was transported from Whitechapel to Westminster by "16 bedecked horses".

The most unusual bells story was a set of 8 bells for St Michael's Church, Charleston, South Carolina. They were installed in 1764. In 1781 during the wars of Independence the City fell into British hands and the bells were shipped back to London as spoils of war where an American businessman bought them and shipped them back to the USA. Then during the Civil War they were taken down and shipped to Columbia for safety but the Union forces took the City and the bells were broken down and melted. After the war the bell metal and pieces were collected and shipped back to Whitechapel for recasting and then returned to Charleston on their 5th transatlantic crossing in 1867. In 1989 the bells were damaged by Hurricane Hugo and went back to Whitechapel for refitting and then finally back to Charleston again.

Whilst there is no direct evidence it is possible that Thomas is descended from Sir Christopher Packe. Sir Christopher was based in London, very well connected and a bell foundry is the sort of worthy occupation one might expect of his family.

In 1752 Thomas was accepted as a member of the Ancient Society of College Youths. This was a society of bell ringers, which was founded in 1637 and still exists to this day. Thomas' interest would have been obvious. In 1712 the Society admitted a George Pack. It would seem highly likely that the two are related and perhaps father and son although no concrete evidence has been traced.

Later in this book we will spend time in a small village in Kent called Egerton. Readers may have noticed that Whitechapel installed 3 bells at St James' church in Egerton in 1759. It is believed that Whitechapel also installed some or all of the bells at St Nicholas' church in Pluckley, which adjoins Egerton, at about the same time and Thomas presumably will have overseen the work. My ancestor, George Pack, was born almost certainly in Pluckley circa 1766. We will return to examine this coincidence in a later chapter.

But for now we must return to the family of Sir Christopher and his youngest son, Simon.

Chapter 7 - Simon Packe (1654-1701) - The Irish Line of Sir Christopher's Family, or is it? - And a Musical Story

Simon was born in London on 31st December 1654, the very same year as his father was Lord Mayor of London and probably at the peak of his power and influence. He initially pursued the traditional family career and joined Sir Henry Goodricke's regiment as a captain in 1678. But the regiment was disbanded a year or so later and it was not until 1685 that he was able to find another posting as a captain in Lord Ferrer's regiment and he used the intervening years to pursue another career as a composer. His father had died in 1682 leaving him £1175 in cash or about £100,000 today (Sir Christopher undoubtedly, as we shall see, also left Simon property and land).

Simon was an accomplished musician and he composed music for a number of shows and collaborated with Henry Purcell on at least one occasion. His music was in triple time, mainly melody and bass and he would have rubbed shoulders with the great playwrights and musicians of the time including Purcell and Dryden. Among fashionable society he had a reputation for being unlucky in love and possessing an "unruly passion" which led to a duel with captain Alan Bellingham in 1686 which both survived.

By 1685 he was back in military work when the War Office issued an order for him to raise a company and quarter and muster them at Derby. Charles II died in that year and was succeeded by his brother, James II, a fervent Catholic. Religious trouble was brewing again and James started promoting Catholics to influential positions in the magistracy, militia and universities. Simon Packe and 5 other officers in the Duke of Berwick's regiment refused to receive Catholic recruits and in 1688 the 6 of them were arrested in what became known as the Revolt of the Portsmouth Captains. They were stripped of their commissions but became national heroes. Before long it became clear that James had overreached himself as the Bishops stared to revolt and James abdicated and William and Mary became sovereigns. The story of the Portsmouth Captains is told in the engraving shown on the following page. Simon is in the middle row on the left.

In December 1688 Simon was made captain in Colonel Solomon Richard's regiment but later rejoined Princess Anne's regiment and he was promoted to Lieutenant Colonel in 1689. He fought at the battle of the Boyne in 1690 and was at the 2nd siege of Limerick in 1691.

The Battle of the Boyne is interesting because it continues themes already started. The battle took place on July 1st 1690 (not the 12th as is commonly assumed). King James had been overthrown by the Glorious Revolution (sometimes called the Bloodless revolution, although it wasn't entirely bloodless) of 1688. He was a Catholic, the last Catholic to occupy the throne, and believed in absolute monarchy and, just like Charles 1st 30 years earlier, this brought him into conflict with Parliament. He was overthrown by William of Orange, who would become William 3rd, leading a parliamentary force.

The Battle of the Boyne, with both armies on either side of the river Boyne, both led by a King, was James' attempt to regain his throne but he was out numbered and convincingly beaten and Parliament would increase its importance and Catholicism further lose its role in England. The battle was the most extensive and bloody in Irish history.

The revolt of the Portsmouth Captains, Simon is middle row, left.

Simon was then stationed at Dundalk camp where he continued to compose music. Some of Simon's works are performed to this day at family concerts at Prestwold. A piece of his music entitled Laurinda, arranged for 4 voices, is shown below. Simon's works are detailed in the New Grove Dictionary of Music and Musicians, Volume 14, 1980.

I have referred in the title above to the Irish story starting. In fact as we saw in an earlier chapter Sir Christopher Packe almost certainly had a relative called Thomas, probably a brother or cousin, born in 1564 and resident in Ballinakill, Queens County, Ireland. Thomas had a son, again Thomas, in 1585 who was then resident in England. It would seem there were already established family groups in Ireland that Simon eventually found when he left the army. A theory suggested by Tom Packe, a descendant of the English Packes, is that the first Thomas, born in 1564 was Sir Christopher's father, the dates would certainly fit. A scrap cutting in Tom's possession reads *"we find among the grants to adventurers under the act of settlement one to Sir Christopher Pack, Bart, of lands in the county of East Meath"*.

After the army Simon settled in the Queens County, Ireland, married, a Miss Kelly (sometimes Kiley), and they had 1 son, Thomas, born just before Simon died prematurely on 2nd April 1701, aged only 47. He died intestate and Letters of Administration were granted on 4th July to his nephews Charles Packe and Robert Wilson (son of his sister Anne). Simon was interred at Prestwold in the family church. In addition to his army service, Simon inherited the land in East Meath that his father, Sir Christopher, had been granted above (presumably by Cromwell who frequently rewarded friends in this way, Meath is close to where the Battle of the Boyne took place). Queens County, referred to above, is the old name of what is now County Laois, which adjoins County Kilkenny, both in the province of Leinster.

In the history books it is frequently stated that the Prestwold/ English Packes have never acknowledged the Irish link and the Packe family file in Leicestershire Records Office gives no mention of it. In this they are obviously not saying that Simon was not part of the family because they interred him at Prestwold but are presumably refusing to acknowledge any descendants of Simon. Details of Simon's marriage and his son are very sketchy and the fact that two of the English Packes administrated his estate when he died, rather than his wife, would seem to cast doubt on these details. Simon may well have had a fortune the size of his brother Christopher's, which would have been considerable. As we shall see in later chapters most of Simon's supposed descendants were middle class working people and do not appear to have been landed gentry with wealth. In the next chapter we will come to Sir Denis Pack, a supposed descendant of Simon, who had a highly illustrious military career. There is a theory that historians, over the years, have tried to invent a link between Sir Denis and the English aristocracy, perhaps not believing that a mere commoner could have achieved what he did and they thus bolted him onto the English Packes through Simon. Then again perhaps the Prestwold Packes did not want Simon's estate to fall into Irish hands? Perhaps Simon's marriage to Miss Kelly (about whom nothing is known) was contested, perhaps it never took place and Simon's son, Thomas, was illegitimate and the Prestwold Packes did not want the family assets dissipated in this way. Simon's supposed son Thomas is recorded as a merchant, which would seem an unlikely profession for a nobleman's son. It would seem the Irish Packs did not benefit from Simon's estate, including the lands in East Meath, and it was all brought back into the English family and that, perhaps, is why the link was not acknowledged in early times and the refusal has carried down the centuries. These are all speculations and we will continue, in the absence of any other certainty, to assume Thomas was Simon's son, acknowledging that there is no certain link between the English Packes and the Irish Packs.

Simon's (possible) son, Thomas, produced 3 children, Thomas again, Richard and Samuel and their stories are described in the next 3 chapters. The 3 sons would all have interesting histories and 2 of them generated significant wealth of their own. The exception was Richard who produced a family of soldiers and clerics.

Simon Packe's memorial at St Andrews church Prestwold is shown below, sadly it is tucked away in a corner of the church and difficult to photograph.

In total there are 18 memorials to Packes in St Andrews church at Prestwold. Many have been shown above in the course of the story so far. There are 4 others who are related to the above but who I have not been able to join up.

Richard Hussey Packe born and died 1874

Edward Hussey Packe

Mother of Richard Hussey above

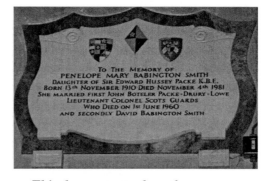

This demonstrates how the surname became so complicated

Somewhere, linked in with the above, is Vere Packe who died 30th September 1866 in Montevideo, South America. His will was in favour of his wife, Caroline Anna Frances Packe and was granted on 5th November 1869, 3 years after his death. She is noted as being resident in Zanzibar. The Packes were truly a family of Empire and this theme will continue in later chapters.

And now we turn to Simon's son, Thomas and his 3 sons; Thomas, Richard and Samuel.

Chapter 8 - Thomas Pack (1700-1758) - A Family of Ecclesiastics, Soldiers and Adventurers

Little is known of Simon's only child, Thomas, except his dates, above, and his children, who follow. He had 3 sons, Thomas (who will be described in this chapter), Richard and Samuel who will be described in the following chapters.

The Very Reverend Thomas Pack (1720-1795)

He was the oldest son of Thomas Pack and was born in Queens County, possibly Ballinakill, in 1720. He started at Trinity College Dublin in 1736, aged 16, and received his B.A. in 1740. He was ordained a clergyman in 1743, became Rector of Nurney, in the Diocese of Leighlin, in 1749 and Dean of Ossory from 1784 until his death in 1795 and was Dean of the Cathedral Church of St. Canice, Kilkenny. This is the start of a long lineage of Pack ecclesiastics. Thomas Pack is pictured below.

THE REV. THOMAS PACK,
When Rector of Nurney.

From "A memoir of Major General Sir Denis Pack KCB" by his Grandson
Denis R. Pack-Beresford (published 1908) courtesy of Tom Packe.

He died 26th May 1795, aged 76 and has a tomb at St Canice. He married Catherine Sullivan (1733 – 1801) of Bere, County Cork on 14th March 1766, when he was 46 and she was 33, and they had 5 children. Catherine was the daughter and heir of Denis Sullivan (The O'Sullivan Bere is an old Irish title) and she died in 1801 and she lies with her husband. Thomas' will was dated 18th June 1783 and it was proved in June 1795 shortly after he died. He left his estate to his wife and made bequests to his children; £400 to Denis, £2000 to Catherine and £2000 to Anne; his son Thomas had already died and presumably so had Caroline. He also left legacies to Jane Lea, Eleanor Pack and Mary Tucker, daughters of brother, Samuel, and to Thomas and Anthony, sons of brother, Richard. A family tree, to keep track of where we are, is shown below.

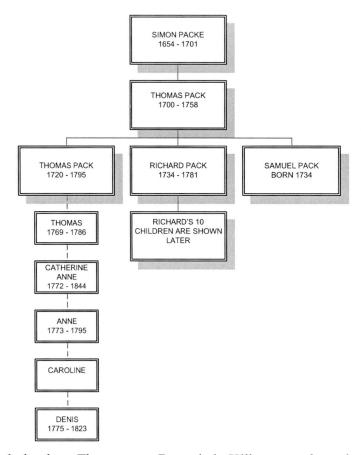

St Canice Cathedral, where Thomas was Dean, is in Kilkenny and was built between 1202 and 1285 on the site of a 6th century monastery founded by Saint Cainnech of Aghaboe, anglicised as Saint Canice. It is pictured below. The round tower was built before the Cathedral in 849, possibly as a place of refuge for people or treasure during Viking raids. In 1332 the central tower collapsed leaving the Cathedral with a very unusual appearance.

The Diocese of Ossory comprises most of modern County Kilkenny plus some parts of the neighbouring Counties of Laois and Offaly. In March 1650 Cromwell laid siege to Kilkenny and eventually captured the Cathedral, which had a Roman Catholic Bishop at the time, and, it is said, used it for stabling horses and caused much damage; the Cathedral remained abandoned and roofless for 12 years. In this he would have been supported and perhaps accompanied by Sir Christopher, as we have seen in his earlier chapter. How strange that Sir Christopher's great grandson, Thomas, is now the Dean of the Cathedral his family helped to wreck.

There is a monument to Thomas and Catherine in St Canice and it is pictured below.

The inscriptions read as follows;

Here lie deposited
The remains of
The Rev Thos Pack
Dean of Ossory
In whom was united
Every virtue
Which could ornament
The Christian
Or dignify
The clerical character.
Having faithfully discharged
The Duties
Of his sacred function
For Fifty Two years
He closed his Ministry and Life
On the 26th of May
In the 76th year of his age
And of our Lord 1795

Within this vault
Rest the remains
of Mrs Catherine Pack
Relict of the Rev Thos Pack
Dean of Ossory
She resigned her soul into her Creators hands
on the 10th April 1801
in the 68th year of her age.
Her life exhibited a uniform scene
of unaffected Piety
And unbounded Charity
She was a faithfull wife
an affectionate parent
And a firm friend
and in the discharge
of every Christian duty
She was equalled by few
She was excelled by none

Little is known of 4 of Thomas' 5 children except that Thomas junior attended Trinity in 1784, aged 15, but died 2 years later on 13th December 1786. His memorial reads "He was the hope of his friends; and ornament of his family. During 2 years continuance in the University he acquired every honor attainable in so short a period and his life, tho' limited was mark'd with every virtue". Anne was born about 1773 and died 6th August 1795, aged 22, her memorial reads " Her disposition was mild and amiable, her manners gentle and engaging; her morning of life was soon overcast, and she fell an early, but not untimely victim to the grave". Caroline must have died young since she is not mentioned in her father's will and Catherine was born about 1772 and died in Harrow, Middlesex in April 1844 but nothing more is known (she may have married John Spencer in St Marylebone in 1808). A considerable amount however is known about the 5th child Denis Pack. Denis' father, Thomas, must have been very proud of his last-born child and this may have helped with the disappointment of 3 of his 5 children dying young and Catherine apparently emigrating to England.

SIR DENIS PACK (1775 – 1823)– a distinguished military history

Denis was named after his maternal grandfather, Captain Denis Sullivan. He attended Trinity College Dublin in 1790 at the age of 15 but a year later he left and entered the army. For most of the next 25 years he would be fighting wars all over the world. His last foreign service was at Waterloo in 1815. After Waterloo Denis' fighting days were over and he married and produced 4 children but only lived another 8 years, possibly as a result of an accumulation of injuries during his military career.

Before we start with Denis' military career a bit of historical background might be helpful. Towards the end of the 18th century France was in economic and political turmoil with an absolute monarchy waging too many wars and impoverishing the populace and this all finally broke loose on July 14th 1789 with the storming of the Bastille and the start of the French revolution which would lead to the execution of Louis 16th, the reign of terror and eventually to the rise of Napoleon Bonaparte, Emperor Napoleon 1st in 1804. The three strongest European powers at the time were Britain, France and Austria and the three would be at war with each other in changing coalitions until the battle of Waterloo in 1815 which would settle things for a while. Britain had a great interest in all this since the ruling classes in England were worried that the revolutionary zeal displayed by the French people would transfer to England and threaten the ruling classes there. Most of Sir Denis' career was spent fighting Napoleon and his allies all over the world.

Denis Pack was appointed cornet in the 14th light dragoons on 30th November 1791 and served in Flanders in 1794. Later he was in Bremen, then Quiberon and by 1798, now with the 5th dragoon guards, he was dealing with rebels in Ireland. On 25th August 1798 he was promoted major in the 4th Royal Irish dragoon guards and just over a year later he was appointed lieutenant colonel in the 71st Highland Light Infantry. At about this time he may well have made the acquaintance of Lord Cornwallis and this will be important later.

Charles, 2nd Earl Cornwallis (1738 – 1805) is best known for his role in the American wars of independence, which ended with his surrender at Yorktown on October 19th 1781 heralding the eventual birth of the United States of America. Cornwallis is sometimes portrayed as the man who lost America. This is perhaps unfair. He was poorly supported by the mother country, which was perhaps more concerned with unfolding revolutionary events much closer to home in France. Their continued faith in Cornwallis was shown when he was next sent to India as Governor-General in 1786 and then was recalled in

1798 to help quell rebellions in Ireland. He was Lord Lieutenant of Ireland from June 1798 to 1801. In 1805 he was sent back to India but died shortly after arriving. Denis Pack and Lord Cornwallis thus were both in Ireland for a three-year period and the relevance of this will become apparent later, as will the fact that Cornwallis had extensive family estates in Kent and Sussex and that he was Member of Parliament for Wye in Kent. Wye is about 12 miles southwest of Canterbury and 10 miles east of Egerton. Cornwallis knew Kent and must have known Denis Pack. Cornwallis was honoured by a memorial in St Paul's Cathedral, which is pictured below together with the inscription.

After Ireland Denis Pack commanded the 71st at the recapture of the Cape of Good Hope in 1806 where he was wounded. A year later he was in South America under General Beresford and was taken prisoner but escaped. He apparently had a fierce temper but was popular with his men and a rhyme after his escape ran " The Devil break the gaoler's back that let thee loose sweet Denis Pack" He was wounded again in Whitelocke's disastrous attack on Buenos Aires.

In 1808 he joined Sir Arthur Wellesley (later the Duke Of Wellington) in Portugal with the 71st at the battles of Rolica and Vimeiro, and then into Spain before returning home. In 1809 he was fighting at Flushing and then on 25th July 1810 he was made colonel and aide-de-camp to the King. Later he would be back in Portugal with a Portuguese brigade under General Beresford and by now he was a brigadier-general. He distinguished himself at the battle of Salamanca and was made major general on 4th June 1813. Later he would fight in the Pyrenees, Nivelle, and Toulouse. He was knighted on 2nd January 1815.

In June 1815 he commanded a brigade of Picton's division at Quatre-Bras and Waterloo where he was again wounded. That was his last foreign service. He was much honoured. He held the orders of the Tower and Sword in Portugal, Maria Theresa in Austria and St Vladimir in Russia and he was invested as Knight Commander and given the Order of the Bath (KCB) and received the thanks of Parliament 5 times for his military service.

Sir Denis Pack © National Portrait Gallery, London.

On 10th July 1816 he married Lady Elizabeth Louisa Beresford, 4th daughter of the first Marquis of Waterford, sister of the second Marquess, and last surviving sister of His Grace the Archbishop of Armagh and Lord Primate of Ireland. She was also a half sister of General Beresford, Sir Denis' commanding officer in South America and elsewhere. However, as General Beresford was an illegitimate son of the first Marquis he was never acknowledged by the Beresford family. He was created Viscount Beresford in 1823 for his military achievements. Denis and Lady Elizabeth had four children and their stories are detailed later in this chapter.

At this point it will be helpful to explain a little about the colourful history of the Beresford family or that part of it that touches on the Pack story. Lord George De La Poer Beresford (1735 – 1800) was the 1st Marquis of Waterford. Waterford is about 30 miles from Kilkenny. He had a number of illegitimate children one of which was William Carr Beresford, Viscount (1768 – 1856). He married his cousin and they had no children. He fought under Wellington and was Sir Denis' commanding officer during some of his career. The 1st Marquis also had a legitimate family of 7 children. One was Elizabeth Louisa Beresford who married Sir Denis. Another was Lord John Beresford (1773 – 1862) who was ordained a priest in 1797, became Bishop of Cork and Ross in 1805, Archbishop of Dublin in 1820, Archbishop of Armagh in 1822 and Primate of Ireland in 1822. The relevance of this detail will become apparent later.

Sir Denis died 24th July 1823 at Upper Wimpole Street, London at Lord Beresford's house. Sir Denis is buried with his parents and other members of his family in the Cathedral Church of St. Canice in Kilkenny, Ireland. In 1828 his widow erected a monument to him surmounted by a marble bust by Chantrey in the church and his portrait, by George Lethbridge (shown on previous page) is in the National Portrait Gallery archives in London. His monument at St Canice is shown below.

The inscription on the monument reads as follows;

Near this place are interred the mortal remains of MAJOR GENERAL SIR DENIS PACK, Knight Commander of the Most Hon. Military Order of the Bath and of the Portuguese Military Order of the Tower and Sword, Knight of the Imperial Russian Order of Wladimer, and of the Imperial Austrian Order of Maria Theresa; Colonel of the 84th Reg't of Foot, and Lieutenant Governor of Plymouth; who terminated a life devoted to the service of his King and Country on the 24th Day of July 1823, aged forty eight years.

The name of this distinguished officer is associated with almost every brilliant achievement of the British Army during the eventful period of Continental warfare between the year 1791 in which he entered His Majesty's service, and the year 1823, in which he ended his honourable career. Throughout the campaigns in Flanders in 1794, and 1795, he served in the 14th Regiment of Light Dragoons; at the capture of the Cape of Good Hope, in 1806, and on the arduous and active campaign which immediately followed in South America, he commanded the 71st Regiment of Highlanders in a manner which reflected the highest credit on his military skill and valour.

At the head of the same Corps in 1808, he acquired fresh reputation in the battles of Roleia and Vimeira; and in the following year in the battle of Corunna. In 1809 he accompanied the expedition to Walcheren, and signalised himself by his zeal and intrepidity at the siege of Flushing. He was subsequently engaged at the head either of a brigade, or of a division of the army in every general action and remarkable siege which took place during the successful war in the Peninsula under the conduct of the great Duke of Wellington. He finally commanded a brigade in the action of Quatre Bras and again in the ever memorable and decisive battle of Waterloo. For these important services in which he was nine times severely wounded, he obtained at the recommendation of his illustrious chief from the foreign Potentates in alliance with Great Britain the honourable titles of distinction above mentioned, and from his own Sovereign, besides the Order of the Bath and a medal in commemoration of the battle of Waterloo, a gold cross with seven clasps, on which are inscribed the following names of the battles and sieges wherein he bore a conspicuous part viz. Roleia, Corunna, Busaco, Cuidad Roderigo, Salamanca, Vittoria, Pyrenees, Nivelle, Nive, Orthes, Toulouse. Upon five different occasions he had also the honour to receive the thanks of both Houses of Parliament. On the 3rd February 1813 for his conduct at Salamanca; on the 10th February 1813 for his conduct at Cuidad Roderigo; on the 8th November 1813 for his conduct at Vittoria; on the 24th March 1814 for his conduct at Orthes; on the 23rd June for his conduct at Waterloo. Whilst these his merits as an officer ensure for him a place in the records of his grateful country amongst those heroes who have bravely fought her battles and advanced her military glory, his virtues as a man, which were securely founded upon Christian piety, are attested by the esteem of his companions in arms and by the love of all who were intimately connected with him.

This monument is erected by his widow, THE LADY ELIZABETH PACK, daughter of George de la Poer Marquess of Waterford, as a just tribute of respect to the memory of one of His Majesty's most deserving soldiers and subjects and in testimony of her own affection.

Several months after Sir Denis died Wellington wrote to his widow as follows. In retirement Sir Denis had been Lieutenant Governor of Plymouth and they had presumably occupied a grace and favour property.

My Dear Lady Elizabeth

I have received your Ladyship's letter; and I request you to give up the house at Plymouth Dock to Mr Ashley – who, it appears, has charge of it – whenever it may suit your convenience to do so.

I assure you that it gave me great satisfaction to be able to contribute in any manner to your comfort, and that of my poor friend; and that I shall always be happy to manifest my respect and affection for his memory by my regard for those whom he has left behind him.

Believe me, ever yours

Most faithfully and sincerely,

Wellington

Sir Denis' 4 children were as follows;

Arthur John Reynell-Pack (1817 – 1860) he was the godson of the Duke of Wellington and became a Lieutenant Colonel in the 7th fusiliers, serving in the Crimea in the 1840s, later Colonel and Assistant Quartermaster General at Cork in Ireland. He was decorated with the Legion d'Honneur by the French and a CB by his own country. He married Frederica Katherine Hely Hutchinson and they had 7 children. He changed his name from Pack to Reynell-Pack in 1847 on succeeding his stepfather, Sir Thomas Reynell, Baronet, whom his mother married after the death of his father. He died on 17th August 1860 at Harley Street, St Marylebone. His will was proved by his brother, below, of Fenagh Lodge, County Carlow on 15th September 1860 and the effects were £12000. He is buried at St Canice and his memorial is below.

The inscription on the memorial reads as follows;

Colonel Arthur John Reynell-Pack
Companion of the Bath
Knight of the French Legion of Honour
5th Class Turkish Order of the Medjidre
Assistant Quarter Master General
Of the South Western District of Ireland
Born May 5th 1817
Died at Cork August 17th 1860
Colonel Reynell-Pack was the eldest son of

Major General Sir Denis Pack KCB
And godson of
Field Marshal Arthur Duke of Wellington
He entered the Army 2nd August 1833
And served with his regiment
In America, Gibraltar and the West Indies
He held the appointment
Of Deputy Assistant Adjutant general
At the Home Guards from 28th Nov 1843 to 25th Jan 1855
Which appointment he relinquished
To join his regiment (the 7th Royal Fusiliers)
In the Crimea
And was severely wounded when in command
In the attack on the Sedan June 18th 1855
Colonel Reynell-Pack married Dec 28th 1850
Frederica Katherine, 2nd daughter of
Colonel the Hon. Henry Hely Hutchinson
And leaves issue 6 daughters and 1 son
His remains rest in the military cemetery Cork.

Denis William Pack-Beresford (1818 – 1881) was a captain in the Royal Artillery. In 1854 he inherited the Irish estates of his uncle, and his father's commanding officer, General William Carr Beresford and then changed his name from Pack to Pack-Beresford. Denis' mother, Elizabeth, widow of Sir Denis, was the daughter of George de la Poer, 1st Marquess of Waterford who had a number of legitimate children but also some illegitimate ones including William Carr Beresford. Carr Beresford married but without issue and clearly decided to leave his wealth to his stepsister's son. He would have known the family well having fought with Sir Denis and possibly with Denis William also. Denis William was High Sheriff and MP for County Carlow and lived at Fenagh Lodge, County Carlow. Fenagh Lodge had land of 5567 acres and may well have been his inheritance from Beresford and is close to Ballinakill. He married Annette Caroline Browne of Browne's Hill, Clonmelsh, County Carlow and they had 5 sons and 4 daughters. He died on 28th December1881 and his will was proved on 14th February1882 by Sir William Reynell Anson, Bt, of Elm Hill, Hawkhurst, Kent, his nephew and a part of the Anson family to be described below. The effects were £20000.

Anne Elizabeth Pack – she married the Rev George J. Mapletoft Paterson in 1869. He was rector of Brome in Suffolk. They had no children.

Elizabeth Catherine Pack – she married Sir John William Hamilton Anson 2nd Baronet in 1842 and they had 11 children. A brief aside on baronetcies may be of interest. Baronetcies are hereditary titles awarded by the Crown. The first ones awarded were in 1611 when James 1st needed to raise funds. They are the lowest of the hereditary titles and have never carried the right of a seat in the House of Lords (which has all changed in recent years anyway). They are no longer created.

The Anson family, which Elizabeth married into, is an interesting one. The family seat is Shugborough Hall in Staffordshire, acquired in 1693 and pictured below. It is now owned by the National Trust and administered by the local council although the family still live there. There has been a strong military and especially naval tradition in the family. George Anson was made first Lord of the Admiralty in 1751 having circumnavigated the globe between 1740 and 1744 and having brought back much treasure, which he used to develop Shugborough. Later there would be at least 2 Rear Admirals in the family one of which was Elizabeth's son. A more recent Anson was Thomas Patrick John Anson, 5th Earl of Lichfield (1939 – 2005), first cousin once removed of Queen Elizabeth II, and better known as Patrick Lichfield, photographer to Royalty and the stars.

Shugborough Hall, where Elizabeth Catherine Pack lived when she became an Anson

Back now to Sir Denis. His will is very short. It is dated 5th August 1816 after his military career was over and in it he leaves everything to Lady Elizabeth except a £200 annuity to his sister Catherine Anne whilst she is unmarried. It is strange that he did not make provision for his wife predeceasing him; was he already unwell and then survived longer than expected? He died on 30th September 1823 and the Lady Elizabeth Louisa Pack realised his entire estate.

After his death Lady Elizabeth remarried, in 1831, Lieutenant General Sir Thomas Reynell KCB (died 1848) who had been one of Pack's majors in the 71st. Sir Denis' children were very young when he died and may have scarcely known him.

Footnote on Waterloo

This was the culmination of Sir Denis' career. There were a number of other Packs involved as well. As we shall see in the next chapter two of Denis' cousins, Richard and Percy, were in the army and may well have served as medical staff at Waterloo and, as we saw in the previous chapter, Robert Christopher was killed at Waterloo and his nephew, George Hussey, was wounded slightly. 3 Pack(e)s for certain and possibly more were involved in the battle which must be an unusual statistic.

And now we turn to Richard Pack, Sir Denis's uncle.

Chapter 9 - Richard Pack (1734-1781)
Priests, Percys, Schools and Sherlock Holmes

Richard Pack (1734-1781) was ordained as a Deacon in 1758 and was then Treasurer of Leighlin Cathedral from 1771 to 1781 and head of Ormonde School (later Kilkenny College) from 1773. Kilkenny College was then and still is one of the most famous schools in Ireland. In 1989 it relocated to the edge of the town but for many years was housed in the fine Georgian building below which is now County Hall.

He married Mary Percy (1720 – 1793) who was 14 years older than him and is believed to be related to the Northumberlands, one of the oldest and most historic families in England, although there is no solid evidence of this. He attended Trinity College from 1748 (aged 14) to 1752 and was aided for his studies, implying he was not from a prosperous family. He and Mary had 11 children as follows;

Mary Pack (Born 1754) married Mr Tucker, a clergyman, nothing else known.

Jane Pack (Born 1755) married Thomas Paul, a clergyman, nothing else known.

Anne Pack (Born 1756) died unmarried, nothing else known.

Thomas Pack (1757 – 1791) attended Trinity from 1774 to 1779 and then became Curate of Inistioge in 1780, Curate of Gowran in 1781 and Treasurer of Leighlin Cathedral, following his father, from 1781 until he died in 1791. The churches at Inistioge and Gowran are pictured below.

St Mary's Church Inistioge   *St Mary's Church Gowran*

Rectors/Curates 1780 - 2009

1780 Rev. T. Pack	1873 Rev. E.W. Hewson	1910 Rev. J. Smyth
1781 Rev. E. Pidgeon	1874 Rev. E.F. Hewson	1925 Rev. H. McClelland
1797 Rev. J.A. Kerr	1879 Rev. W.A. Nevill	1941 Rev. W.B. Stack
1818 Rev. T. Cuffe,	1883 Rev. R. O'Connor	1941 Rev. C.M. Stack
1820 Rev. C. Bradshaw	1885 Rev. J. Madden	1947 Rev. T.S. Devlin
1824 Rev. Parker	1887 Rev. L. Nixon	1950 Rev. J. Palmer
1840 Rev. R.D. Parks	1888 Rev. C.E. Keane	1960 Rev. D.T. Young
1842 Rev. S.S. Mounks	1891 Rev. J. Leslie	1974 Rev. H. Thompson
1855 Rev. Th. Hewson	1892 Rev. J. Halligan	1976 Rev. C.A. Cripey
1856 Rev. T. Hudson	189? _ _ _ Besford	1984 Rev. J. _ _ _
1858 Rev. J.W. Lanster	18_ _ _ _ _ Crostwait	1988 Rev. W.E. Brown
1863 Rev. T. Hatchel	1903 Rev. _. Butler	1991 Rev. W.J. Richie
1869 Rev. T. Townsand	1906 Rev. R. Warren	1992 Rev. D. Sandes
1873 Rev. M.N. Kearney	1906 Rev. W. Briggs	2008 Rev. J.P. Kavanagh

Thomas' Curacy at Inistioge in 1780 is noted in the church above.

Anthony Pack (1758 – 1842) attended Trinity from 1774 to 1777. He was ordained a priest in 1781 and was Vicar of Dunmore for 30 years from 1782 – 1812. St Andrews Church in Dunmore is pictured below.

There was an interesting and possibly quite rare discovery in Dunmore and this is pictured left. Edward 7th was King from 1901 to 1910. When the Irish gained independence they removed as many vestiges of their colonial past as possible so the discovery of an old British post box was a surprise.

After Dunmore Anthony was Prebendary of Blackrath 1812 – 1821, briefly a schoolmaster at St Patricks, Kilkenny in 1815, Dean's vicar of St Canice 1816 – 1823 and finally Prebendary of Clonmeany from 1821 to 1842 when he died. He married Sarah Blount in 1795. They had 12 children and I will just mention one **George Denis Pack** (1811 – 1841). After Trinity, in 1825, aged 14, he joined the 80th Army regiment. In 1836 he was in Canberra, part of the Mounted Police, responsible for discipline amongst male convicts deported to Australia. He died in New South Wales, Australia in 1841, aged only 30.

Richard Pack (1759 – 1815) was a doctor and staff surgeon in Kilkenny. He married a Miss Gould and they had 6 children. One son, Anthony Pierce Pack became a soldier and served as Aide de Camp to Sir Denis Pack from 1819 until 1823 when Sir Denis died.

Percy Pack he married a Miss Crawford of County Waterford. He was a surgeon serving in 40th Regiment.

William Pack (Born 1760) He married Katherine Scott (1785 – 1863) in 1802 and he was apparently a Grocer and Wine Merchant in the High Street, Kilkenny, the first non-military and non-ecclesiastic in the story. His wife, Katherine, opened a school in Kilkenny in 1813 and by 1831 she had built a very impressive school on St. John's Quay. In 1995 the building housed the Home Rule Club, which is a poetic twist for what was an Anglo-Irish family. The language of the school was French, which makes it sound like a sort of finishing school, and the income, apparently, was considerable. The Home Rule Club today, school as was, is pictured below.

William and Katherine had 4 children. ***William Denis Pack*** enlisted into the army and died, unmarried, on the Island of St Catherine. ***Maria Angela*** married Daniel Cormac of County Kilkenny and that is all that is known of these 2 children. The other 2 children were ***Anne*** and ***Katherine*** who were both educated at the school above and later helped to run it, and later still ran schools of their own. The date of William's death is unknown but his wife, Katherine Scott Pack married a 2nd time, sometime before July 1836, to a Mr St. John (born 1773), who also ran a school! Sometime after 1847, and for reasons unknown, Katherine and her 2 daughters, Anne and Katherine, moved to Edinburgh. She used her experience to run a boarding house and it was there in 1849 that one of her tenants was Charles Altamount Doyle, of whom more in the next paragraph. Katherine died in 1863 and must have been considerably younger than William who was born in 1760.

Daughter ***Anne*** married a Mr O'Neill and daughter ***Katherine*** (1808 – 1862) married William Foley (born 1807) of Trinity College, Dublin in 1835 but he died in 1840. They had just time for two daughters; Catherine Foley, born May 1st 1839, nothing else known, and Mary Josephine Elizabeth Foley (1837 – 1920) who married Charles Altamount Doyle (1832 – 1893), a tenant at her mother's boarding house. They had 10 children and one of these was Arthur Conan Doyle (1859 – 1930) and this will become relevant later in this story (Conan was the maiden name of his grandmother, it is not known why he adopted this and none of his siblings used it).

So Katherine Pack who married William Foley was Arthur Conan Doyle's maternal grandmother and she was a relation of Sir Denis Pack from the previous chapter. Ely Liebow, Associate Professor of English at Northeastern Illinois University, USA, wrote a book proposing that a Dr Joe Bell (of whom more later) was the model used by Conan Doyle for the character of Sherlock Holmes. In his book he quotes from "The Life of Sir Arthur Conan Doyle" written by John Dickson Carr in which Conan Doyle's mother says " *My mother, please observe, was born Katherine Pack. Her uncle (sic) was Major-General Sir Denis Pack, who led Pack's brigade at Waterloo. And the seventeenth-century Packs, as everyone knows or ought to know, were allied in marriage with Mary Percy of Balintemple, heir of the Irish branch of the Percys of Northumberland. In that wooden chest are the papers of our descent for six hundred years; from the marriage of Henry Percy, sixth Baron, with Eleanor, niece of King Henry the Third*". Sadly there is no sign of the wooden chest. More of this connection later in the book

Samuel Pack (1760 – 1815) he attended Trinity in 1774 and later emigrated to the USA (although, as we shall see in the next chapter, there is some confusion as to whether it is this Samuel or his uncle, of the same name and covered in the next chapter, who emigrated; suffice to say that a Samuel Pack emigrated).

George Helsham Pack (born 1764-66) married Emily Mathews of Bonnetstown Co Kilkenny and died in 1821 having produced no children. He was an attorney and had a law practice (in Dublin, at 45 Mount Street) and a wealthy wife.

Bartholomew Pack (1769 – 1849) Priest and Schoolmaster, he attended Trinity from 1787 to 1791. He was the Rector at Ettagh, Kings County, Ireland. He married Barbara Harty 18th July 1800. They had 11 children 5 of whom died in infancy. There are details of only 2 of the children. ***Bartholomew Ponsonby Pack*** (1811 – 1890), believed to have married Jane Salisbury, he emigrated to New York in 1860, and had 7 children one of which was another Bartholomew (1852 – 1946) who is pictured below. He was born in Portumna, Galway, Ireland.

Bartholomew Pack (1852 – 1946)

Bartholomew's second child was ***Anne Catherine Pack*** (1805 - 1866)- she married George Washington Brasier-Creagh in 1822, he was a Lieutenant in the Royal Navy and they lived at Creagh Castle, County Cork. One of their children was also George Washington Brasier-Creagh, 1832 – 1900, he married Averina Purdon Bevan Sherlock, and they produced 12 children including Kilner Charles Brasier-Creagh (1869 – 1956, married Agnes Denny) who produced Kilner Rupert Brasier-Creagh (1909 – 2002) and the tribute to Sir Rupert Brasier-Creagh when he died reads as follows;

Knight of the Most Excellent Order of the British Empire, Companion of the Most Honourable Order of Bath, Companion of the Distinguished Service Order, Officer of the United States of America Legion of Merit, Sir Rupert graduated from the Royal Military Academy, class of 1929, first in his class. He was commissioned by the present Queen's grandfather, King George 5th, as an officer in the Royal Artillery. At the age of 36, Sir Rupert became the youngest 2 star general in the British Army. He served as Chief of Staff of the Eastern Command, Director of Staff duties at the War Office and was aide to General Montgomery. Queen Elizabeth knighted Sir Rupert in February 1962 after his retirement from the Army.

Prior to coming to the United States, he owned Tarbrook Stud Farm in Croom County, Limerick, breeding championship thoroughbreds. After relocating to America Sir Rupert became a United States citizen. He addressed the U.S.Army Corps of Cadets at West Point on April 19th 1982.

He is survived by his loving wife, Lady Marie Helen (Nelson) Brasier-Creagh; 2 daughters, 1 son, 6 grandchildren and 3 great-grandchildren, all of England, and 3 stepchildren and 5 step grandchildren. His first wife, Molly Major died in 1967 and his second wife died shortly after him in July 2004.

We have already seen that the Packs and descendants migrated regularly in both directions across the Irish sea, now we find a similar migration across the Atlantic and that will increase as the story unfolds and this couldn't be a better introduction to the next chapter on Samuel, the third son of Thomas, after Thomas and Richard.

Chapter 10 - Samuel Pack (b. 1734) - The Packs Discover America - But Can We Believe Jake Hatcher?

Christopher Columbus (1451 – 1506) "discovered" America in 1492; he was trying to find a westward sea passage to the Orient when he bumped into America, although some Native Americans might disagree about this being his discovery. It would take more than 100 years before English settlers arrived to colonise the discovery; the Mayflower landed at Cape Cod on November 11th 1620 and colonists of all nationalities, British, French, Spanish, Dutch, Swedish, Russians and others would start to flood in.

Just over 100 years after the Mayflower the first known Pack travelled to America and after him there would be many waves of emigration. Before we start the family history a little American history will help to set the scene. This is not a comprehensive history; it merely sets some time lines to assist the family story.

Spanish and English settlers, including Walter Raleigh, had attempted to establish colonies from 1520 onwards but they all failed usually being under resourced, although Raleigh famously did discover tobacco. The first successful colonisation was from the Mayflower and at Jamestown, Virginia exploiting the tobacco crop. All of this early colonisation was on the eastern coast. The settlers were often escaping religious persecution in their home countries but also over half of European migrants arrived as indentured servants and the first convicts shipped to America predated the Mayflower.

Gradually the growing success and prosperity of the American colonists began to cause difficulties with the mother country. The colonists objected to taxes being levied ("no taxation without representation") and objected to the order not to expand westwards because of the military costs of doing so.

This would lead to the American wars of Independence and the defeat of Cornwallis at Yorktown in 1781 and in 1789 the first Congress met and George Washington became the first President of the United States of America (then only 13 states down the eastern seaboard not the present 50 states). Now immigration and westward expansion would really take off. In 1803 Napoleon agreed to sell Louisiana, which would become the 18th State, for $15m. American troops would take Texas in 1836 and California in 1848 both from Mexico. Oregon joined the Union in 1859 and 5 States joined in the 20th century; Oklahoma in 1907 and Arizona and New Mexico in 1912 and Alaska and Hawaii in 1959.

So, let us resume the family story with Samuel Pack and just to help you keep your bearings I will repeat an earlier chart on the next page. Simon, at the top, was the youngest son of Sir Christopher Packe.

Samuel was born in 1734 in Ballynakill and married Jane Caddell (sometimes Caldwell) of Lancashire. It is stated, in some sources, that he emigrated to the US in 1740 (aged 6). For this to be true he must have emigrated with his parents and married in the US, neither of which appear to have been true. This is an appropriate place to properly introduce Peggy Dolan, who I have mentioned before. Peggy is an assiduous Pack researcher and has given me much help in the course of this book. She is a descendant of Bartholomew Pack who we met in the previous chapter. She is certain that Samuel and Jane did not emigrate but Samuel may well have made business trips since he worked for the East India Company, a connection which may have passed down the years since, as we have seen in an earlier chapter, Sir Christopher Packe, Samuel's great grandfather, was also a member over 100 years earlier.

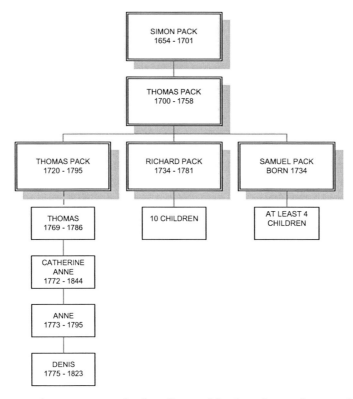

One of the sources stating erroneously that Samuel had emigrated was a book published in 1908, "A Memoir of Major-Gen Sir Denis Pack" by his grandson Denis R. Pack-Beresford which contains a family tree. But it does also record that another Samuel Pack, the 6th son of Richard Pack, who we met in the previous chapter, went to America and so we must assume that he simply got the wrong Samuel.

Another piece of research was done by a Jake Hatcher of Princetown, West Virginia. The research came into the possession of Alby Pack's brother Thomas (more of them later) and is also in the possession of Frannie Pack (more later). Jake Hatcher may well be part of the story – Lucy Pack married Wesley Basham and their daughter Eula married Lester Hatcher. I have not been able to link this up but there must be a link.

Jake Hatcher's account starts as follows; "*The Packs came from England where, for several centuries, they were a distinguished family. Alderman Pack, an ancestor, was a member of the Long Parliament during Cromwell's time. Another ancestor was General Pack, who served in the English Army under Lord Wellington. From those Packs were descended three brothers whose given names are not known to this compiler. They came from England to this country in 1740. Two of them settled in South Carolina, while the third settled in Virginia*"

Peggy Dolan's comments on the above are unprintable. How can 3 brothers "descended" from Sir Denis Pack emigrate to the US in 1740 when Sir Denis wasn't born until 1775? How can he be sure that the US Packs he then goes on to list are related to Alderman Pack or General Pack when the names of the original three brothers are unknown? One can only assume that Jake Hatcher did do some proper research of the US Packs and then bolted on some instant English history to try and glamorise his work. We will thus proceed by accepting that some Packs came to the US and that his US history is accurate but the English source is uncertain.

The Jake Hatcher account starts with the 3 Pack brothers coming to the US from England (and this could well have been Ireland which was part of England then) in 1740. Two settled in South Carolina while the third settled in Virginia. Samuel Pack (probably the 6th son of Richard in the previous chapter) appears to be the brother who settled in Virginia.

The Packs colonise Virginia – extracts from Jake Hatcher

By 1763 Samuel Pack (even though he was only born in 1760!) together with 2 other hunters, Swope and Pittman, was on the New River, at the mouth of Indian Creek, in what was then a wilderness part of Virginia, and is now Monroe County, West Virginia. He had 2 sons one of which was also Samuel, born in Augusta County in 1760. He almost certainly returned to Ireland to attend Trinity College in 1774 before returning to the US. Samuel Pack junior married Mary Farley, a daughter of Captain Matthew Farley, and it was in the New River Valley (in Virginia) that they settled. Samuel and Mary were among the most thrifty of the first settlers in that region. They owned all of the fertile bottomland along New River, from the mouth of Greenbrier River to Warford. The couple had seven sons, one after the other, and then three daughters: John, Matthew, Samuel, Bartley, Lowe, William, Anderson, Betsey, Polly, and Jennie.

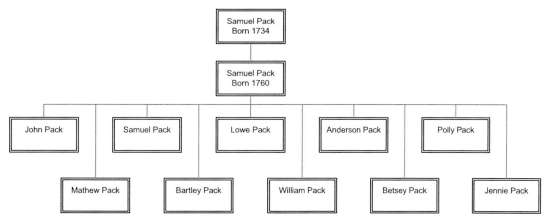

John and Bartley settled at Pack's ferry, now Summers County where for some time they had problems with the Indians, John married Jane Hutchinson and they accumulated a large fortune, he was a large land and slave owner. They had 3 sons and 3 daughters. John was taken prisoner on Flat Top Mountain during the Civil War, and Colonel Hayes, who would later become President, claimed a relationship with John and told him that his wife's mother was a Pack (this was Jennie, who married Jonah Morriss) and by reason of this John was allowed the privilege of the camp. Rutherford B. Hayes became President in 1876, he only served 1 term.

Mathew settled on the west side of the New River, opposite Pack's ferry and at the mouth of Big Bluestone River, he married twice and had 7 children.

Samuel settled on Glade Creek, in what is now Raleigh County.

Lowe lived on Brush Creek, in what is now Monroe County.

William went west

Anderson married Rebecca Peters and they settled on the New River also and he was a very wealthy and prominent man at the time of his death in 1858. They had 9 children, 6 boys and 3 girls, 3 sons moved to Kansas (Conrad, Samuel and Allen) and 2 moved to Oklahoma (John and Charles). Lowe and the 3 girls lived and married locally.

Polly married Joe Lively and *Betsey* married Jacob Dickinson and both families lived in Monroe; and *Jennie* married Jonah Morriss and they moved to Missouri (their daughter would marry Colonel Hayes (see above) a future President).

After this Jake Hatcher gives a highly detailed family tree right up to the early 20th century, which is too large to include here, but is shown in full in appendix 1. The original Jake Hatcher account shows the Pack family from chapter 9 page 75 so it was part of a larger work, perhaps a history of many Virginia families. In the attachment I have edited the page and chapter headings out to shorten it.

The Packs are numerous in Virginia and especially in a town called Streeter, which is where Pack's Mill is sited, built by John Pack, and one of the streets is named after Rhoda Anne Pack, wife of Samuel. Streeter is almost the American Egerton although Syracuse, as we shall see later, also has a claim.

And Carolina

The names of the 2 brothers who came to South Carolina are unknown. However there are a large number of Packs in that state. Alexa Pack has provided the author with details of her husband's ancestry, which starts in the early 19th century about 80 years after the unnamed brothers arrived.

Her first Pack is **Jeremiah** (born 1821), a farmer, who married Sarah (born 1822) and they had 10 children. Margaret (born 1839 married Samuel Melton 1866), John (1841 - 1918 married Martha Price 1866) Thomas (born 1846) Angelina (born 1847 married C. Blackwell 1866) Myrna (born 1850) Jonathan (1851 – 1935 married Anna Shehan then Mary Willis Mathis, lived at Coxe Plantation) James Madison (born 1852) Sarah (born 1854) Eliza (born 1857) and Amanda (born 1859). Most of the family lived around Inman, South Carolina, and most were Baptists.

Alexa's antecedent above was **James Madison Pack**, who would become Madison Pack and he and Martha Ann Blackwell would have 8 children. Taylor Madison, Isaac Logan, Pinckney Thomas, James Lucas, Ella Margaret, Avery Huston, Peter Chesterfield and Lewis Madison.

The next stage in Alexa's history is **Isaac Logan Pack** (1879 – 1953). He and Mary Ella Hester (1886 – 1969) had 10 children. When Mary Ella died in 1969 she had 26 grandchildren, 35 great grandchildren and 2 great great grandchildren! Their children were; Annie (born 1907) Maude (1908 – 1984 married James Cecil Shetton 15 grandchildren, 23 great grandchildren) Mattie (1911 – 1999, married a Shetton brother as well) Raymond Earl (born 1914) Walter Rufus (1916 – 1970 married Lovadia Welborn) Otis Albert (1918 – 1973 married Effie Savannah Clark of Georgia) Millie Naomi (1920 – 2005 married Robert Lowe) H.Odell (1923 – 1987 married Rhobelia Bishop) Howard L. (1926 – 1999 married Pearl) and James Carroll.

Summary

So what does all this add up to and do we believe Jake Hatcher? One way or another the Packs got to America and there are a lot there now and they must have come from England or Ireland. Jake Hatcher seems to have a Pack connection, which presumably means he has taken the trouble to at least do the US research right.

The population of the USA was 76 million in 1900 and there were 4,600 Packs. The US population was 281 million in 2000 and so by simple extrapolation there are probably about 17,000 Packs there now. The same figures for the UK are 1,800 Packs out of a total population of 30 million in 1900 and therefore about 3,600 Packs today out of a total population of 58.8 million. This may be slightly simplistic since immigration to the US since 1900 has been disproportionately from other countries than the UK compared to before 1900 but it is still likely that there are nearly 3 or 4 times as many Packs in the USA as in the UK despite the fact that the US Packs all came from this country. Readers may draw their own conclusions about US productivity.

There will be more Pack migration to the US in later chapters. Continuing with our Pack eclecticana there is another Pack to mention who lived more or less contemporaneously with Samuel although on the other side of the Atlantic.

Faithful Christopher Pack (1760 – 1840) was a painter. He was born in Norwich the son of a Quaker merchant whose family claimed a connection with that of Sir Christopher Packe. He moved to London to pursue his painting career and studied under Sir Joshua Reynolds. He exhibited at the Royal Academy in 1796. In 1802 he moved to Dublin and taught and exhibited widely. Later he returned to London and died aged 81 at 20 Sandwich Street, Gray's Inn Lane, London. He married but the names of his wife and any children are unknown. His claimed connection with Sir Christopher Packe has not been traced. In the next chapter we come to George Pack and my certain history begins.

Chapter 11 - George Pack 1766/7-1824
My Family Story Begins

Contemporaneously with the last few chapters (Richard Pack 1734-1781 in Ireland, Thomas Pack of the Whitechapel bell foundry who died in 1781 and Samuel Pack, either born in 1734 or 1760, depending on which one it was that went to the US) another Pack was born in 1766/7 and George Pack is my certain ancestor; my great-great-great-great grandfather and most of the rest of this book describes his descendants leading eventually to me. He is not certainly related to the other Packs already covered in this book; as we have seen simply having the same surname does not mean you are related. But some very unusual things happened to George and his family that make it possible that he is related to one or more of them and this will be explored in depth in this chapter. George had 1 son, also George, and 3, possibly 4, daughters. Because there is a lot of overlap between the 2 Georges, father and son, and to make sense of certain developments, George junior's story is partially told in this chapter and then completed in the next.

George senior was buried in Egerton on March 20th 1824, aged 57 and so was born 1766/7. He is noted in the parish records as a "bricklayer" although this may have been a generous description. He was probably the son of Lucy Pack of Pluckley. Pluckley is very close to Egerton. From the Pluckley parish records at Maidstone Lucy Pack was "buried in woollen" on December 1st 1793.

Lucy Pack and the Pluckley records

"Buried in woollen" came about from the Woollen Acts 1666-1680, which required that the dead should be buried in shrouds of pure wool (excluding plague victims). The reason for this was to help the woollen industry, which was in decline, by creating a new market for them. An affidavit had to be sworn in front of a Justice of the Peace confirming that the body had been buried in wool and there was a penalty of £5 if any other material was used. If the family could not afford the wool then "naked" would be entered into the records. The law was rescinded in 1814 but was usually ignored after 1770 (although not in Pluckley). In the parish records the word "affidavit" or "A" or "Aff" would follow the deceased's name to confirm that wool had been used, and this was so for Lucy's entry. Interestingly Mrs Dering, in the Pluckley records, was "buried in Linnen(sic)". The Derings were a prominent family in Pluckley and they presumably paid the £5 penalty to see off their loved one in style.

Also in the Pluckley records there is a baptism on 27th October 1765 of a George Peck, son of Lucy Peck. No father is recorded. Was "Peck" a mistake for "Pack"? "Peck" could well be how "Pack" would sound in a broad Kentish accent. One wonders who could spell or enunciate better, Lucy when announcing her son's birth in 1765 or George when announcing his mother's death in 1793 when she is definitely Pack not Peck in the records.

The dates don't quite work out. George Pack is recorded in the Egerton records as having been buried on March 20th 1824, aged 57. If he was born on 27th October 1765 then he was 58 in early 1824 but this is pretty close for those inaccurate times and it could be that the family member registering his death did not know his exact date of birth.

There are a number of intriguing things about this. Firstly there are no other entries for "Pack" or "Peck" in the Pluckley records for 100 years or more before 1765. No births, deaths or marriages, no siblings or parents, aunts or uncles. There is no record of Lucy being born there or married there. Lucy could be a diminutive of Louisa and she may have been born there as Louisa Smith, or some such, then married a Pack elsewhere and then came back to Pluckley. Secondly there is no record of a father on George's baptism. Did he die shortly before George was born or was Lucy an unmarried mother? There is no record of a Pack death in Pluckley shortly before 1765. There are records of numerous unmarried births (including some on the same page as George) and each time the name of the child is followed by "bastard". George's name is not so followed. And if Lucy was an unmarried mother she would have been a burden on the parish who would normally return her to her parish of origin, yet Lucy died in Pluckley which was almost certainly not her parish of origin. How did Lucy survive with a son and no husband for another 30 years or so after George's birth? Thirdly the name "Lucy" is interesting. Having ploughed through many parish records I don't ever remember seeing a Lucy before, and very few Louisas. The name is common now but I don't think it was common then, in fact the only place I have seen it is in aristocratic circles. If Lucy was helped in some way then one local family of prominence was the Dering family as we have seen above and an even more well connected one was the Cornwallis family but more of these speculations later.

George's marriage

George married Elizabeth Ann Battlemore (nee Sedgwick, daughter of Joseph and Elizabeth Sedgwick) on 27th July 1788, both marking the document with a cross in the presence of Joseph Sedgwick (Elizabeth's father) and John Coppins, just 7 months after Elizabeth's first husband died (he was buried 23rd December 1787). Elizabeth had married Richard Battlemore on 5th November 1774, both marking with a cross, and they had had one child, Peter Battlemore. Elizabeth was born on 24th January 1753 and was buried 30th October 1829, aged 76.

George and Elizabeth married in Egerton and they are noted in the records as "*George Pack, bachelor, **of this parish** and Elizabeth Battlemore, widow, **of the same**"*. Banns had been published on 6th, 13th and 20th July in the conventional way. Oddly she is noted as *Elizabeth* Battlemore in the banns and *Anne* Battlemore in the wedding entry. When she married a second time she was aged 35 and George was 22 or 23.

The words "*of this parish*" might seem inconsequential today but in those days they were very important. Social security (or charity) in the 18th century was administered by the parish and to be able to access it you had to be an accepted resident of the parish. More of this later but George was certainly not born in Egerton. There are no Packs in the Egerton parish register until his marriage, and no Packs in any other of the surrounding parishes except for Pluckley (as above). George certainly wasn't a resident of Egerton by birth and yet he is noted as "*of this parish*" when he is married. It is also interesting that present at the wedding were Elizabeth's father but none of George's family. His father may well have died just before George's birth but Lucy, his probable mother, was still alive. Also present at the wedding was John Coppins who signed his name properly and who may have been the parish overseer and the relevance of this will come out later.

The Battlemores

A brief aside on the Battlemores; the family of Elizabeth's first husband. The surname does not sound unusual but a search of the name in Ancestry for the whole of Great Britain for 1841 to 1901 gives just the following 5 entries (a similar search for Pack, not a common name, for the same period produced nearly 10,000, many duplicated for the 6 censuses, and Smith produced 2.8 million). There was another Elizabeth Battlemore who married Richard Burchat on 30th May 1706 in Steyning, Sussex (and presumably took his surname), a Steven Battlemore is shown aged 20 in the 1841 census, an agricultural labourer with the Coppins family in Headcorn, Kent, but then there are no further records of him in later censuses, Charles Battlemore was born in Dartford, Kent in 1843, but then no further records, Louisa Battlemore was born in Rye in 1851 but then no more records and Frances Battlemore was noted, aged 40, in 1861, a servant in Hastings but then no more records. But Peggy Dolan found some others – one Battlemore, born in 1809, was transported in 1841 for sheep stealing, another was imprisoned for larceny in 1814, another acquitted of larceny in 1826, one married in Tonbridge in 1804 and one was under life sentence in Australia in 1828.

The search referred to above was for all of Great Britain and the only entries found were in Kent or Sussex. One possible explanation of this is that the Battlemores were a travelling family in this area, of no fixed abode, perhaps gypsies, taking temporary or seasonal work here and there and somehow missing most of the censuses which were conducted in early Spring when perhaps they were en route to the next job? As we shall see the Sedgwicks were a distinguished family and an itinerant Battlemore would seem an unlikely match for their daughter and it must be possible that Elizabeth was made pregnant by a travelling Richard Battlemore who was then forced to marry her. Elizabeth and Richard had been "married" 13 years when he died. I have been able to trace no other offspring than Peter Battlemore; this would seem to support the forced marriage theory.

The Sedgwicks

The Sedgwicks feature prominently in the Smarden Parish records. Smarden, Egerton and Pluckley all adjoin each other. The family appear to have been very active in the Smarden Baptist church and Robert Sedgwick, an uncle (?), appears to have been in charge of accounts and disciplinary matters. So George seems to have married into a highly religious and disciplined family except that Elizabeth had a transgression and when Richard Battlemore died they were determined that someone else would take responsibility for their daughter.

Did George willingly agree to marry Elizabeth Battlemore?

It goes without saying that a marriage between a 22-year-old bachelor and a 35-year-old widow with one child might be considered unusual. But this can perhaps be explained by the fact that Elizabeth was pregnant when they married. They married on 27th July 1788 and their first child, Charlotte, was baptised (date of actual birth unknown) on March 1st 1789, 7 months later. When they married Elizabeth will almost certainly have known she was pregnant and it is likely that it will have suited her, her father and the parish to then rush someone up the aisle to make an honest woman of her and so relieve the parish and her parents of the responsibility. It may be that Charlotte was not George's daughter and so the parish now would have had a widow and soon to be 2 children to support. When they married her father was present to witness the marriage; George's family were not.

George signed the marriage register with a cross. Does the cross possibly show that someone else made the entry for him! The same may be true of Elizabeth who, as a Sedgwick, presumably was educated. And could the confusion between the name "Elizabeth" being used in the banns and "Anne" in the wedding entry also indicate the involvement of others in the process; would she have made this mistake about her own name? The other witness was John Coppins who is apparently unrelated to either of them and is presumably an educated man since he signed his name properly and he may well have been the parish overseer. This will be a little like having the local mayor present and he will have been keen to have someone take responsibility for Elizabeth and perhaps to make sure George went through with it. There are some additional reasons for believing this may have been a forced marriage but first let us look at their children.

George and Elizabeth's family

They had at least 4 children

- **Charlotte** (baptised March 1ˢᵗ 1789, about 7 months after they married)
- **Silvestris** (baptised May 22nd 1791)
- **Harriet** (baptised September 1ˢᵗ 1793)
- **George** (born March 19ᵗʰ 1797 baptised 21st May 1797).

There is also a **Mary Pack** in the parish records who died 5ᵗʰ October 1821 aged 22, therefore born 1798/9 who was probably their last child (no parents were given but she was a Pack and she was mentioned in the poor book which we will come to). Elizabeth was 44 when George was born, and 46 if Mary was also her child, so it is highly likely that there were no further children.

There are a few interesting things about the above. Firstly, the parish records in those days typically showed the date of baptism and not always the date of birth, it is almost as if you only existed once you had entered the church and that entering the world was not enough.

After their births there is no trace in the records of Charlotte, Silvestris or Harriet. Most likely is that they were sent away to work as maidservants in large houses in Kent. In those days, and for a hundred or more years to come, there was very little if any education and children were expected to quickly become economically active. Sons would normally work with their fathers. Daughters would become domestics, often living-in, often far away. The three sisters may well have married but this could have been in parishes far removed from Egerton and parish records would be the only way of tracing their marriages. Since there are 106 parishes in Kent tracing them is very difficult.

Silvestris is a very unusual name both then and now. Today it is the Latin genus name for wild felines such as bobcats. Another possible derivation is from the Roman name Silvester "of the forest", its female form being Silvestra. The other names are quite traditional but note how George (senior) gives his name to his son, this will occur regularly throughout this story and especially with Georges.

There is also one very interesting anomaly with the above. For 2 of the 4 recorded children, Harriet and George, the parents are noted in the parish records as being Geo and Eliz Packe, with the trailing "e", not Pack. Could this be a link to some Packes we have already seen or was it just a mistake? We shall see that as a family they had a difficult time, although this would change, but first it is appropriate to explain the system of parish support for the needy.

The Poor and the Poor Laws

The original Elizabethan Poor Laws were passed in 1601. Paupers were to be a charge on their parish of settlement, either the parish of birth or of the husband's birth. Parishes levied a poor rate on local landowners to pay for their parish poor and these support arrangements were administered by parish overseers and were essentially informal and discretionary. It was a system of outdoor relief for the deserving poor and Houses of Correction for the undeserving.

This system changed in the 1830s. Agricultural unrest and acute concern over the spiralling numbers of claimants, and therefore costs, led to the appointment of a Royal Commission in 1832 to investigate. The main recommendations were incorporated into the New Poor Law Act of 1834, which introduced the workhouse system. A new administrative unit called the Union replaced the parish for poor relief purposes. Unions were groupings of 6 or more parishes and were run by an elected board of guardians with representatives from each parish. Indoor relief in workhouses replaced outdoor relief and workhouses were made as repellent as possible to discourage people from applying for help and as a disincentive to idleness. Parish discretion was gone forever.

The act also sanctioned a concerted effort to reduce surplus labour by assisted emigration but this time not to the US, which a number of parishes had done before the act, but only to the colonies and mainly Canada, Australia and New Zealand. In 1828 the parish offered assisted emigration to the US to George junior which may have been motivated by wishing to get rid of one of the parish's most expensive burdens, as we shall see, but it could also indicate that the parish were acting in George's interests since they would have known about the changes in the Poor Laws that would soon take place. It does not appear that George junior (his father was dead by then) ever had to endure the workhouse, indeed his fortunes would change dramatically for the better, as we shall see. The following chart shows the extent of assisted emigration from Egerton and Kent for a 10-year period. The population of Egerton at the time would have been about 800 so nearly 10% of the population emigrated. Between 1825 and 1846 over 600,000 emigrants landed in Canada (mostly assisted).

	Egerton	Kent	Destination
1837	26	320	Canada and US
1838	20	156	Canada and US
1839		251	Mainly Australia
1840	6	307	All Australia
1841		329	Mostly Australia
1842		298	Australia/New Zealand
1843		327	Australia/ New Zealand and Canada
1844		297	Mostly Canada
1845		193	All Canada
1846		62	Mostly Canada

Source; Farewell to Kent by Helen Allinson

By the early 1880s orphans and Barnados children were being sent but by the mid 1880s free and assisted passages ceased. At least 4 Packs emigrated from Egerton to North

America and their stories will be covered in later chapters. One was George junior's son, the others his grandchildren. Three certainly did not have assisted passages, the fourth might have done. Back now to George's family.

George and Elizabeth's family and the parish

George and Elizabeth and their family appear to have had a difficult time. About 150 years later another George Pack, of whom more later, began researching a history of Egerton, and particularly St James' church and the operation of relief for the poor and needy. In a later chapter there is a fuller description of how this system worked. George's widow, Pam, has kindly given me access to George's papers and the voluminous research and detail he amassed. Sadly George passed away in 1986 before his book could be finished. With such a profusion of Georges I shall call this one George the historian.

From the Poor book from 1804 onwards Elizabeth Battlemore and George Pack were regularly receiving amounts from the parish for subsistence, often specifically for Elizabeth's son (I do not know if their subsistence started in 1804 or predated this back to their marriage in 1788; it may be that George the historian only had access to books from 1804). In 1804 she received 10/- for 5 weeks for "Elizabeth Battlemore's child". By 1808 George Pack is receiving 3/- a week to have "Elizabeth Battlemore's boy" and this continues regularly from then until May 25th 1813, which is the last entry for Peter Battlemore. There is no record of Peter Battlemore's birth date but it will have been sometime between 1774 (when Elizabeth and Richard Battlemore married) and 1787 (when Richard Battlemore died) Thus by 1804 when the support starts he is at least 17 and possibly older, and the support continues until he is at least 26. Then there is no further record of him after 1813 and no census information either. Perhaps he died or perhaps he was sent to America, possibly in 1828 when, as we have seen, George's son was approached, or perhaps he resumed the itinerant life of his father's family?

Peter Battlemore did however do some work. In 1809 the Poor Book records a receipt from James Coppins for work from "Elizabeth Battlemore's child" 24 weeks, for £3/5/-. He was also assigned from the workhouse to work for 6 months for Richard Jennings of the Red Lion, Charing Heath, and in April 1817, George, his stepfather, also does some work; he was paid £1/8/- for repairing the poorhouse window.

The Poor book records extend up to 1830 for the name George Pack but George senior died in 1824 and thus some of the records are in respect of George junior. In 1828 he was given £1 for clothes and later received £5/17/6d to cover subsistence from 26th September 1828 to 27th March 1829. He does also claim lodging money (4/-) for working away. It was not uncommon for men working away to be given an allowance for their families, which presumably was repayable on return. In 1828 George junior received relief for 13 weeks at 2/6d and then a further 13 weeks totalling £4/4/6d and by now the two George Packs had cost the parish a considerable amount of money and in the same year the Vestry tried to persuade George Pack and his family to go to America. This would have been George junior since George senior passed away 4 years earlier. George junior was 31 and already had 6 children and was presumably becoming very expensive. There is a note in the parish records that he would go to America if the parish gave the same as Westwell parish, namely £20 (as opposed to the £10 offered) to land with. This clearly proved too expensive for the parish but it could have shown a certain confidence about his position that George had tried to negotiate, a point we will return to.

The 30-year period when the two Georges were receiving parish support was a dark and dismal time throughout the country. England was at war with Napoleon's France (in which, as we have seen, another Pack, Sir Denis, was very prominent) for much of this period and the cost to the country was substantial. Between 1801 and 1831 the population of Britain soared from 10 million to 16 million and in Kent the population increased by 56%. Infant mortality was decreasing and people were marrying younger and thus having larger families. Add to this the returning troops from the wars plus more efficient farming methods (which would lead to the "Swing" riots of 1830/1; spontaneous outbreaks of lawlessness and machine breaking – especially threshing machines which were replacing labourers) and unemployment increased dramatically especially among farm labourers. The rural poor were increasing and in Egerton George the historian notes that numbers receiving parish charity nearly trebled from an average of about 8 fifty years earlier to nearly 30 by the time the system changed (see next paragraph). There were nearly 300,000 inmates of workhouses in 1841 in England and Wales (this was in the middle of the 1837 – 42 trade depression, one in 50 of the total population), and by 1851 the figure was still nearly 130,000. Despite this the Georges, father and son, were remarkably well treated and their costs must have been a considerable drain on parish resources. For a number of reasons there must have been something unusual about George senior and his family to warrant this largesse and/or he must have had some substantial and influential support from the authorities. One small example; in 1828 there is a parish note "George Pack wants 2/- for an axe, 3/- granted"!!! The exclamation marks were added by George the historian. It should also be noted that if Lucy Pack was George's mother then she must have received support in Pluckley if she had no husband and at least one child to bring up. As a rough guide to monetary conversions £10 in 1830 is the equivalent of £760 in 2008. Much of George's support was before 1830 and, bringing the index up to 2010, a factor of 80 would appear appropriate.

More on George and Elizabeth's family

As we saw above the parish, in their records, continued to refer to Elizabeth as "Battlemore" after she had married George in 1788 and become a Pack. This could have been to link her with their charge, Peter Battlemore, or was it that the marriage for some reason was disputed? This is compounded by an entry in the Poor book for 1804 recording 2 trips to Charing and the expenses and carrying home of Mary Battlemore, who had presumably been ill. This Mary was born in 1798/9 and was certainly Mary Pack, daughter of George, so why is she recorded as Mary Battlemore? Could it be that the marriage with George was only ever a marriage of convenience enforced by the parish in an unsuccessful attempt to try and keep Elizabeth and her son off their books. If the Egerton parish did force George into marriage with Elizabeth Battlemore then he may have made such a fuss that the parish then overlooked the forced marriage and continued to treat Elizabeth as a Battlemore until many years later when George appears to have accepted the situation. Then even more intriguingly in 1793, when the third child, Harriet, is born, 5 years after they "married", the parish do recognise the marriage and George and Elizabeth are recorded as parents but they are recorded as "Geo and Elizabeth Packe", and this was also the case for George junior.

The parish support given to George was highly unusual

In those days there were very strict parish rules about recipients of parish charity and the fundamental one was that you had to be an established resident. George was not an established resident and was certainly born elsewhere, possibly Pluckley. In normal circumstances he would have been escorted back to where he came from if he could not support himself. There is one exception to this - apprentices. If a craftsman takes on an apprentice and the apprenticeship lasts for at least 40 days then that apprentice becomes resident in the parish of his Master. There were cases of parents prepared to pay money to get rid of their children, sometimes as young as 7, in this way and evidence of severe mistreatment of apprentices. But this is unlikely for George in view of what happens later. The research done by George the historian confirms the incredible generosity of the parish in supporting George and Elizabeth and their family for the best part of 30 years. Of course the parish overseers were Christian and charitable men but their funds came from local landowners who might take a different view of this drain on their resources and the overseers were only appointed for 6 or 12-month periods to prevent favouritism. In those difficult times parishes only took responsibility for their own needy parishioners and not for others, who were returned to their own parishes. Given that George was a discretionary cost, since he did not come from Egerton and could have been returned, the landowners who paid the rates must have agreed to support George and his family and the largest landowner by far and thus the largest contributor to parish funds was Lord Cornwallis and his consent must have been active and not merely passive. We will return to this later but there must have been something exceptional about George for this to happen and soon something rather extraordinary happens to George's son, also George, as we shall see next.

Things look up for George junior

In the early 19th century most sons took their father's trade; with virtually no formal education your father was your only source of career's advice. George junior's father had existed for most of his working life on parish support and the occasional odd job and thus had few skills to pass on. Yet in 1841 George junior is noted in the census as a farmer living at Borehill with 7 of his children. In the census Borehill is marked as Egerton but there is nowhere in the village today with that name. By the 1851 census George and family are living at Link farm and he is a farmer of 60 acres, which in those days was a considerable size. Let us first look at Link House and Link Farm.

Link House and farm in Egerton

Link House was built in 1420. Originally it would have had 2 living areas at each side and a central common area. There were no chimneys originally only an opening in the roof for smoke from the fire to escape. There would have been no glass in the windows either. Chimneys, fireplaces and glass for the windows would be added about 100 years later. Link House was owned by the Pemble family for many years, then Mary Dadson and John Gladdish. By 1817 the Cornwallis estate had bought it and it appears in the secretary's accounts.

England, in the early 19th century, was not a land of opportunity, unlike the USA, which is why so many went westward, and by and large whatever social station you were born into was where you remained. It would have been almost impossible to go from the Parish poorhouse to the prosperity of Link house without some help and the help must have come from the Cornwallis estate.

In the early 1830s the system of poor support changed in England and parishes no longer made discretionary bequests and instead the Victorian system of residential workhouses was introduced. Something had to be done or George junior and his family would end up in the workhouse. As we saw earlier in 1828 the Parish tried to persuade George junior and his family to go to the USA (probably with the best of motives realising the threat of the workhouse) without success, and so something now had to be done. With the change in the Poor laws whoever was sponsoring George would lose their influence. Sometime before 1817 George junior married Keturah (Palmer) who appears to have been a highly practical woman (by the 1861 census when George had died, Keturah, at the age of 63, was the farmer of 60 acres).

Link House today.

In the 1853 report to the Trustees on the estates in Kent and Sussex of the late Earl Cornwallis there is an account of George Pack renting Link house and part of Goodale (72 acres) for £60 p.a. Goodale is the former name of Egerton House so the land must have been between Link house and Egerton House. "The farmhouse is old but in good and substantial repair, as are all the farm buildings. The land requires draining. It is well farmed."

Cornwallis must have been the hidden hand behind the parish support given to George senior and junior, and perhaps Lucy in Pluckley, but with the change in the system support could no longer be given through the parish and a different way had to be found and that was Link House. George senior died in 1824 and was certainly receiving parish support until the end. His son George was born in 1797 and was receiving parish support until about 1830 when the system changed. But then by 1841 George junior and his family were resident at Borehill and then by 1851 they are in Link House and George is a farmer of 60 acres. Where did George get his farming skills from, perhaps his wife's family? As we shall see next Link farm was a prosperous farm so how did this remarkable transformation in fortunes come about? We will speculate later on the Cornwallis link but first the value of the help given to George junior is then demonstrated by what happened when he died, as described below.

The "Battle" for Link House

George junior got very lucky sometime between 1841 and 1851 (and perhaps before 1841 if Borehill is anything to do with Cornwallis), when he and his family moved into Link house, which was the property of the Cornwallis estate. George died in November 1860, aged 63. The reactions of his family to his death are very interesting. We are jumping generations a bit here and will come back properly to George junior's family in the next chapter; this just describes what appears to have been a family battle for George's inheritance, which must have been quite considerable.

Of George's children James, the eldest, a builder, having moved out of his parent's house to marry in 1840, and having lived for 10 years or more at Pack cottages, then moved back into Link House with his family. George, the second born son, showed no interest, having moved away to Sheerness. Charles, third born son, was nearly 40 and still living at home in Link House and unmarried when his father died. 3 years later in 1863 he married Sarah Hopkins. Nathaniel was 35 when his father died and already had 6 children and had left home but then he moved back into Link House with his family.

Edward had emigrated to the US in 1852 and returned in 1857 to marry and then return to the US with his new wife shortly afterwards where their first daughter was born, but they then returned to Egerton sometime before 1861 and were resident at Link House by 1861. By 1871 they have moved out to Maidstone and then later still Edward returned with his family to the US. William was 36, unmarried and still living at home when his father died. A year later he married Susannah Charlotte Hopkins and they are living at Link House and then in 1871 they are at Baker farm and by 1881 at Newland Green Farm with 13 acres. With many of the family moving back into Link House, and quite a few who haven't yet left, it must have been pretty crowded! The 1861 census records 25 adults and children resident there. The writer has had the privilege of visiting Link House and whilst it is a big property this will have been a considerable squeeze.

In the 1861 census, after George had died, Keturah, his wife, is shown as head of the family and the farmer of the 60 acres. By 1871 she has moved out and is living in Pleasant valley and she died in 1876. George and Keturah never owned Link House and farm. How then to explain the return of many of the family? Could it have been just to help Mum in her hour of need and to help with the farm? But James, a builder, and Nathaniel, a butcher, and Edward, a carpenter, had no farming skills. It is difficult to avoid the conclusion that they all came back to make sure that they got their share of their parent's prosperity and that none of their siblings, Charles or William in particular, who were still living at home in Link House, benefited unduly at their expense. This could indeed have been a family battle. What else could explain Edward, in particular, returning from the US only a couple of years after he had married and emigrated and then sticking around for the best part of 20 years before returning again to the US? And presumably Charles and William, who have been helping their father on the farm, and are therefore best placed of all to inherit it, now realise that they had better get married too; both are in their late thirties and have left it late, but if they are to inherit Link farm they will need a wife and family (it may even have been a condition of the lease that there had to be a married couple). They both then visit Newland Green to find a Hopkins daughter, there being no better farming pedigree than a Hopkins.

The winner of the "battle" is Charles who becomes the farmer of Link farm and resident of Link House. But in fact most of the children seem to have benefited from their parents. George and Keturah left modest amounts when they died. This must mean that George had left everything to Keturah before he died, including his farming rights to Link farm. And then Keturah must have distributed her assets before she died. James started a building business, Charles continued to farm Link farm, Nathaniel started a butchers business and William ended up with his own farm in years to come. Edward, by 1881 is a Master

Carpenter and has also apparently done well. They may well have helped their daughters as well but I have no details.

George and Keturah must have generated some reasonable wealth to have helped their children in this way. Only 30 years earlier George was dependent on parish charity. How did this remarkable transformation occur? Considerable prosperity was generated by George junior and this would have been inconceivable without some sort of help. A name that has cropped up several times is that of Cornwallis and he must have been involved in the happenings above but there is no evidence that he knew George Pack and one can only assume that someone else pleaded George's case with him. We will look first at Charles Cornwallis and then speculate on what the link may have been.

The Cornwallis connection

Charles, 2nd Earl Cornwallis (1738 – 1805) is best known for his role in the American wars of independence, which ended with his surrender at Yorktown on October 19th 1781 heralding the eventual birth of the United States of America. Cornwallis is sometimes portrayed as the man who lost America. This is perhaps unfair. He was poorly supported by the mother country, which was perhaps more concerned with unfolding revolutionary events much closer to home in France. Their continued faith in Cornwallis was shown when he was next sent to India as Governor-General in 1786 and then was recalled in 1798 to help quell rebellions in Ireland. He was Lord Lieutenant of Ireland from June 1798 to 1801. During this period a certain Denis Pack was also in Ireland and would have almost certainly known Lord Cornwallis. Sir Denis Pack, as he would become, has been described in an earlier chapter. In 1805 Cornwallis was sent back to India but died shortly after arriving. The Cornwallis family was a very distinguished one. Charles' uncles, who were twins, were Frederick, Archbishop of Canterbury and Edward, (1713-1776) Lieutenant General and Governor of Nova Scotia, and his brother was Admiral Sir William Cornwallis, prominent in the Napoleonic wars.

Cornwallis had extensive family estates in Kent and Sussex and owned a substantial amount of the land and property around Egerton and he was the Member of Parliament for Wye in Kent. Wye is about 12 miles southwest of Canterbury and 10 miles east of Egerton. His uncle, Frederick, was Archbishop of Canterbury from 1768 to 1783. Lord Cornwallis knew Kent and must have known Denis Pack.

Cornwallis died in 1805 and the parish support for the 2 Georges extended beyond this until about 1830 and then George junior's occupancy of Link house took place sometime after 1841 and so one assumes that the Cornwallis support continued beyond the 2nd Earl and through his family and successors. But who pleaded George's case with the Cornwallis family? Later we will speculate on some possible candidates. The Cornwallis family have been generous in many ways over many years. Some small examples in Egerton were the donation of land for the building of the village school (now replaced by a more modern school in 1971) and the donation of a village hall and recreation field in 1920. Cornwallis was honoured by a memorial in St Paul's Cathedral, which is pictured below together with the inscription.

Next we will examine George junior's Baptist connections.

Charles Earl Cornwallis (1738-1805) in St Paul's Cathedral

TO THE MEMORY OF
CHARLES MARQUIS CORNWALLIS,
GOVERNOR GENERAL OF BENGAL,
WHO DIED 5TH OCTOBER 1805, AGED 66 AT GHAZEEPORE IN THE PROVINCE OF BENARES,
IN HIS PROGRESS TO ASSUME THE COMMAND OF THE ARMY IN THE FIELD.

THIS MONUMENT
IS ERECTED AT THE PUBLIC EXPENCE
IN TESTIMONY OF HIS HIGH AND DISTINGUISHED PUBLIC CHARACTER,
HIS LONG AND EMINENT SERVICES BOTH AS A SOLDIER AND A STATESMAN
AND THE UNWEARIED ZEAL WITH WHICH HIS EXERTIONS WERE EMPLOYED
IN THE LAST MOMENT OF HIS LIFE
TO PROMOTE THE INTEREST AND HONOR OF HIS COUNTRY.

George's Baptist connections

George junior was certainly a Baptist. After the original Baptist church in Egerton Forstal burned down in 1824 it would appear George junior attended the Smarden Baptist church but then later returned to Egerton, as there are records from October 26th 1836 of the formation of the Particular Baptist Church at Egerton Forstal. George Pack was one of the members "dismissed" from Tilden Smarden specially for the purpose of refounding Egerton. On January 5th 1840 George Pack was appointed Deacon, a position he held for most of the next 20 years. At a church meeting held on March 15th 1868 to discuss fees for the graveyard, Charles Pack, George's son, was the church secretary. Most of his descendants for the next 50 years would be Baptists. When George became Deacon in 1840 this was only 10 years or so since he had been dependent on parish support and was about the time that he and his family were moving into Link house. It was truly a transformation in fortunes. George senior was also a Baptist and is noted in the "transcribed" church book of the Smarden Baptist church 1640-1845 as being present at communions. George senior's burial place has never been found. He is recorded in the parish records as having died in 1824. The Baptist chapel at Egerton Forstal burnt down in 1824. Was George senior's burial place destroyed or was he reburied somewhere else?

There are several things that may have attracted the Georges, father and son, to the Baptists. George senior's wife, Elizabeth, was a Sedgwick by birth and her family were prominent in the Baptist church. But there could also have been another reason.

The Church of England is described as the established Church. This means that it undertakes some semi-official state functions. In years gone by it had many more of them than today. In George's time it would have been effectively the local council, social services and the police and we have seen that it was responsible for the raising of funds and then their distribution for the poor and needy of the parish. George senior may well have preferred not to mix with his paymasters. If the parish also originally forced him into marriage with Elizabeth Battlemore he will have had an additional reason to go elsewhere.

Who pleaded with Cornwallis on behalf of the two Georges, father and son?

As we have seen George senior was very generously treated by the parish, as was his son who then, when the Poor Laws were about to change, was given the use of Link house and farm. Cornwallis will have been the largest single contributor by far to parish funds and was the owner of Link farm. So somehow the fortunes of the 2 Georges were intertwined with those of Cornwallis, but how? There is no evidence that either of them knew Cornwallis. I must emphasize that at this point we enter the world of conjecture; there are a number of fanciful theories but no certainty.

In the parish records there is an entry for a James Pack in 1817 paying £3/4/4d *into* the Egerton parish accounts. And then again in 1823 he is paying rates for property with a rateable value of £8/10/-. There is also a James Pack who is recorded as buried in Egerton on March 31st 1844 aged 84; he was thus born in 1760, 6 or 7 years earlier than George. Could he be George's brother or a relation? There is also a James Pack born to James and Elizabeth on 1st January 1762 who might just fit the dates. He was born in Huntingdonshire, which means he could be a descendant of Sir Christopher Packe and this might explain 2 of George's children being noted as having Pack**e** parents. As we have seen this was a spelling adopted by Sir Christopher and not, so far as I know, used by any other Pack families. Sadly there is no further information to be found about James Pack but it would be rather odd for 2 brothers or cousins to be living in the same village one living wealthily and the other on the bread line. Is it possible that James was bankrolling the parish for his relation? And if James was part of Sir Christopher Packe's family then he may well have known the Cornwallis family through the public lives of distinguished families and connections.

In a previous chapter we looked at the distinguished military career of Sir Denis Pack. Sir Denis Pack would have certainly known Lord Cornwallis during their military careers, they were both stationed in Ireland for a time. Cornwallis was Lord Lieutenant of Ireland from 1798 to 1801 a time when Sir Denis was also there. Were George, or Lucy or James (above) related to Sir Denis in some way that I haven't found, and Sir Denis pleaded their case?

Cornwallis' uncle was Frederick, the Archbishop of Canterbury from 1768 to 1783, was there some ecclesiastical link? In an earlier chapter we met Richard Pack, Dean of Ossory. As head of the Anglican Communion Frederick will surely have known Richard Pack. Were George, or Lucy or James (above) related to Richard in some way that I haven't found, and Richard or his family pleaded their case? Frederick's accession to Canterbury was, apparently, largely due to the support of the 3rd Duke of Grafton, Augustus Henry Fitzroy. The family seat of the Graftons is at Wakefield Lodge, which is part of the Grafton estate and very close to Prestwold, family seat of the descendants of Sir Christopher Packe, as we have seen in a previous chapter. Is it too much to believe that all these family connections were in some way used to help George and his family?

But with all these distinguished names possibly helping George how does he end up possibly in a forced marriage and certainly living on parish charity? It seems quite likely that he was totally impractical and perhaps naïve and possibly simple. And there is another variation on this and that is that George, or perhaps Lucy, was a "Remittance man". If wealthy families had a troublesome child they would often send the child away, often to North America or Australasia, with a periodic remittance to sustain them and make sure they did not come back. It is all conjecture and all I have done is to hopefully prove that the Cornwallis family were behind the generosity shown to George and his family and then try and find links between other Packs and Cornwallis but without a shred of proof.

There is yet another piece of the jigsaw to mention. George J.E. Pack (1926 - 1987), George the Historian, spent much time researching the parish records with a particular interest in the operation of poor relief. I never met him but am told, by Tony Turner, that he expressed the view that the Packs came originally from Scotland. This view came, I believe, from his contacts with Eli Liebow, mentioned in an earlier chapter, and the quote from Arthur Conan Doyle's mother:

"My mother, please observe, was born Catherine Pack. Her uncle was Major-General Sir Denis Pack, who led Pack's brigade at Waterloo. And the seventeenth-century Packs, as everyone knows or ought to know, were allied in marriage with Mary Percy of Balintemple, heir of the Irish branch of the Percy's of Northumberland. In that wooden chest are the papers of our descent for six hundred years; from the marriage of Henry Percy, sixth Baron, with Eleanor, niece of King Henry the Third".

Arthur Conan Doyle was born in 1859 in Edinburgh where his parents had lived for some time. Eli Liebow spent much time in Edinburgh researching his book and wrote frequently to George the Historian. I believe it was this connection that led George to conclude that the Packs came from Scotland. The full history of Conan Doyle and his Pack connections is covered in a later chapter. Suffice to say for now that George the Historian, who had spent many years going through the parish records, had concluded that the Packs, and George, were not originally an Egerton or Kentish family.

We saw in an earlier chapter that Richard Pack's son, William, was the great grandfather of Arthur Conan Doyle. Doyle had a number of links with the Egerton area. He is reputed to have lived for a while in Tenterden, which is close to Egerton. He also studied to be a doctor under Dr Joe Bell at Edinburgh. Bell is acknowledged as the model used by Doyle for Sherlock Holmes with his forensic approach to investigation. Bell and Doyle knew each other well. Egerton House was owned and occupied until the 1950s by Major and Mrs Stisted. Mrs Stisted was the daughter of Dr Joe Bell.

Is this simply a remarkable coincidence? Is it possible that Doyle's ancestor, William Percy Pack had some connection with Egerton, perhaps through George or Lucy and somehow 100 years later the Bell/Stisted family pursued the connection, perhaps at Doyle's suggestion, and through a family link for Mrs Stisted bought Egerton House? This connection is explored further in the chapter on local personalities.

There is one final connection to explore; Thomas Pack of Whitechapel, bell founder, described in an earlier chapter. Whitechapel installed 3 of the 6 bells at St James' church in Egerton in 1759. They almost certainly installed the bells at Pluckley because Whitechapel was engaged to service the bells in the 19th century and it would be unusual to use another bell founder. The date of the installation at Pluckley is unknown but may well have been at about the same time, as Whitechapel was very active in Kent generally at that time, as we saw in an earlier chapter. Thomas Pack is thus likely to have been in the area at about the time that George was born in 1766/7. Thomas Pack is believed to have married Elizabeth Oliver in 1754 and he died in 1781. When Thomas died George would have been about 13 or 14. If George and/or Lucy are in some way related to Thomas then Thomas would have had the wealth and position to support George and/or access Cornwallis. Beyond this we can all speculate about things that might have happened; all your writer can do is point out all these remarkable coincidences.

There are some other Packs around in Kent

In the course of this research I have come across a number of other Packs not connected, as far as I know, with any of the foregoing and I mention them here just for the record and in case we can ever join them up via the web site.

The first arises from a note made by George the historian from the Expense book of a James Masters Esq in **1657-8** "Given to Mr ffurner for drawing ye lease and release from John Pack to me, for a cottage and 4 acres of woodland which cost me £11 05 00". This could have been John Packe, son of Sir Christopher Packe. I have no birth date for him but it will have been sometime after 1638 when Sir Christopher's first wife, Jane Newman died. If this is him then by 1682 he must have died since he is not mentioned in Sir Christopher's final will.

There is a Thomas Pack who married Katherine Dimont on 19th October **1671** at Brenchley, Kent, could these be the grandparents of George? I have found no further details.

Then again readers may remember in an earlier chapter that Christopher Pack, had a son Christopher, who also had a son Christopher, born about 1685, and he married Mary Randolph in **1726** in Canterbury. In **1734** an Isaac Pack is recorded in Ashford.

There was a John Pack who married Margaret Jeffrey (born 1723) round about **1740** in Tonbridge. They had 4 children; Elizabeth (born 1745) John (1744) Mary (1745) and James (dob unknown).

Then there is a George Pack, discovered on the CLDS website, who married Ann Waghorn in Tonbridge, Kent on 27th December **1756**. Was this George the son of Christopher (above) and the father of Egerton George? Sadly there are no further details.

Then there is a James Pack who was christened in Chatham, Kent on 15th April **1770**. His parents were Thomas and Elizabeth Pack (nee Baker) who married on 30th December 1751 at Pembury, Kent. Thomas and Elizabeth had a remarkable 17 children but none of them was a George.

There is a Thomas Pack who was born in **1789** in Harrietsham, Kent. His wife was Keturah, she was 5 years younger than him, and they had at least 6 children; Henry (1825), Jane (1827), Charles (1829), Harriet (1843), George (1846) and another Henry (1848). George (who was born in Frinstead) would marry Mary Anne (born in Egerton) and in 1871 he had a stepson Edward Hopkins (born 1859 in Lenham) implying Mary Anne was the widow of a Hopkins.

In the **1790** poll books for Kent Tony Turner found 3 Packs; George (from Yalding), William (Braestead) and Thomas (Wye). There are no further details. This George is certainly not ours since the poll books recorded election results and only landowners could vote. It appears this George had land at Yalding but was resident in Tonbridge.

In **1802** a Hercules Packe is recorded in Canterbury and then again in **1832**, the same person or his son?

The Archdeaconry court of Canterbury Index of Wills contains the following and they are all exceptionally difficult to read and for now are just noted for the record.

Surname	First name	Parish	Date range	Ref	Page
Pack	Ann	Bobbing	1768-72	98	549
Pack	Eleanor	Bobbing	1796-06	103	541
Pack	Elizabeth	Stockbury	1712-17	82	298
Pack	Isaac	Bobbing	1796-1806	103	324
Pack	James	Frinstead	1849-1853	112	189
Pack	John	Chartham	1715-19	83	41
Pack	John	Borden	1768-72	98	355
Pack	John	Lenham	1849-53	112	383
Pack	Thomas	Faversham	1828-31	108	219
Pack	William	Borden	1778-83	100	296
Pack	William	Chilham	1807-12	104	146
Packe	Christopher	Canterbury	1796-06	103	321

In the Tonbridge parish records there are a number of Packs

There were **John and Mary Pack** to whom were born James (born November 26th 1792) Joseph (August 14th 1794) Samuel (December 7th 1796) and Phoebe (March 10th 1797).

And **Thomas and Mary Pack** to whom were born George (February 17th 1793) and Edmund (April 1801)

And **Richard and Priscilla Pack** to whom were born Harriet (3rd July 1803)

And **James and Cecilia Pack** to whom were born Charlotte (4th June 1807)

And **Philip and Elizabeth Pack** to whom were born and Edward (30th November 1803) and James (8th November 1807).

James Pack was baptised in Chatham 15th April 1770. Thomas and Elizabeth Pack were married 30th December 1751 in Pembury. And in Harrietsham the Thomas Pack born in 1789 and noticed by Tony is actually Peck in 1788.

And **George and Maria Pack** to whom were born Anna (1st January 1809) and Susannah (12th May 1811)

And **William and Hannah Pack** to whom was born Maria (23rd January 1811)

And finally **Sarah Pack** bore Elizabeth (Oct 22 1797) by Nathaniel Tompsett.

Summary

Of necessity this has been a long and dense chapter containing a number of suppositions that have tried to explain what happened. A brief summary may help to keep the big picture in mind. George was born in 1766/7 probably the son of Lucy Pack. He was probably born in Pluckley. His father is unknown and it is arguable that his mother was unmarried. He married Elizabeth Battlemore in Egerton in 1788. There are reasons for believing this was a forced marriage arranged by the parish or possibly by Elizabeth's father. George and Elizabeth then lived most of their married lives on parish support. Their son, George, also lived on parish support but then, just as parish support was about to change to a much harsher regime, he and his family moved to Link House and became farmers, something he had no experience of. The common factor behind all this must have been Cornwallis who was the largest contributor to parish funds and was the owner of Link house and farm. This generated considerable prosperity for the family as was demonstrated by the battle for Link farm. We then tried to speculate on why the Cornwallis family might have been so generous to George and his family.

Now we move on to the rest of George junior's story.

Chapter 12 - George Pack Jnr and Keturah
The Family Take Off Begins

Newspapers began in England in about 1717 but would not become mass circulation until literacy increased and it is unlikely they were read widely in Egerton for another 200 years or so, indeed Charles Hooker (of whom more later) notes that there were only three people taking newspapers in the village in December 1898. Radio broadcasting did not begin until 1926 and television in 1936. Thus the sources of names tended to be either the Bible (the church was a much more significant part of everyday life then), prominent national figures or family names. The most popular name in the Pack family, and probably throughout the country, was George. This cannot be unrelated to the fact that over the 238 years between 1714 and 1952 there was a King George on the throne of England for 158 years of that time. Indeed from 1714 to 1830 there were four King George's in a row. In Egerton even the local pub is The George. If George was good enough for the Royal family then it was clearly good enough also for the Pack family and we move on in this chapter to the next George Pack, his story having been partially told in the last chapter, and there will be many other Georges following him.

George (senior) had 3 daughters, about whom little is known, and only 1 son but now George (junior) has 8 sons and 5 daughters! In the 1841 census George and Keturah and family are the only Packs in Egerton, George's parents having both died by then, but now they and their children are about to correct that.

George Pack (junior) was born on March 19th 1797 and died November 19th 1860 aged 63. His will was proved by oaths from Thomas Fowle and John Turk on 21st March 1861 and his effects were under £600. He married Keturah (Palmer, daughter of Nathaniel and Barbara Palmer, they had 12 children and Keturah was their last-born) who was born on 2nd April 1798 and died on 30th September 1876 aged 78. Her will was proved on 10th December 1876 by Edward White, carpenter, and David Sands Davis, farmer, and her effects were under £300. There is no trace of their marriage in the Egerton (Anglican) records; they were both Baptists but the omission from the official records is strange.

The name "Keturah" is from the bible. Keturah was the second wife of Abraham whom he married after Sarah died. Keturah had 6 children by Abraham. Biblical names were commonly used in earlier times. Keturah is pictured below. The picture was probably taken sometime after 1860 when George died otherwise he would surely have been in it. There will be a number of family pictures from Elsie Mackethan's collection. As we shall see a number of Packs emigrated to the USA (Elsie is part of one such family) and they probably wanted to keep in touch and asked for the pictures to be sent to them. They will have left a peaceful village where everyone knew everyone else for a bustling metropolis where no one knew anyone else. The large-scale immigration to the USA brought Russians, Irish, Jews and nationalities from all over Europe and communication must have been a problem. In these circumstances some pictures from the Old Country may have been reassuring.

Modern black and white photographic techniques were available by the 1820s and by the 1860s there had begun a boom in portrait studios. The first Kodak camera appeared in 1888 and finally in 1907 commercial colour film had been invented. It will have been fairly unusual for a family to be as well documented as the Packs have been and even more unusual that so many of the pictures survived.

Picture of Keturah courtesy of Elsie Hopton MacKethan

George and Keturah had 13 children (2 of whom died young and strangely it was their namesakes that died) and set up the following production line with a new child every 2/3 years for 24 years. Their first-born son was called James, and it is said that he was born out of wedlock. George and Keturah were approximately 19 and 18 when they married. Did they call their first-born James because he was illegitimate and then wait for their first legitimate son before conferring the traditional family name of George? And then when the first George dies young, the name is given to the next born, to ensure a George continues in the family? Their 13 children are set out below.

- James (baptised May 4th 1817)
- George (born 31st Jan 1819 died 2nd Feb 1819)
- George (born 6th Jan 1820)
- Charles (born 12th Dec 1821)
- Nathaniel (born 1st May 1825) – named after Keturah's father?
- Sophia (born 2nd Feb 1827)
- Harriett (born 13th March 1829)
- Edward (born 28th April 1831)
- Keturah (born 8th Jan 1833 died 11th Sept 1833)
- Horatio (born 25th Sept 1834)
- Mary (born 18th July 1836)
- William (born 25th June 1838)
- Elizabeth (born 10th June 1840).

At that time, in the early 19th century, most sons took their father's trade; with virtually no formal education your father was your only source of careers advice (compulsory

78

elementary education in England started in 1870 up to the age of 10. It was increased to age 11 in 1893, 12 in 1899, 14 in 1918, 15 in 1947 and 16 in 1974). With his lack of practical skills, George's father had existed for most of his married life on parish charity and the occasional odd job and thus had few skills to pass on. Yet in the 1841 census George junior was a farmer living at Borehill with 7 of their children. In the census Borehill is marked as Egerton, but there is nowhere in the village today with that name. The entry for Borehill immediately follows Court Lodge, which is in Stonebridge Road, the other side of the village from Link farm. By the 1851 census they were living at Link Farm with 6 of their children and he is a farmer of 60 acres, which is quite a large farm for those days and they will have been prosperous and almost wealthy. In fact there is an interesting twist in 1848 when the tables appear to have completely turned and George Pack is paid 4/6d for conveying Selina Ann Ashbee to the Union Workhouse. He is described as a "constable" which probably means rate collector. This is about 20 years after he was dependent on the parish and now he is working for them.

Link House and farm were rented by George from the Lord Cornwallis estate. We have speculated in the previous chapter as to how this came about. Keturah was the last born of 12 Palmer children and neither her background nor George's seem appropriate to running a large farm and they would surely not have been the obvious tenants. The only possibility is that George and Keturah were favoured by the property owners, the Cornwallis estate. By the 1861 census George had died and Keturah was the farmer of 60 acres with many of her family to help.

By 1871 Keturah is living on her own at Pleasant Valley. Pleasant Valley is an area of Egerton about a mile by road from Link farm, and is where most of the Egerton-based Packs lived for some time to come. The original name for this area was Little Houses and this name is occasionally still used today. The history and reasons for the name of Little Houses is set out in a later chapter where it is more appropriately explained.

George's father was certainly not a farmer and many later Packs were builders, carpenters or labourers. Did George (junior) get farming knowledge from his wife's family, the Palmers? The farming knowledge acquired by George is not then passed on, for the most part, to their children, most of whom did not pursue farming careers. This is actually not surprising. The farm would almost certainly have been arable. It would need large numbers of seasonal workers for sowing and harvesting but probably only 1 or 2 permanent labourers throughout the year. With such a large family most of the children appear to conclude that they will have to pursue other trades. There are some exceptions, as we shall see below.

Many of their children were just as productive in their families as George and Keturah, as we shall see, and when she died in 1876 Keturah had at least 50 grandchildren and at least 10 great grandchildren. In fact it could have been considerably more than this because I have not been able to find any marriage details for Sophia, Harriett or Elizabeth, for reasons explained elsewhere. If they were as productive as their siblings then the totals could be half as much again. In the space of 50 years the Pack population in Egerton had gone from 1 to possibly nearly 100.

There were also some curious family relationships. James 's first born was George and he was born in the same year, 1841, as his aunt, Elizabeth, James 's sister. In later generations, as the family tree becomes more complicated, this will become more pronounced. And with the same names cropping up time and again it must have been very difficult to know who was who. Add to this the fact that the Packs mostly were builders and labourers, and thus in competition with each other, and my father's comment about "the other Packs", two unrelated families with the same name, becomes understandable.

Note also how evenly spaced the children are. In those days there were of course no modern birth control methods. What there was in most villages was a herbalist who could mix concoctions for all sorts of ailments including unwanted pregnancies. The favourite for this was apparently a concoction based on birch bark. In this way the mothers could decide which pregnancies to keep and which to abort so as to keep the spacings consistent with housing space and resources.

So far telling the story has been relatively easy, when information has been available, but it now gets far more complicated with 11 surviving children to account for above, and some more large families to come. The following chart explains how this will be dealt with.

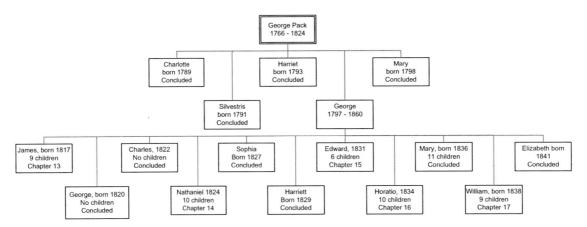

"Concluded", in Charlotte's box, and others, indicates that their story is now told as far as possible and is pursued no further. For Nathaniel and his 10 children Chapter 14 will explore his family tree as far as possible and for as many generations as possible, and the same for Edward, Horatio and William in their chapters. The following generations of James, my ancestor, will be explored in later chapters with another chart to assist understanding. The task is simplified somewhat by the fact that 2 sons, George and Charles did not have any offspring and for three of the four daughters, Sophia, Harriett and Elizabeth, it has not been possible to trace marriages or children. The fourth daughter, Mary, is described below. The following thumbnail sketches of all 11 children are followed by more detailed trees in later chapters for James, Nathaniel, Edward, Horatio and William, who are all the second generation after George senior.

James (1817 – 1890) married Frances Page in 1840 at the Baptist chapel. Over the next 21 years they had 9 children as follows; George (1841) Frances (1843) Charles (1845) Eliza (1847) Edward (1850) Robert (1852) Maria (1855) Elizabeth (1858) and Ezra (1861). There are some interesting stories in their family, 3 children emigrated to the USA, George, Edward and Maria, and three, Charles, Frances and Ezra, met with serious misfortune. James' story is continued in the next chapter.

George (1820 – 1901) married (date unknown) Maria Warren (1813 – 1888, born in Portsmouth). George is noted in the 1881 census living in Gravesend with Nathaniel Palmer, uncle, while Maria is living at 137 Shortlands Road Sittingbourne; it sounds as if they have split up. In 1901 he is living in Sheppey, aged 81, with Horatio, his brother, 66, and Harriett, 40, Horatio's daughter. In this same census he describes himself as "pensioner". It is difficult to know what pension this was as State pensions and company pensions would not appear until the 20th century. George and Maria did not have children. Maria may have been a widow, she was 7 years older than George, and she could have already raised a family before they were married. This George is now the third in a row.

Charles (1822 – 1897) does not appear to have had children either. He married Sarah, probably in 1863 when he was 41 and she was 33 (almost certainly Sarah Hopkins, since in the 1891 census Frances Hopkins, niece, is staying with them). There were several Pack/Hopkins marriages, as we shall see. We have seen how Charles becomes the tenant of Link house and farm sometime before 1871 and he and Sarah then occupy the property for the next 30 years or so; Charles died in 1897 and is interred at the Mount Zion Chapel and by the 1901 census Sarah is living on her own at Link Farm although she died very shortly afterwards and was interred at Mount Zion on April 30th 1901.

In the 1875-6 Report and rental valuation of the estates of the Right Hon Viscount and Viscountess Holmesdale (Cornwallis' successors) Link farm is "in fair repair. The buildings consist of very old Barn, Yards, Stable Piggery etc and the Rental valuation is £128 10s less tithe rent charges of £16 18s giving a net rental of £111 12s. The account in the report is shown below.

Link Farm — Charles Pack

Nos	Name or description				Egerton A	R	P	Intaunels A	R	P	Outbou[…] A	R
1655	Footway Field	Q. A	Q.	A	9	3	33	9	2	7	9	3
1656	Link Meadow		Q.	P	3	2	6	3	1	17	3	2
1657	Hopgarden & Footway Field		Q.	A	5	3	0	5	2	7	5	3
1658	Peartree Field		Q.	A	5	3	33	5	2	22	5	3
1659	Road Field		Q.	A	4	1	31	4	„	24	4	1
1660	Gage Meadow		Q.	P	2	3	14	2	2	27	2	3
1661	Lower Calves Field		Q.	P	3	3	„	3	2	16	3	3
1662	Baker Hilly Field		Q.	A	5	3	10	5	2	17	5	3
1663	Banky Field		Q.	P	7	„	34	6	3	23	7	„
1664	Orchard		+	P	„	3	2	„	2	27	„	3
1665	Roundabout		Q.	H	2	1	23	2	„	29	2	1
1666	Homestead				„	3	0	„	„	„	„	3
1667	Barn Field		Q.	P	4	1	„	4	„	13	4	1
1668	Orchard		+	P	„	1	22	„	1	11	„	1
1669	Palmer Field		Q.	A	8	1	20	8	„	5	8	1
1670	Cottages & Garden				„	1	0	„	„	„	„	1
1671	Orchard Plat		+	P	2	„	2	1	3	8	2	„
1672	Cottage & Garden				„	„	34	„	„	„	„	„
1673	Lane Meadow		+	P	2	3	14	2	2	20	2	3

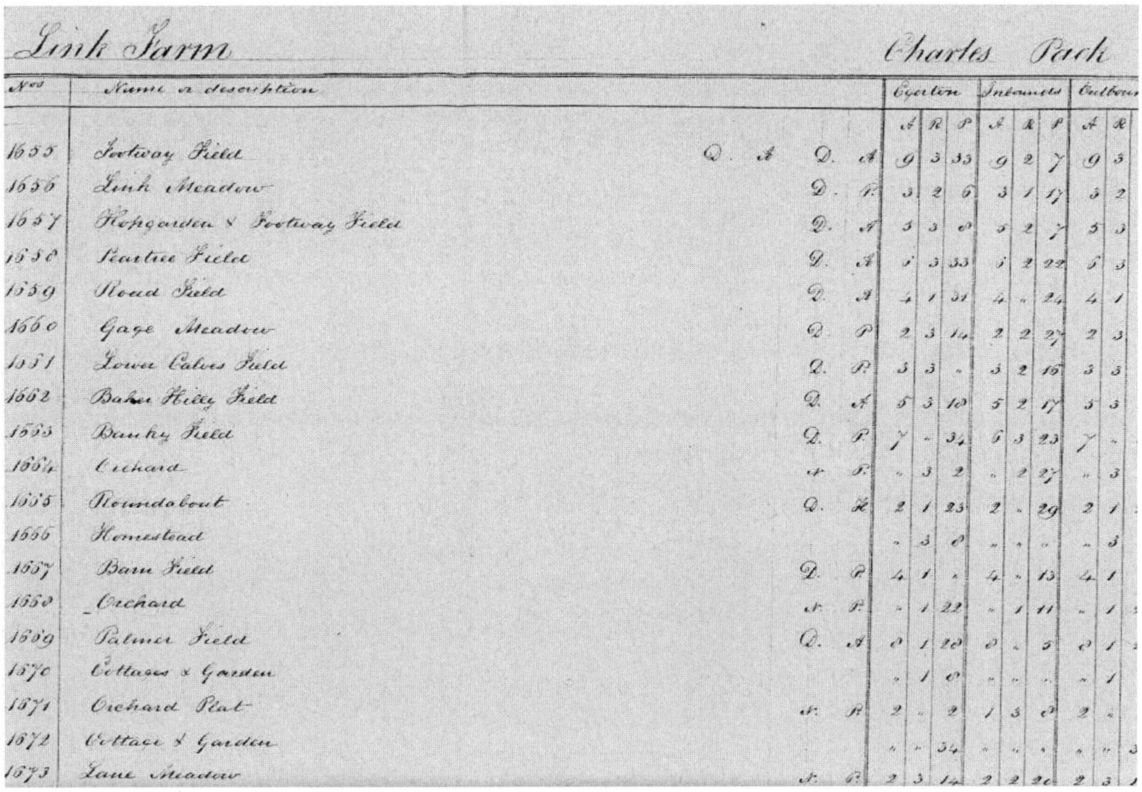

My grandfather, also Jeffrey, will have known Link House well, he was born in 1885 and became a builder and worked several times on Link House and it may be that the property in some way entered the Pack consciousness since much later he built a model of the property, shown below. The model was given by the author to the current owner of Link House to remain there as a memory of my grandfather.

Whilst not having children Charles and Sarah appear to be family oriented since in the 1871 census Albert, 14, and Eli, 12, nephews, are staying with them and in 1881 Stephen; all Nathaniel's sons. In 1891 Frances Hopkins is back with them.

Nathaniel (1824 – 1877) married Mary Ann Dawson and they had 10 children, 7 boys and 3 girls. Alfred (1854), Edwin (1856), Albert (1857), Eliza (1858), Elias (1859), Edward (1860), Stephen (1863), Leonard (1866), Elizabeth (1868) and Emma (1870). Nathaniel was a butcher and his story continues in chapter 14.

Sophia (born 1827) In the 1841 census she is living with Sarah and John Evenden, age 14, probably as a maid. On 6th November 1852 she married James Coppins at the Tilden Baptist Church in Smarden and they had at least 3 children; Keturah (1854), Anne (1858) and William (1863). By 1881 Sophia had a granddaughter, Barbara, aged 6, but it is not known whose daughter she was. There are no further details.

Harriett (born 1829) No details whatsoever. Possibly died young since she does not appear in the 1841 census when she would have been an unmarried 12 years old.

Edward (born 1831). In the 1851 census he is resident at the George Inn working for Edward and Sarah Amos as a butler and by 1871 he is a carpenter. In 1852 he emigrated to the US and then returned to Egerton in 1857 to marry Elizabeth, and then they both returned to the US. They had 4 sons and two daughters. The first daughter, Mary, was born in the USA; all the other children were born in Egerton. After Mary was born in the US they then came back to Egerton sometime before 1861 where all their other children were born. Their children were Mary E. (1859 in USA) Everett G. W. (1862) Charles Edward (1864) J.Earnest (1872) J. Mathew (1875) and Anne (1878). By 1881 Edward was a Master Carpenter employing 1 man and 1 boy and apparently doing quite well but he later returned again to the US with some of his family. Edward's story and the reasons for his transatlantic perambulations are explained later.

Horatio (born 1834) married Jane probably in 1856 and they had 10 children – Caroline (1857) George J (1858/9) Harriet Ann (1861) Horatio (1863) Alfred C (1868) William (1870) Kate (1872) Ada K. (1877) Charlotte S. (1879) and Albert E. (1881). Horatio's story continues in chapter 16.

Mary (1836 -1890) In 1841 she is aged 4 living at Borehill with her parents and Charles, Edward, Harriett, Horatio and William In the 1851 census she is a servant with John and Sarah Evenden at Headcorn where she appears to have taken over from her elder sister, Sophia, above, when Sophia married. She almost certainly married John Collins from Lenham in 1860. She was 23 when they married and he was 33 and they set up house in Lenham, about 3 miles from Egerton. They had 11 children Edward (1858 – before they were married), Sophia (1861), Dinah (1862), George (1864), William (1867), Margaret (1869), John (1873), Nathaniel (1873 – were they twins? Or 2 sons in one year?), Ester (1876), Keturah (1878) and Louie A. (1881). Mary lived to a reasonable age for the times, 64, and was still producing children until 9 years before she died, and will scarcely have known a life without children, especially as before she married and started her own family she was probably looking after the Evenden children. We will not pursue this lineage any further because they now have the wrong surname but simply acknowledge another amazing feat of childbearing.

William (1838 – 1915) married (1861?) Susannah Charlotte (almost certainly) Hopkins born 1841, and they had 5 sons and 4 daughters. In 1841 he is resident with his family at Borehill, Egerton. In 1871 he is an agricultural labourer at Baker farm and by 1881 he is farmer of 13 acres at Newland Green farm (although the Packs did not have a history of farming the Hopkinses certainly did and it sounds as if they have given him a small holding from their lands) and by 1901 he is still at Newland Green farm living with Edmund, son, road engine driver, and Albert and Selina. Their children are William Norton (1862) Amy Elizabeth (1864) Harriett (1865) George (1868) Joseph James (1870) Sarah (1872) Edmond (1875) Whitfield Albert (1878) and Elizabeth Selina (1880). William's story continues in chapter 17.

Elizabeth (1841 -?) In the 1841 census she is 11 months and in the 1851 census she is 10, at Link farm and a scholar. After that there are no details and she has probably followed the traditional route of domestic service then marriage.

The 2 Pack families

It was the view of my father (shared by his sister Meg and others) that there were two (by implication unrelated) Pack families in Egerton during his childhood. I believe this can now be explained. George junior had 11 children but a) his sons George and Charles didn't have any children b) there are 4 daughters who would change their names presumably when they married or if they didn't marry then probably didn't have children c) Horatio moved to Sheerness d) Edward emigrated to the US e) Nathaniel's children for the most part moved away elsewhere in Kent … so this only left 2 Pack families in Egerton to compete – the families of William and Robert – this may well be where they all start thinking they were different. Another differentiating factor is that William is a farmer and his family mostly follow him in this and Robert a builder. It could well also be that William and Robert both felt somewhat bruised towards each other after the "battle of Link farm". Perhaps one benefited more than the other? Certainly William continued the farming tradition his father had unexpectedly come into while Robert became a builder and perhaps this contributed to the division as well. It is also interesting that both families were, in part, Pack/Hopkins families. William married Susannah Hopkins and Joe's father, Jeffrey, Robert's son, married Edith Emma Hopkins. I would love to be able to tell my father that there were not 2 separate families and in fact the 2 families were only one generation apart.

The religious divide

George senior may have developed an aversion to the Anglican Church in Egerton after they tried to force him into marriage with Elizabeth Battlemore. He may also have found it difficult attending the same church as his parish paymasters whilst he was living on charity and with the family connection with the Sedgwicks the Baptists were his obvious choice for a church. This Baptist tradition continued in the family up to the 20th century but gradually various family members drifted away to the Anglicans and a bit of a divide opened up.

There were, and are now, no great theological differences between the Baptists and the Anglicans, both are Protestant; most of the differences are procedural and ceremonial. Compared to the Anglican church Baptist churches tend to be more evangelical, less centrally organised with each church having a lot of local autonomy, more democratic and less structured, more non-conformist with most Baptists strongly preferring not to be an established church. Baptists do not allow baptism, entry into the church, until adulthood thus ensuring people actually know what they are signing up for.

In the 19th century your choice of church was quite important. The church was a social centre as well as a religious source. This was where you met your friends and possibly where you conducted some business and you would look for like minds in your congregation. If the Church of England is often called "the Conservative party at prayer", praying perhaps for nothing to change, then the Baptists, and other non-conformist Churches, may be thought of as the labouring classes at prayer, praying, perhaps, for the opposite. The Anglican Church, as the established Church, was where the local nobility would go as well as the middle classes and trades people. The Baptists would tend to be the labourers and workers who would prefer a non-conformist environment that partly rejected the status quo. Geography was also important. In Egerton the Baptist church was just down the road from Pleasant valley and you did not have to climb Egerton hill to get to it

George's son, George junior, was certainly a Baptist. After the original Baptist church in Egerton Forstal burned down in 1824 it would appear George junior attended the Smarden Baptist church but then later returned to Egerton as there are records from October 26th 1836 of the formation of the Particular Baptist church at Egerton Forstal, George Pack was one of the members "dismissed" from Tilden Smarden specially for the purpose of refounding Egerton. On January 5th 1840 George Pack was appointed Deacon, a position he held for most of the next 20 years. At a church meeting held on March 15th 1868 to discuss fees for the graveyard, Charles Pack, George's son, was the church secretary. This is an interesting link with the senior ecclesiastical positions held by Richard Pack and his sons in Ireland in an earlier chapter. As we have seen above many, if not all, of George's family were Baptists, either baptised or married or buried at Mount Zion Baptist church Egerton. This began to change towards the end of the 19th century as they all became more successful and middle class and perhaps began to align themselves as part of the establishment. But Jeffrey, great grandson of George, and my grandfather, and born in 1885 notes in his diary;

My father and mother went to Chapel, my father used to play the flute. Of course I had to go, in fact I went each Sunday. But what I detested most was that I had to wear a sort of straw hat with a broad brim which had a band around it and what annoyed me was that there were two ribbons floating about at the back. When in Chapel the preacher took a long time over his sermon there was fidgeting because I thought he would never stop and I wanted my dinner badly.

Jeffrey's brother, Victor, was also a very strict Baptist, as we shall see in a later chapter.

There was one important factor which would hasten the move to the Anglican church in generations after George. My immediate Pack ancestors loved campanology; bell ringing. In Egerton this was only available at St James' Anglican church and that may have clinched it for them. Whether they knew that the bells they were ringing were installed by Thomas Pack of Whitechapel, and whether he is a possible relation is unknown.

Although it is barely readable, George and Keturah and their entire family are commemorated on this stone in St James' Church, Egerton.

Now we move on to James, George junior's first born and my great great great grandfather, his siblings having all been taken as far as possible in this chapter.

Chapter 13 - James Pack and Frances
The Take Off Continues - Plus Five Sons

James and his brothers, Nathaniel, Edward, Horatio and William, who follow this chapter, are all the second generation after George senior.

James Pack was George junior's first-born child and was baptised on May 4th 1817. He married Frances Page (born 1818) on 26th February 1840 at the Baptist chapel in the district of West Ashford. The marriage certificate is signed by James Pack and noted by the mark "X" of Frances Page. James was a bricklayer and the witnesses were George Pack (his father) and James Page (Frances' father). James and Frances are pictured below.

Pictures courtesy of Elsie Hopton MacKethan.

Over the next 21 years they had 9 children.

- George W (1841)
- Frances (1843)
- Charles (1845)
- Eliza (1847)
- Edward (1850)
- Robert (1852)
- Maria (1855)
- Elizabeth (1858)
- Ezra (1861).

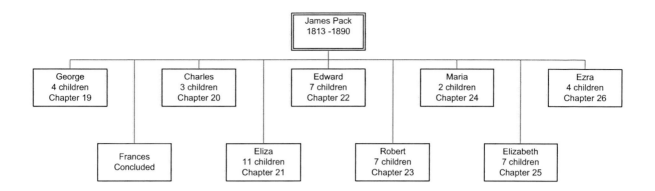

```
                          ┌─────────────────┐
                          │   James Pack    │
                          │   1813 -1890    │
                          └─────────────────┘
```

George	Charles	Edward	Maria	Ezra
4 children	3 children	7 children	2 children	4 children
Chapter 19	Chapter 20	Chapter 22	Chapter 24	Chapter 26

Frances	Eliza	Robert	Elizabeth
Concluded	11 children	7 children	7 children
	Chapter 21	Chapter 23	Chapter 25

The same conventions are used here as in the previous chart. All the offspring are taken as far as possible in their chapters except Robert, who is the continuing ancestor, and Frances who died young.

Five of their children were named the same as James' brothers and sisters – James, George, Charles, Edward and Elizabeth. Frances was obviously named after her mother. The new names they chose for their children were Eliza, Robert, Maria and Ezra and perhaps these came from Frances' family. Note also that the name George has now been running for 4 generations.

Frances died in 1883 when their final child, Ezra, was 22 and so she and James can only have had a few years together after the family had grown up and gone.

In the 1851 census James (33) and Frances (32) are shown as living at Pack Cottages with George (10), Frances (8), Charles (6), Eliza (4) Charles (1) and Eliza Smith (23) a niece. Nowhere in Egerton is now called Pack Cottages and it is believed that this is what is now Water Villas in Pleasant Valley, pictured below (more of this later in the chapter on Pack Properties).

In the 1861 census they are at Link House with Charles (16) Eliza (14) Edward (11) Robert (9) Maria (6) Elizabeth (3) and Ezra (2m).

In the 1871 census they are shown as having a family of Charles, 26, a bricklayer, Edward, 21, Robert, 19, a bricklayer, Maria, 16, Elizabeth, 13, and Ezra, 10. Keturah, James' mother, is also living with them. Frances had died in 1862 and George had left home by then, aged 30, but they still had 8 children at home! In 1871 James was 52 and Frances 51. 10 years later in the 1881 census they are shown as living at Pleasant Valley but now with only 2 children left, Elizabeth, 23, by now a teacher and Ezra, 20, a carpenter, but they do now have George, a grandson (believed to be the son of William and Charlotte Pack).

Of their 9 children 3 would emigrate to the US, George, Edward and Maria, 3 would meet with serious misfortune, Frances, Ezra and Charles, and 3 would have normal lives, Eliza, Robert and Elizabeth.

James Pack was a builder. His grandson, Jeffrey, notes in his diary that *"in 1899 I followed my father in the building trade and my grandfather was also a builder employing up to 30 men at times"*. Employing such a large number of men will have made James one of the largest employers in the village. His son, Robert, and grandson, Jeffrey, continued the building career and between them they may well have built quite a good percentage of the buildings in Egerton. I will try and trace how many in a later chapter. James made a will dated 16th October 1890 shortly before his death and he appointed Ezra William Weeks, son in law, and George Langley (solicitor?) of Langley as executors, and he left quite a considerable estate.

Frances died on March 29th 1883, aged 64, and was buried 7th April 1883 in St James' churchyard next to her daughter, pictured below. It is strange that having married in the Baptist Chapel James and Frances decided to bury their daughter in the Anglican Church and then, when his wife dies; James decides to bury her beside their daughter.

Frances, died aged 64   *Frances, died aged 19*

But stranger still, James was interred at the Mount Zion Baptist chapel at Egerton Forstal on November 6th 1890, aged 73, separately from his wife and daughter. His gravestone is shown below and the reason for being buried here becomes obvious when the stone is inspected closely.

James is buried with his wife Mary. James remarried, after Frances had died in 1883, to Mary Millen in 1885. He was 68 and she was 56. Mary was born on April 28th 1828 and was the widow of John Millen. After their marriage they had about 5 years together before George died and she must have been a Baptist and insisted that James was interred at Mount Zion with preparations for her to join him later. This does seem rather wrong. He surely should have joined his wife of 43 years at St James' rather than his second wife of only 5 years? In 1891 Mary was living in Folkestone with her sister-in-law Harriett Millen and she died on February 4th 1898 and joined James.

The Mount Zion church records note that both James and Mary became members of the church by baptism on February 8th 1861. It may have been completely coincidental that they both joined on the same date but it is strange. James' first wife, Frances, did not die until 1883 and their last child, Ezra, was born in 1861. Did they become estranged at this time and James took instead to Mary only to have to wait another 22 years until Frances died before they could marry?

As can be seen in the above chart whilst James and Frances had 9 children their offspring were gradually becoming less productive or, perhaps, more careful, although Eliza sets up a family record with 12 children.

We now move on to Nathaniel, George junior's second son and James' brother.

Chapter 14 - Nathaniel Pack - Seven More Boys

Nathaniel was the 4th son of George junior; James was covered in the last chapter, then came George and Charles who had no children but now comes Nathaniel who makes up for that by having 10 children including 7 sons. He was born on 1st May 1825. The name Nathaniel is not common today but was common back in the 19th century. Nathaniel was one of the twelve apostles and the name is Hebrew meaning Gift from God. This Nathaniel probably got the name from his maternal grandfather, Nathaniel Palmer. He married Mary Anne Dawson at the Tilden Baptist Chapel in Smarden on 16th October 1852. She was born in 1828 and was from Ewhurst in Sussex. Why didn't they marry at the bride's home town?

Thanks to Albie Pack (a descendant now living in New Zealand and more of Albie later) there is an intriguing twist to this. In the records there are 2 Nathaniel Pack marriages in Q4 1852, one to Mary Anne Dawson and the other to Mary Anderson and they have identical references, 2A/847. Since there was only one Nathaniel Pack in Egerton at this time the only explanation for this is a mistake of transcription or communication. Mary Anndawson might have been misheard as Anderson and wrongly entered and then corrected without deleting the error.

Nathaniel was a butcher. It is not known where he found the skills of his trade. His father was a farmer and his grandfather had no known trade. To set up as a butcher would have required some capital for a shop, stock and equipment and this was presumably courtesy of the legacy from his parents and the prosperity generated by Link farm. It may be that his butchery skills were acquired from his wife's family. Nathaniel and Mary had 10 children, 7 boys and 3 girls. It was quite difficult collecting all the details as in several censuses they are recorded as "Puck". Whether this was due to their writing skills or the enumerator's mistakes is unknown. Two of the children, Alfred and Eliza, were found quite by chance. Nathaniel's family is the first Pack family so far to not have a George!

- Alfred (b.1854)
- Edwin (b.1856)
- Albert (b.1857)
- Eliza (b.1858)
- Elias (b.1859)
- Edward (b.1860)
- Stephen (b.1863)
- Leonard (b.1866)
- Elizabeth (b.1868)
- Emma (b.1870)

Nathaniel died on February 13th 1877, aged only 51, and was interred at Mount Zion, as was Mary Anne on April 17th 1881, aged 54. They were both Baptists and spent their lives in Egerton. In the Mount Zion Chapel burial ground is a gravestone to Nathaniel and Mary Ann which also refers to their 8 surviving sons and 2 daughters and which has the following inscription.

Tis religion that can give
Sweetest pleasure while we live
Tis religion must supply
Solid comfort when we die.

This is a verse from Hymn 590 in the Stevens selection of hymns in common use among Strict and Particular Baptists for many years.

The reference on the headstone to 8 sons and 2 daughters includes a Henry who I have not been able to trace and must mean that one of the daughters died very young and was not recorded. As we shall see below they have some unconventional offspring most of whom began to move out to other parts of Kent and eventually further afield and it is difficult to avoid the conclusion that they may have been escaping Nathaniel, possibly a difficult man to live with. A potted history of each of the children follows the route map below; I have numbered the children to keep track of some of the quite dense stories. The longest stories are those of Albert (the 3rd child) and Leonard (the 8th).

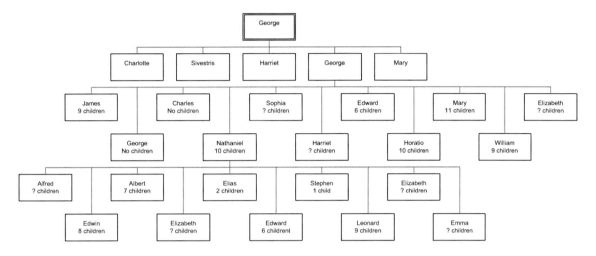

1) Alfred Pack

In 1881 he is a 28 year old labourer at the Ironworks in Dartford and living at 149 Longfield Street as a lodger with James Pack, age 34 and an ironmonger, and Charlotte Pack, his wife, aged 46, together with William Hands, 23, stepson, Charles Hands, stepson, 11, Mary Ann Hands, stepdaughter, 8, and James Pack, son, 1. By 1897 Alfred was in Australia but no further details have been found. There is also no indication of his relationship with the family he was lodging with in Dartford and note also the age discrepancy of his married Pack landlords.

2) Edwin Pack

Edwin, a bricklayer, married Harriett Hales (born 1857 in Sittingbourne) in 1876 at Hollingbourne in Kent. They then produced 8 daughters (at least until the census runs out in 1901) many of whom ended up in London and thus the Pack name does not survive in Edwin's line. *Phoebe* Emma (?)(born 1878) - there is an Emma, aged 13, in the 1891 census, possibly married 1906 in Camberwell, *Minnie* (1880), by 1901 she is 21 and a servant to the Cockings family, *Amy Florence* (1883), living, as a niece, with the Hales family in Battersea in 1901, *Edith* (1886), in 1901 , age 15, she is a servant with the Sharp family in Rusthall Avenue, Acton, and probably married in 1910, *Daisy* (1889), *Ethel* (1893), born in Rainham, Kent, probably married Taylor in 1919, *Hilda A.*(1897), possibly married Lowrey in 1918 and *Emily* (aka Lily) (1900) she married Fuller in 1925. An interesting genealogical challenge arose with this family. Three of their eight daughters were called Edith, Ethel and Emily. Edwin's cousin, Joseph James (see later) also had three daughters called Edith, Ethel and Emily. Their dates of birth were also similar; Edith (Edwin's daughter 1886, Joseph's daughter 1901) Ethel (1901 and 1903) and Emily (1900 and 1905). Unravelling this took some time! We now turn to the 3rd child Albert, on the next page.

3) Albert Pack

Albert married Elizabeth Vousden (born 1860, her parents were William Vousden (born in 1840) and Rebecca Potter (born in 1834)) on January 25th 1879. Like his brother Edwin, Albert was a bricklayer living in Sittingbourne. They had 8 children; George Henry (born 1880), Alice (1882), Ernest (1884), Kate Elizabeth (1887), Eddy W. (1889), Mabel Florence (1890), Stanley Arthur (1894 but died 1898) and Hilda A. (1897). I am grateful to Hilary Burley, great granddaughter of Albert and Elizabeth, for discovering that 6 of the children (except George Henry and Hilda, who wasn't yet born) were baptised at the same time on October 20th 1895. It is thought that the local vicar rounded up families that weren't baptised and processed them as a job lot. Little is known about Alice (she married a Frederick Black and had 2 children; David and Alice), Ernest (married and had a son; Archie), Kate (died in 1901, aged 14) or Mabel (married William Taylor and 1 son; Gordon). Hilda was born in 1897; she never married and worked for the Singer Sewing Machine Company until she died prematurely aged about 40.

The two of their children about whom more is known, George Henry and Eddy W. are featured later. Elizabeth is pictured below with two of her daughters, Hilda (on the left) and Mabel. In the picture the girls appear to be about 14 and 7, which would make the date of the picture about 1904.

Picture courtesy of Hilary Burley great granddaughter of Albert and Elizabeth

Another picture of the family is shown below. This was found in Audrey's papers and must have come down from her father, Jeffrey; he was a distant relation of Albert and Elizabeth but still seems to have been in touch. We will come to Audrey and Jeffrey in later chapters.

Albert and Elizabeth appear to have had a difficult life together. I am grateful to Hilary Burley, great granddaughter for the following information.

Around 1896 Albert was admitted to an asylum leaving Elizabeth with 7 children to care for. They owned 2 cottages which made Elizabeth ineligible for poor relief but she couldn't pay the interest on them. She tried to make ends meet by renting a shop which sold ginger beer, coffee and sweets but the profits barely covered the rent. Her eldest son, George Henry, was unhelpful and did not seek work. Things were apparently so bad that Elizabeth applied to Barnados to give up 2 of her youngest children, Eddy and Mabel. In the end Mabel did not go but Eddy, as we shall see later, did. The above picture may well have been taken after Albert had left for the asylum and in the midst of their difficulties. Albert did come home in 1901 but was then readmitted and eventually died in the asylum aged 57, in June 1913. When he was working it appears to have been from the Milton workhouse.

The other 2 children about whom we do know something are George Henry and Eddy W.

George Henry Pack (1880 - 1969)

He married Edith Cordelia Jones (1880 – 1956) in 1899. They had 6 children

1) **Stanley Maurice Pack** (1899 – 1935) he had 7 children, the sixth birth was twins, a large family in a short life. The descendants live in Ashford.

2) **Albert Edward Pack** (1900 – 1979) Albert Edward and Ellen had eight children. Two daughters died young. One son was another Albert Edward ("**Albie**" with whom the author is in touch, living now in Christchurch New Zealand. Albie had made a trip to Egerton and left his e-mail address in the visitor's book at St James' Church and thus we made contact. Alby was born in Faversham and emigrated with Ivy and their daughter,

Yvonne, to New Zealand on 20th May 1959 on the SS Captain Cook. Like many other Packs Albie was a builder and his grandchildren, Tyrone and Ciara have followed the tradition in the property markets). Albie's older brother, Thomas, served in the Navy in WW2 and emigrated to the USA after family friends invited him and his family to come. The other children were Jean, Sheila, Stanley (living in Brighton) and Brian (living in Bearsted, Kent). Thomas persuaded his parents, Albert and Ellen, and Jean, Sheila and Barrie (Harry Richard's son, their grandson, adopted when Harry died) to also emigrate to the USA. Thus of the six surviving children three plus Barrie went to the States, one went to New Zealand, and only two remained in England.

3) **Ernest Frederick Pack** (1904 – 1924) he joined the army, lying about his age, and was sent to India where he joined the cavalry. In April 1924, during a charge, his horse tripped and he fell, breaking his neck. He is pictured below as well as his memorial in India.

Pictures courtesy of Alby Pack, nephew of Ernest

4) **Phyllis Pack** (1914 – 1997), her descendants still live in Faversham,

5) **Harry Richard Pack** (1918 – 1945) he was in the Navy in WW2 and

6) **Edith Mary Pack** (1919 – 1998) she emigrated to New Zealand with Albic and Ivy, then moved to Australia in 1973 and then back to Kent.

Eddy W. Pack (born 1889)

In the 1901 census Eddy W. is recorded, age 12, as an inmate at the National Incorporated WAIFS association, Mile End Road, London. This Institution was later to be taken over by a Dr Barnardo. Thomas Barnardo was an Irish doctor who arrived in London in 1866. A few months after he arrived an outbreak of cholera swept through the East End of London leaving many children destitute. In 1870 he founded an orphanage in Stepney and then progressively expanded the organisation, which was to become Barnardos Homes today. The word WAIF is believed to come from the Old French word "guaif" for stray beast. In English it referred to an orphaned, homeless or forsaken child. It did not usually refer to a runaway child since they would have exercised free will. Eddy was given up by his mother to Barnardos in 1897 at the age of 9. On the application form he is recorded as a Baptist, and baptised and there was a Canada clause, which Elizabeth agreed to and which meant that after his education Eddy would be sent to Canada. Elizabeth saw Eddy once or twice a year when he was allowed home for a few days but then in 1905 he was sent to Ontario where he worked on farms and apparently did quite well. In 1908/9 he returned to England on an old boys trip and then never returned to Canada to work. He joined the crew of the White Star liner Laurentic (which sailed into Montreal) and then served on the Marlborough and Revenge in WW1 being at the battle of Jutland. After the war he managed the estate of his ship's captain in Scotland and then settled on the outskirts of Glasgow where he was steward of a golf club for many years. Later still he managed a pub in Wales called the George and Dragon. Eddy is pictured below, firstly as a Barnardos boy, then a young man and finally as the golf club steward.

Back now to Nathaniel's children and after Alfred, Edwin and Albert we have 7 more to go and a very interesting story to come.

4) Eliza Pack

In the 1861 census she is aged 3 living with her parents but then no further trace

5) Elias Pack

Elias married Jane Brenchley (born 1858/9) from Pluckley on 10th March 1883. He is also a bricklayer. They had 2 children *Edith Mary* (born 12th February 1883), married 1905, and *Alfred Nathaniel* (born 30th November 1885), married 1915 Howland from Sheppey. In the 1891 census the children are living with their mother and Eli was a lodger in Rochester. He must have been working away from home because in the 1911 census Elias and Jane are living together in Strood, Rochester.

6) Edward Pack

Edward was also a bricklayer and married Jane Turk on 2nd December 1882. They had 6 children *Charles* (born 25th September 1884), married Davis 1915, *Edward* (born 29th August 1888), married 1907, Milton, *Percy George* (born 3rd December 1890, died 8th November 1954, in St James' churchyard records) He would have a son, also Percy, who married Nora May Smith, 22, domestic at Ragged House, Egerton, on 9th September 1935. *Alfred Leonard* (born 30th December 1892) married Howland in Sheppey in1915 (note that his cousin Alfred Nathaniel, 10 lines above, also married a Howland at the exact same time, two Alfreds marrying two Howlands!) *Phyleus* (1896), daughter, no other information, and *Doris* (1889), no other details. In 1881 Edward is living at Grove Cottage with his mother and brothers and sisters. Also living with them in 1891 at Little Chart were Stephen (Edward's brother) 28, and Samuel Sank 15. The family were resident in Little Chart

7) Stephen Pack

Stephen (born 1863) married Sophia Turk (born 1863) on 4th February 1893. Note that Stephen's brother, Edward above, also married a Turk 11 years earlier. The Turks are an old family in Egerton. He was buried 24th April 1929 aged 65. They had 1 son *Frank* (born 28th March 1892). Frank married King in 1921. Stephen started as an agricultural labourer but by 1901 was a Bailiff and Farmer in Pluckley. Now we turn to the second interesting story in this family; Leonard Pack.

8) Leonard Pack

Leonard Pack was born in 1865 and married Emma Jane Foreman on the 18th February 1888. But Leonard appears to have fathered three children before this marriage and may have entered an unofficial marriage. The first-born was *George* (born 1881, Leonard would have been 16, the birth was registered in Blackfriars, London; by 1901 George is in the Navy and on board ship on the night of the census), then *Elizabeth* (1884), her place of birth is noted as the Old Kent Road Lds branch. The third born is then *Olive B.* (1886).

Elizabeth's place of birth - the Old Kent Road Lds branch - required a lot of searching but it is believed that Lds is the Church of the Latter Day Saints, often known as the Mormons. The Mormons were founded in 1830 by Joseph Smith and are based in Salt Lake City, Utah. Adherents are called Latter-day Saints, or Mormons, and they were conducting missions to Britain from 1839. The Mormons believe in polygamy. It appears that Leonard may have been an adherent and had 2 wives and 2 families. After formally marrying Emma Jane Foreman he then went on to produce 6 more children. *Lilian May* (born 26th April 1889), married William John Cox September 20th 1913, she died 8th February 1974, he died 30th May 1977 *William Leonard* (7th April 1890), married Rose Pendleton from Canterbury and they had 4 children *Frederick* (1891, probably died later that year since no further trace), *Percy* (1891 – were they twins?), *Sydney Robert* born 3rd August 1899 at Quay Lane, Rainham, died October 7th 1918, aged 19, buried Arras, France and *Leonard A.* (1901) married Lilian Dunk May 14th 1929, he was a bus driver for Maidstone and District buses, they had 2 daughters; Joyce and Alice Emma (born 17th May 1904), married Leonard Goodwin 3rd February 1929, she died 26th September 1979, no children.

The mother of Leonard's first 3 children is believed to be Olive Croucher, variously described in the records as Pack or Croucher. In the 1901 census the family are living at Rainham St Margaret in Kent and Leonard is 36, Emma 34, Lillian 11, William 10. Percy 6, Sydney 1 and Leonard 4months. Also living with them is Olive Pack, aged 33, and noted as "wife" of Leonard. It is believed that there were 2 households in Rainham St Margaret and that on the night of the census Olive just happened to be at Emma's house. There is no trace of a formal marriage between Olive and Leonard and Olive appears to have been married to Abraham Croucher, and how he fits in is unknown, so there is no case for charges of bigamy. But with 2 households to support and 9 children Leonard must have been a very strong man. The above is all that can be gleaned from census information and is necessarily somewhat conjectural and I would be delighted to hear from any descendants what actually happened and how it all panned out.

Per Leslia Thauoos, a descendant, Leonard died at the Kent County Asylum at Chartham . Leslia also reports that 2 of Leonard's children, Percy and Alice (the reader will not find an Alice above so she must have been born after 1901), were very odd, but that Emma Jane, Leonard's wife, or one of them, was saintly! Emma Jane's obituary in the Chatham News read as follows following her death on October 30th 1937, 16 years after Leonard.

"The sudden death of Mrs Emma Jane Pack of 62, High Street, Rainham, who has passed away on Saturday in her 71st year, has deprived Rainham of one of its best known residents. Although she had been in failing health for some years her death came as a shock, as she had only taken to her bed two days previously. Mrs Pack was born at Folkestone, and came to Rainham 44 years ago. Since then she had become well known and liked. She is survived by two daughters, Mrs A E Goodwin, with whom she had been living, and Mrs L Cox of Upchurch, also by three sons, Messrs William, Percy and Leonard Pack, seven grandchildren and one great grandchild (This was Leslia, aged 3 months). The funeral took place on Wednesday afternoon at St Margaret's Parish Church and was conducted by the Vicar, the Rev A D Hodgson."

9) Elizabeth Pack

Elizabeth was born in 1868 and in 1891, aged 23, was a servant with the Sellers family in Hampton Wick. There are no further details.

10) Emma Pack

Emma was born 31st July 1870. In 1891 she was a servant with the Hall family in Folkestone and in 1892 she married James Frederick Hales. They had at least 1 child; Sidney Frederick Hales was born in 1901. Emma's brother, Edwin, also married a Hales, Harriett, in 1876.

And now we turn to Nathaniel's younger brother, Edward Pack, 8th born and 6th son of George junior.

Chapter 15 - Edward Pack - The USA Story Starts

Edward was born in April 1831 and in the 1851 census he is shown as resident at the George Inn working for Edward and Sarah Amos as a butler. The George is the local pub in Egerton and is still there. It will not have escaped the reader's notice that there are a lot of Georges in the Pack family and now we find that even the local pub has the same name. The original pub was built on the site in 1576 and has been much changed and altered over the years. During the 2nd World War 127 Wing of the RCAF was based nearby and the George was their regular local.

The George with St James' church in the background

Edward married Elizabeth Day at the Tilden Baptist Church in Smarden on 30th August 1857. They had 6 children. The first *Mary Ellen.* according to the 1871 census, was born in the USA in 1859. Mary Ellen married in 1878 in Maidstone, aged 19, spouse unknown. The other 5 children were all born in Egerton – *Everett G.W* (1862), *Charles Edward* (1864), *J.Earnest* (1872), *J.Mathew* (1874) and *Anne* (1878). They may have had a further daughter, Frances Edith, born in 1884 shortly before they returned again to the US.

Edward was the 8th of 13 children (11 surviving) and the 5th surviving son; of his older brothers James had started a building business, Charles had inherited Link farm and Nathaniel had started a butchers business and Egerton may well have been very crowded with Packs and opportunities may have been scarce and so Edward probably used his inheritance to emigrate to the USA in 1852 aged 21. He may well have started a small exodus from Egerton. The Coppins family emigrated in 1855 and Edward's nephew, George W. Pack emigrated in 1866 (at which time Edward was temporarily back in Egerton as we shall see later) and Edward's other nephew, again Edward, emigrated in 1890, all to the same approximate area. After emigrating in 1852 , and presumably now well established in the USA, Edward then came back to Egerton to marry Elizabeth in 1857 when she was 21 and he was 26 and took her back to the US and in the 10th July

1860 US census they were resident at Sangerfield, Oneida County, New York with Mary Ellen who is 8 months old. He is 28 and a carpenter, she is 24. They then returned to Egerton because in the 1861 UK census (UK censuses are usually in the spring, so they returned just a few months after the US census) they were resident at Link Farm. All the rest of their family were then born in Kent. In the 1871 census they were living in Mole Road and later, in 1881, at 16 Marsham Street, both in Maidstone. In the 1881 census Everett G.W. (George Washington?) has become plain George. He was an apprentice house painter and Everett might have been too exotic a name for that job.

Edward and Elizabeth then returned to the US in 1884 just after Frances was born. Edward appears in a trade directory in 1887 living at Yates Terrace, Syracuse, as a carpenter. They then appeared in a later directory at 333 Renwick Avenue, Syracuse. The USA census of 1890 was lost in a building fire and the next entry is the USA census of 1900 and they were resident in Syracuse, ward 14, Onondaga County, New York State, together with James E. (in the UK birth records he was J.Earnest, but has obviously now decided he wants to be James E.) and in 1910 they are still there (interestingly 8 out of the 9 families on the relevant US census page are from England, the 9th is Italian), he is 75, she is 70 and living with them is their son George W.E., aged 48 and a labourer, unmarried. They are also still there in 1913, well into their 80's, but then no further details. As we will see there were 2 Edward Packs who emigrated from Egerton, and this Edward's nephew will appear in a later chapter.

We have speculated at length in an earlier chapter about the reasons for Edward's transatlantic hyperactivity but some general comments may be of interest.

The first known emigration from Egerton to the USA occurred in 1828 when the Parish offered three families free passage in order to relieve ratepayers of their costs from parish charity. These were the families of John Landen, William Turk and James Palmer. More followed the next year; three families and a single man and woman. It is not known what became of them when they arrived in the USA. There is a longer description in a later chapter of the operation of the workhouse and the Parish Overseers who operated it.

Edward emigrated in 1852 and the next known migration was when John Coppins and his family emigrated in 1855. In 1834 the Poor Law changed the system of workhouses and John Coppins' emigration will have been voluntary. John Coppins' daughter was Ursula who will become Mrs George W. Pack in a later chapter. From all of these emigrations there will undoubtedly have been a grapevine feeding back to Egerton of the boundless possibilities on the other side of the Atlantic and Edward will have also assisted this by returning often to Egerton.

Elizabeth was born in England from her US census returns. Thus it would appear that when Edward emigrated in 1852 (when Elizabeth would have been 16) he must have kept in contact with her, waiting until she came of age, and then returned to marry her in 1857 when she was 21. They then returned to the USA intent on starting a new life but, as we have seen all of this was interrupted when Edward's father, George, died in 1860.

One explanation for Edward's perambulations can be considered and then discarded. The USA had a civil war from 1861 to 1865. Southern States which supported slavery had declared their secession from the US and formed a Confederacy and it took 4 years of fierce and bloody fighting before Lincoln and the Unionists prevailed and it is conceivable that Edward saw this coming and decided it was too dangerous for him, or perhaps he was worried about being conscripted, and that this was the reason he returned to Egerton with his family, as we have seen, in late 1860. This is however unlikely. Whilst the fighting was bloody – 620,000 killed and 400,000 wounded out of a population in 1860 of 31.5 million - there was no fighting around Syracuse, it was all much further south, and there was never much likelihood of fighting in the north-east with the relative armies so heavily skewed in favour of the unionists and why anyway would Edward remain outside the US for a further 15 years or more after the fighting was over?

As well as the disruption of all of this to Edward and Elizabeth it must have been quite confusing for their children. James Earnest and George W Everett certainly followed their parents back to the US after 1881 because they feature in US censuses, Mary Ellen had married in Kent in 1878, aged 19, and may have stayed there; the other three were still young in 1881 and almost certainly went with their parents but by the 1900 US census will have grown up and moved out.

It is difficult to avoid the conclusion that Edward must have been disappointed with how his life turned out. He probably emigrated to the US, aged 21, with high hopes of making his fortune, came back with hopes of a different fortune, waited nearly 20 years to realise that fortune and was perhaps partially successful and then went back to the USA, now well over 50, probably too old now to be successful again there. One of Edward's children, Charles, committed suicide in 1894, and James Earnest died in 1901, aged 30 and both are buried in the Syracuse graveyard but I have not been able to trace any of the other children any further but if any of them, or their descendants, read this I would be interested to hear how things turned out for them. Edward died in December 1917 and Elizabeth in June of the same year, he was 86 she was 81.

The final piece of conjecture is why Edward (in 1852) and then later his nephews George (in 1866) and Edward (in 1890) chose Syracuse to settle. Syracuse is situated between Albany and Buffalo in New York State and is on the Erie Canal, which was built between 1817 and 1825 to connect the Hudson River with Lake Erie. This would create an important route for commerce and for migration and there will have been much activity and opportunity. It was described as the pathway to the West, but this was not yet the West Coast since California was only taken from the Mexicans in 1848, and the rush there would start later. President Zachary Taylor sent Ed Mackethan's great-great-grandfather to California in 1849 to evaluate the situation and urge settlers to apply for statehood, which they duly did in 1850. He then stood as US senator for California but lost. Ed's family history could have been completely different if the family had settled in California. The "West" of the USA in the 1820s was a line broadly from the Appalachians to the Great Lakes. Perhaps the first families in 1828 started out intending to cross the USA to these Western parts but found work and a future in Syracuse and went no further and perhaps they kept in touch with Egerton by letter passing back news about the opportunities, which Edward and then George, Maria and Edward then followed?

The next chapter brings us to Horatio Pack, George junior's 8th surviving child and 6th surviving son.

Chapter 16 - Horatio Pack and a Branch of the Family Moves Elsewhere in Kent

Horatio was born in 1835 in Egerton and was a farm labourer in 1851, aged 16.Horatio is an old English name with Latin and Greek origins and appears in Shakespeare's play Hamlet. In later times it became very popular because of the deeds of Horatio Nelson.

Nelson is regarded as Britain's greatest naval officer; to Byron he was "Britannia's God of War". He was born in deepest rural north Norfolk in Burnham Thorpe where his father was Rector of All Saints Church. He was from a large family with 3 children who died in infancy and Horatio was the 4th of 8 surviving children. To his father Horatio was always Horace but to no one else. He joined the Royal Navy at the age of 12 in 1770, was promoted to Captain at the age of 20, lost an eye in battle in 1793, then lost his right arm in battle in 1797, then, following a succession of successful battles, he was promoted to Vice Admiral in 1803 and in 1805 defeated the French at the battle of Trafalgar but in so doing lost his life. He was as famous also for his affair with Emma, Lady Hamilton living openly together and having a child, Horatia, despite both being married to others. He is celebrated by a column in Trafalgar Square. For more than a century after Waterloo Britain was supreme on the world's oceans.

The country's gratitude to Nelson also displays an interesting story of Britain's approach to the honours system. Nelson left no legitimate children when he died in 1805, aged 47, so his eldest brother, the Reverend William Nelson, was created the 1st Earl Nelson by George III and given £90,000 (£100 million in today's monetary values) to buy an estate (Trafalgar Park in Wiltshire) and a pension of £5000 a year (£3.7million in today's prices) to last for as long as there were Lords Nelson.

By 1946 the family could no longer afford to maintain the estate on the pension granted (whose value had not been increased for the intervening inflation) and a deal was done cancelling the pension but allowing the 4th Earl to sell the estate. Estate duties meant that the family realised very little of the value of the property and by 1981 when the 9th Earl assumed the title there was nothing left of the family fortune, only the right to sit in the House of Lords. This right was then withdrawn in 1999 following reforms of the House of Lords. The 9th Lord Nelson died in 2009 and had been a policeman in CID and the Flying Squad. He is succeeded by his son, also a policeman.

The Nation obviously felt obliged to do something for Nelson after his exploits and could think of nothing else in the circumstances than to shower it's gratitude on his brother who had played no part in Nelson's exploits. The Nation then spent the next 150 years clawing back the cost of all its gratitude. William Nelson is commemorated in St Paul's Cathedral, pictured left, as is his illustrious brother.

Following Nelson's exploits many families chose to call their sons Horatio, after the national hero, and it is surprising that it was not until 1835, thirty years after his death, that the Packs chose to name one of theirs after him.

Horatio Pack married Jane Elizabeth (from Minster in Sheppey) in 1856 and they had 10 children. By 1881 he is 46 and living at 29 Lower James Street, Minster in Sheppey, Kent, and is an assistant engine fitter. Of all George junior's offspring Horatio seems to have benefited least from the family fortunes. When his father, George junior, died in 1860 all Horatio's other brothers came home to Link House and I have characterised this as a battle for the family legacy. Horatio did not come back to Egerton. All of Horatio's brothers started trades of their own, Horatio appears to have missed out on this perhaps because he was not on the spot when things were happening?

He would have been working at the naval dockyard in Sheerness, on the Isle of Sheppey, about 25 miles from Egerton. How often did he get his leg pulled about his name as he worked in a naval establishment? The original dockyard was established in 1665 by, among others, Samuel Pepys (1633 – 1703, he worked for the Navy Board and was instrumental in creating the Admiralty and much else). It was a subsidiary dockyard to the larger Chatham dockyard, 15 miles to the west. From 1813 to 1823 a major overhaul of Sheerness was undertaken to enable it to build small to medium sized ships and the shipyard would have been buzzing with activity in the 1850s when Horatio would have been looking for work. This was also the time when wooden ships gave way to iron ships and then later, by the 1890s, to steel. The naval dockyard closed in 1962 after 290 years of service to the Navy and it is now a commercial port.

By the 1901 census Horatio, 66, is living in Sheerness at 9 James Street with daughters Harriet (40, single) and Charlotte (21, single, dressmaker) as well as his brother, George, aged 81, but Jane had died in 1894, aged 55. Their 10 children are shown in the chart below and then some brief descriptions follow.

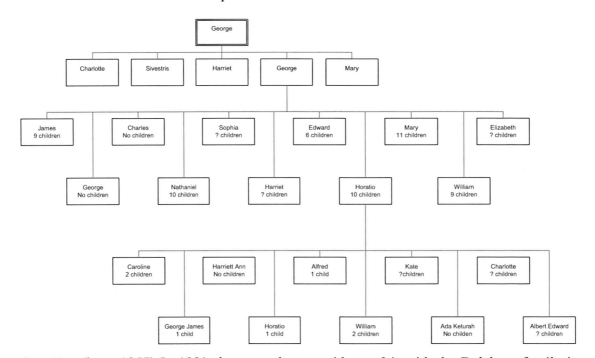

Caroline (born 1857) In 1881 she was a housemaid, age 24, with the Delabere family in Camberwell, London. Shortly after, in 1883, she married John Hail Luscombe (born 1857 in Sheppey). They had 2 children **Ada Mary** (born 1886), married Green in 1920 in

Islington, and *Amie J* (1888), married Gibbs, 1912, Sheppey. John Luscombe died in 1889 just after the birth of their second child and aged only 32. The family lived in Croydon, London where both children were born but both daughters by 1901 were living in Sheerness.

George James (born 1858/9) In the 1881 census he is living with his parents at 29 Lower James Street, Sheerness, a coppersmith, probably in the dockyard. In 1883 he married Annie (born 1858) and they had 1 child, *George William* (born 1884). George James died in 1904, aged 46 and Annie died in 1914 aged 56. In the 1901 census the family are in Sheerness but are recorded as Annie Tack and George J Tack!

Harriett Ann (born 1861) In 1901 she is living with Horatio, George and Charlotte in Sheerness, aged 40, so presumably never married

Horatio (born 1863) he married Elizabeth and produced *Douglas Horatio* in 1896 in Chertsey. By 1901 they are living in Weybridge, Surrey. Note the run of 3 Horatios.

Alfred C (born 1868) he married Alice (born 1869) in 1892 and produced *Lilian E* in 1901 when he is a shipwright worker in Sheerness

William (born 1870) married Eliza M (born 1868). He is also a shipwright in Sheerness and they had 2 children *Eva Gladys* (born 1895), married Joynes 1918, and *William H S* (born 1897), married Reynolds 1915, Malling, Kent (was the "H" in his middle name another Horatio?).

Kate (born 1872) In 1891 aged 19, she is living with her sister, Caroline Luscombe who is described as a widow (her husband died 2 years earlier) and general dealer. Kate is a dressmaker. Possibly married in1901 in Sheppey.

Ada Keturah (born 1877) died 1890 aged 13.

Charlotte S (born 1879) In 1901, aged 21, she is living with Horatio (66), George (81, brother of Horatio) and Harriet (40, sister of Charlotte). No other details.

Albert Edward (born 1881) In 1901 he is aged 20 at Aldershot as a private in the Seventh Queens Own Hussars. This regiment was formed in 1690 and was originally Scottish. It had a long and dashing history. In 1901 it was sent to South Africa for the closing phases of the Boer war, this posting must have been just after the 1901 census. He clearly survived since he married Henrietta M. Owen in 1916.

The next chapter is about William Pack, George junior's last son. In between Horatio and William is Mary, about whom I have found nothing and the same applies to Elizabeth who follows William. Thus we have nearly finished George junior's progeny although, for special reasons to be explained, following William there is a chapter on one of his sons, Hubert. After that we will explore the children of James, George junior's first-born child.

Chapter 17 - William Pack - The First Hopkins Wedding, the Advent of Traction Engines and the 'Other Packs'

William was born in 1839. He married Susannah Charlotte Hopkins (born 1841) in 1861. They had 6 sons and 5 daughters and there is a tombstone in the Baptist Chapel recording this. They are both buried at the Mount Zion Baptist Chapel, Egerton Forstal. He was interred August 10th 1915, aged 77, she was interred on January 24th 1898 aged 57. Most of the Packs until now have been Baptists but this will change. Their tombstone is shown left.

This is the first known Pack/Hopkins marriage but is quickly followed by another when William's brother, Charles, married Sarah Hopkins in 1863. There are further unions of the two families yet to come and there may be previously undiscovered ones. This is not surprising. The Packs lived mostly in Pleasant valley, which is very close to Newland Green farm, where the Hopkinses lived. There were several local families which crop up all the time – the Turks, Coppinses, Hopkinses, Days and so on. There were probably as many Pack marriages with these other families as with the Hopkinses. But since my grandmother was a Hopkins this family gets a special mention.

In 1861 William is living at Link farm with his mother, Keturah. Later that year he married and by 1871 he is a labourer (presumably agricultural) at Baker farm. As we have seen, his brother, Charles, inherited the rights to Link farm even though William married first. But by 1881 William is a farmer of 12 acres at Newland Green and in 1901 he is still there. Later he would live at Shaw farm and later still he appears to have given up farming to become a carrier. He will have benefited in some way from his parents and also from his in-laws, the Hopkins.

My father and my aunt both referred frequently to there being another Pack family living in Egerton which was unrelated to them, the "Other Packs". There was even the mildest hint of disapproval. As we have seen the "Other Packs" must surely be William Pack and his descendants.

William and Susannah had eleven children, 6 sons and 5 daughters, although 1 son and 1 daughter died very young, and the children are all listed below. They are numbered to assist the reader since some of the descriptions contain quite a lot of detail. The route map below may also help.

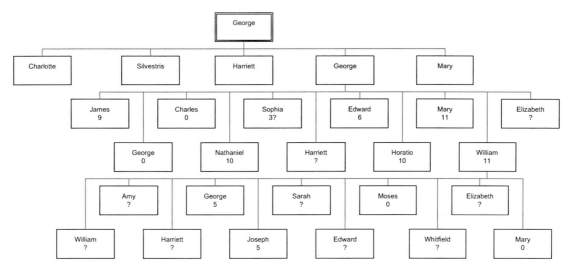

1) William Norton (born 1862) married Ellen (born 1858) in 1886. They do not appear to have had any children. By 1901 he is an "engine driver on the road" (the meaning of this will be explained later) at Brook Gates, Egerton.

2) Amy Elizabeth (born 1864) married Frederick William Vane (34), a labourer from Biddenden, on July 2nd 1892 at St James' church Egerton.

3) Harriett (born 1865) married Major Day at the Tilden Baptist Chapel in Smarden on 13th June 1885. Major is not a rank but an unusual first name. The Days came originally from Sussex but sometime between 1861 and 1871 the entire family, grandparents included, moved to Egerton. In 1871 they were in Newland Green, by 1891 they are in Bedlam lane and in 1901 in Stonebridge green. As a farming family they presumably move around to where the work was, living in tied cottages. Major and Harriett had 3 children; Ellen (born 1886), Caleb M. (born 1887) and William (born 1893). By 1901 Caleb M. has become Major C. and is a servant/waggoner at Link farm for his grandmother, Sarah, who is noted in the census as being a farmer, aged 71. Harriett died in 1918, aged 53, and Major died in 1941, aged 76 and they are buried together at the Baptist chapel left.

4) George William (born 1868, died 12th September 1934, aged 67) In 1881 he is a farm servant (indoor) aged 13 living with James and Frances, his uncle and aunt, at Pleasant valley. He married Sarah Ellen (born 1869, daughter of William and Anne Buckman of Bethersden, died 21st September 1930, aged 62) in 1890 in Sevenoaks and by 1891 they are living at Water villa (previously known as Pack cottage). By 1901 he is still at Water villa living with Ida Buckman, sister in law. He also became an engine driver per his daughter's marriage certificate. George died 12th March 1934 aged 67 and Sarah Ellen died 21st September 1930 aged 62, and they are buried together in St James' and their monument is below.

George and Sarah Ellen had 5 children.

The first was **George William** (born 12th December 1891). He married Henrietta Hopkins on 27th December 1919, he was 28, she was 31 and had an illegitimate child called Joyce, who would marry George Turner eventually producing Anthony and Monica Turner. Tony Turner has given the author much help with the Egerton part of this story. George William started work as a stable boy in 1905 (age 14), joined up in 1914 and was injured and after the war became head gardener and chauffeur at Egerton House working for Major Stisted and living in nearby Egerton Cottage (in November 1956 Henrietta was given one months notice to quit what was presumably a tied cottage following the sale of Egerton House – presumably both George and the Stisteds had died by then). George died suddenly while assisting a friend to feed stock at Greenhill Farm. He had been captain and secretary of the Cricket club and a playing member into his 62nd year. He was employed by the Stisteds for 48 years. He was a keen bellringer, a member of the gardening society and served with

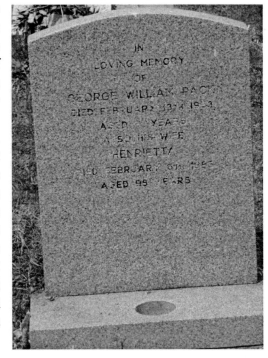

The Buffs in the 1914/18 War (The Buffs were the Royal East Kent Regiment, one of the oldest regiments in the British Army dating back to 1572. They were called The Buffs because of their original buff coats). George and Henrietta produced George Joseph Edward (born 18th July 1926), who married Pamela (Hargrove) in 1951 and they had 2 children Colin George and Julie. There is a memorial plaque in the choir at St James' to George J.E. Pack 1926-1987 Church Warden 1976-1987 a "respected and much loved servant of the parish". George Joseph Edward died 2nd.March.1987 aged 60 and is in the St James' churchyard records but as George Edward Joseph, not George Joseph Edward! George William died 13th February 1953 aged 62 and. Henrietta died 2nd February 1984, aged 98. Their tombstone, in St James' churchyard, is right.

George and Sarah's second child was **Flora Annie** (born 1st July 1893) she married Mr Cole in 1916. An extract from the local paper of December 1919 read "Corporal Reginald Cole, 9th Lancers, son-in-law of Mr G Pack, of Egerton, has safely reached home after being a prisoner in the hands of the Germans for nine months. He was taken prisoner at Hesbecourt in March and arrived at Leith, via Vibourg, Denmark, on December 26th – From Leith he was sent to Ripon for medical inspection and finally reached Egerton on December 30th. He had been confined in the prison camps of Dulmen, Limburg, Parchim and the Springhirch NCO Straffe camp. The food supplied was very bad consisting chiefly of sauerkraut, a small quantity of black bread and so-called coffee. Corporal Cole has won the Military Medal for conspicuous bravery at Nouef Wood, Marcoing. He speaks very feelingly of the splendid reception accorded the freed prisoners at Leith" Extract courtesy of Renee Weeks.

Their third child was **Victoria Eve** (born 1896) she married Frank Troy, 8th September 1919; he was a 27-year-old commercial clerk from Wolverhampton.

Then came **Edward Edmund** (born 1900) no other details and finally **Hubert Spence** (born 7th September 1906). The next chapter is devoted to Hubert for reasons that will become apparent. The three brothers George, Edward (Ted) and Hubert are pictured below.

5) Joseph James (born 1870) married Rose Emma Smith (born 1872) from The Old Harrow, at the Tilden Baptist Church in Smarden on 30th April 1894, as "most of the Packs were Chapel" (a comment that crops up regularly but does not appear to be true, except perhaps in this part of the family). He died 21st June 1950, aged 80, and, despite being Chapel, was buried in St James' church! She is also in St James'; she died 31st August 1949, age 77 and their tombstone is below.

Kath Hilder has written the following about her grandfather:

"Elm Meadow was the site of the local cesspit serving properties at the top of the hill. It frequently gave trouble and had to be cleaned out. In 1922 the local roadman, Mr J Pack, was contracted to take on the job of keeping it clear at 30 shillings a year ("As Joseph Pack's granddaughter I feel sure he managed it very well"). Sewer rents of £2 per annum were paid by the school and 2 nearby property owners. There was also a spring on Elm Meadow which supplied some houses in the Lower Street, so all these drains and sewers were running under the village playing fields. Thank goodness they were taken over by professionals in due course."

Joseph James started as an agricultural labourer and later became a Road Foreman. . In the 1901 census they are living at The Old Harrow with 4 of their children, and a fifth, Emily, yet to arrive in 1905. They were living with Jane Smith (64, farmer) and her other children (Rose's brothers and sisters Alice, 27, George, 24, Albert, 21, and Emily19). Their 5 children were ***Albert Joseph*** (born 1896). He served in the 1st World war and was gassed and never recovered and died February 6th 1923 aged 27 per churchyard records, buried 12th February 1923. His picture is left.

The local paper reported in February 1923 that *"he had been suffering from tuberculosis for a long time, contracted while on war service. He joined the Royal East Kent Mounted Rifles in the early days of the war, and served in France where he was wounded and gassed. After recovering from his wounds he was sent to India and then on to Mesopotamia. The deceased's favourite hymn "Abide with me" was sung and as the coffin left the church the Dead March in "Saul" was played"*. Extract courtesy of Renee Weeks.

Charles Earnest (born 1898) He was a groom at Munday Bois at the time when the Slaughter family lived there, he is shown below in smart attire and also washing his dog. He died 4th August 1948, aged 50, his wife was Pearl Caroline (nee Blackford from

Headcorn, they married 11th April 1931) and she died February 1978, they are both in the churchyard records at St James and the tombstone is shown below. In later years they had lived at Belhams Grove.

Edith Jane (born 1901) She married Arthur William Gardner 16th June 1923. They were about the same age. He was an engineer from Ashford. Charles (above) and Emily (below) are present at the wedding.

The photo above is the wedding of another Pack.
This time its Edith's turn and the groom is Arthur Gardner.

Ethel Rose (born 19th October 1903) married David Richard Wickens on 15th November 1924 at Egerton Church; they went to live in Boughton Malherbe parish where they had 5 daughters, Nora, Molly, Kath and 2 others.

Emily May (born 13th March 1905, died 1986) who married Edward Arthur Wickens (born 1907 died 1991, aged 84), brother of David, above, on 27th February 1935, she was 29 and a domestic, he was 27 and a shepherd from Broughton Malherbe. Two sisters marrying 2 brothers, albeit 11 years apart, is unusual.

Two brothers married two sisters. Pictured left are David Watkins and Ethel Pack, who married at Saint James church, Egerton on 15th November 1924. Pictured right are Edward Watkins and Emily Pack, who also married at saint James' church.

Emily May is on the left, Molly Wickens, her daughter in the middle and Ethel Rose is on the right; note the flasks, cans and saucepan all needed for a long day hop picking

6) Sarah Ann (born 1872) in 1891 she was a servant at Boughton Malherbe with the Cheeseman family. She married on Christmas day 1919 William Frederick Hills, a bricklayer. He was 51 she was 47 so it is unlikely there were any children.

7) Edward Edmund for reasons which will become apparent his full story will follow his remaining siblings below.

8) Moses C. (born 1875) died February 11th 1876, aged 13 months. There is a tombstone for him in the Mount Zion Chapel at Egerton Forstal. The engraving reads July 1876, which is an engraver's error.

9) Whitfield Albert (born 1878) In 1901 he was living with his father, William, Edmund and Selina at Newland Green. No other details. Perhaps he became known as Albert?

10) Elizabeth Selina (born 1880) By 1901 she was known as Selina not Elizabeth, a common problem for genealogists and a common trait amongst the Packs. She is pictured below, from a History of Egerton 1900-2000, outside Shaw Farm, where the family lived for a while, in 1910, thus aged 30 and unmarried. No other details have been found.

11) Mary J. (born 1882) died August 13th 1882, aged 5 months. There is a tombstone for her in the Mount Zion Chapel at Egerton Forstal.

7) Edward Edmund (names sometimes reversed) (born 1874) Edmund married Julia, they had a daughter Dorothy Mary who was baptised 18th April 1909. Edmund was a traction engine driver.

On the left, with a pipe, is Edmund Pack, in the middle is his mate and on the right Walter Hooker, brother of Charles Hooker junior.

Mr. Hooker's traction engine.

Traction Engines

Today Traction engines are viewed as lumbering amusing giants at village fetes but in their time they were revolutionary. In 1859 Aveling and Porter modified a portable steam engine which had to be hauled from job to job by horses into a self propelled one by fitting a driving chain between the crankshaft and the rear axle and the self propelled steam traction engine was born. They revolutionised agriculture and road haulage at a time when the only alternative was the draught horse. By the early 20th century they were progressively replaced by internal combustion engines powering much lighter tractors. Their uses in Egerton would be road laying, rolling broken stone with earth and water, threshing, in Egerton the seasonal threshers, according to Charles Hooker (see later) were brought to this casual labour by "an uncontrollable craving for strong drink. They spent the winter months in the workhouse, early spring and summer picking flints on the hills or farm work, returning to the threshing when the season started with the harvest. Many of these men were known only by a nickname such as Doggy, Jacko, Swimmer, Bob the Devil, Nelson, Croutty, Funny Eye and so on", pumping water, sawing, haulage, this was the most difficult, the driver had to maintain the engine and steer and manoeuvre in difficult terrains as well as having regard for horses, and ploughing (see picture below)

Steam ploughing at Court Lodge, Egerton, autumn 1938.
Photograph taken by E.Botting (of whom more later)

The firm of Charles Hooker and sons was founded by Stephen Hooker and his son Charles in 1888 and then continued by his sons Charles junior and Edward (who is on the engine above). At it's peak the firm had 17 Traction engines working all over Kent and Sussex. Charles junior wrote a book of his experiences entitled "My Seventy Years With Traction Engines", details are in the appendix. In it he refers to four brothers who all worked for the firm. *"After some years one left to work for a Scottish firm who specialised in bulky haulage, such as boilers or tanks, two remained with us until they died; the other, Edmund Pack, remained until Father died and the stock-in-trade was sold."* The four brothers were of course Edmund (shown in previous picture), George William, William Norton and Whitfield Albert. Note in William Norton's census return his occupation is given as "engine driver on the road". I am grateful to Renee Weeks for access to the Hooker book and much else to do with her family. The resourcefulness of traction engines is shown by the following picture of her great grandfathers wedding party.

Wedding conveyance for Charles Hooker and his bride with friends and relatives at Egerton, Easter 1906. The engine is an 1874 Aveling driven by Charles Hooker senior

Extract from a local newspaper in May 1906

... a novel wedding took place at the old parish church, the contracting parties being Charles Ernest Hooker and Miss Alice Winifred Wilkins. The wedding party were drawn to church in a traction engine and truck, the truck being prettily decorated for the occasion. The bride was attired in a pretty cream dress trimmed with satin ribbon and lace. She wore a veil and orange blossoms and carried a bouquet of choice white flowers. She was attended by two bridesmaids, Miss Rosie Hooker and Miss Emily Hooker, sisters of the bridegroom. They wore pretty dresses of pale grey, trimmed with satin lace. Mr Jeffrey Pack (the authors grandfather) acted as best man. Large crowds gathered to witness the ceremony. Extract courtesy of Renee Weeks.

We have already encountered Hubert Pack above but, for special reasons, the next chapter explores his story in greater depth.

Chapter 18 - Hubert Pack - A Catalyst for this Story

Hubert Spencer (sometimes Spence) Pack deserves a chapter for himself for a number of reasons which I will explain below. He was born on 7th September 1906. He married Elizabeth (Stella) R Knight. She was born in 1897 in Bramley, Yorkshire and was thus 9 years older than Hubert. She was a schoolteacher. My father, Joe, wrote:

"On one occasion at Egerton school a new teacher was selected to replace a retiring teacher. Her name was Miss Knight and she came from the north of England somewhere. Miss Knight fell in love with Hubert Pack (no relation – there were a cricket team of Packs in the village). I was not the easiest of boys and frequently received a blow around the head. Any slight movement by a teacher and I would put my arm up to ward off any blow I might receive.

When dancing around the Maypole one day to the music of the school gramophone, I found myself opposite the teacher, Miss Knight, and arm in arm I had to twirl around with her – which I did, but swept her off her feet! When the music stopped, she gave me such a clout on my head that I saw sparks! It was shortly after this that I found myself in favour with her, as my name was the same as her boyfriend, Hubert; she thought we must be related! It didn't last for long."

A picture of the school is shown below. It was built in 1846 and enlarged in 1884. The school was given to the Parish by the then Lord Cornwallis for as long as it was used for the education of village children. The property reverted to the Cornwallis estate when a new school was built in 1972.

The School, Egerton

Note my father's comment "she thought we must be related!" implying that they were not related. My father always said that Hubert was one of the "other lot" and unrelated to him. In fact he would have been a second cousin to Joe's father or a second uncle to Joe. One can only speculate as to why this family link was denied, Hubert and Joe lived just a few houses apart in Pleasant valley.

Hubert Pack

Hubert and Stella had no children and she eventually became headmistress of Leeds school (the one in Kent not Yorkshire). Stella is just visible in this picture from 1939. As we shall see in the next chapter Stella met Elsie Hopton during Elsie's visit to England in 1977, when they were both 80 years of age.

The Archbishop of Canterbury at the 1939 May festival. Also pictured are the Rev. Luckraft Mrs Stella Pack, Miss Gladys Bolton and attendant Jim Homewood.

Stella with schoolchildren

Perhaps Hubert deserved his own chapter above all because he and Stella were my Godparents. So the Lady who was always bashing my father about the head in school would later become my godmother! Except on December 1st 1946, when I was baptised, I don't remember, sadly, ever meeting Hubert or Stella.

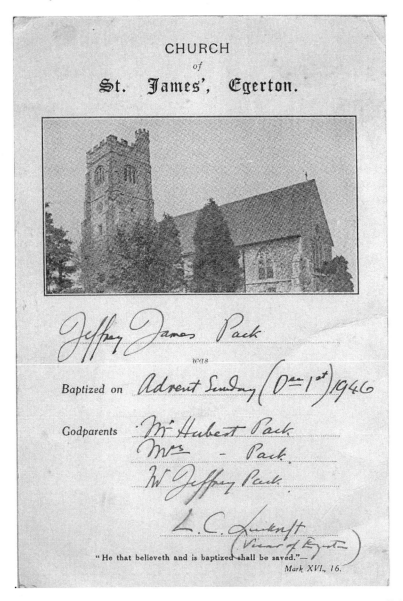

We have now traced as many of George junior's offspring as possible. The next generation, the third after George senior, are the offspring of James, George junior's first born, and Frances. James and Frances had 10 children. Of one of them, James (born 1839) nothing is known. Another, Frances, died aged 19. Robert (born 1852) is my direct ancestor and so will continue, as before, to further generations. The other seven will be taken as far as possible in the following chapters, starting with George (born 1841).

Chapter 19 - George W. Pack (1840-1913)
Another USA Story and Four Trips to the Old Country

George was born on July 28th 1840 and is recorded in the 1851 and 1861 UK censuses (in 1861 he is a lodger at Charlton, Dover, a bricklayer) and then he emigrated to the USA in 1866, aged 26, possibly following the lead of his uncle, Edward, who had originally emigrated in 1852 and again in 1857. George went to Syracuse, New York, where he married Ursula Coppins (born 10th August 1848, daughter of John Coppins and his second wife Eliza (Smith) Coppins, also of Egerton) The Coppins family had emigrated in 1855, John Coppins was running a public house in Syracuse, and George must have discovered them in the USA when he went over in 1866. They married in 1867 when he was 26 and she was 19. What are the chances of finding an Egerton family in the USA? It is quite possible that the families kept in touch after the Coppinses emigrated. George was not the first Egerton Pack to emigrate. In 1852 his uncle, Edward, as we have seen, emigrated to Sangerfield, Oneida County, NY. Edward's story of transatlantic perambulations is told in an earlier chapter but it would appear highly likely that he encouraged George to come to the same area; Sangerfield and Syracuse are about 40 miles apart and when Edward returned for the last time to the USA it was to Syracuse. Syracuse is about 250 miles North West of New York City and about 150 miles from the Canadian border.

George W. Pack in youth and later in life – pictures courtesy of Elsie Hopton MacKethan

In the 1870 US census George and Ursula were living at Syracuse, Onondaga County, New York with Harry Selding, miller and presumably a lodger and Charles Coppins, age 35, labourer and uncle or brother? In three US censuses George is progressively recorded as a brick mason, then a contractor and then a builder contractor. Later still he is a building materials manufacturer with his own company called George W. Pack and son, and his son, Charles, did indeed work with him and eventually take over the business. He had clearly prospered. George's father, James, had been a builder in Egerton, as were most of his brothers and many later Packs. Indeed the writers father, grandfather and brother were or are all builders and it would seem this is part of the Pack genes. There will be at least 5 different Pack companies, either building or building materials or contracting, during the course of this book.

George and Ursula had 4 children; John G. born and died 1868, Charles Henry (1871 – 1944) Frances Maude (1874 – 1880) and George J (1884 – 1901) Only 1 of their 4 children, Charles Henry, reached adulthood and his story is told below. George and Ursula visited Egerton in 1910, this was *the first of the 4 trips* referred to in the title, they would both have been in their late 60's, and the pictures below, all courtesy of Elsie Hopton MacKethan, great granddaughter of George and Ursula Pack, show them with Harry and Eliza (Pack) White (covered in chapter 21). Both George and Ursula died in 1913, Ursula on January 20th and George on July 15th, 3 years after their trip.

Pictures courtesy of Elsie Hopton MacKethan

Charles Henry Pack (1871 – 1944)

George and Ursula's only surviving child, Charles Henry Pack, married Harriet Gertrude Frost (1874 – 1941, always Gertrude) in 1897 in Syracuse New York. Gertrude had come from Kings Cross, London with her parents in 1887. Her father, Thomas Robert Frost, had owned paint and grocery stores in London and would do the same in Syracuse. Her maternal grandfather was apparently a gunmaker to the King and descended from Robert the Bruce. I have no proof of this. Charles and Gertrude had 4 children; Elsie Frances, Harold Charles, Phylis Maude and Ralph William and their stories will be described below. But first, in 1926, Charles and Gertrude followed Charles' parents from 16 years earlier and visited Egerton to discover their roots, and extracts from this are quoted below, courtesy of Elsie Hopton Mackethan; *this is the 2nd of the trips referred to in the title.*

H. Gertrude (Mrs Charles H.) Pack's 1926 Trip book

When they made their trip Gertrude would have been 52 years old and Charles 55. Their daughters (Elsie and Phylis Pack) came with them. Since Gertrude's ancestry was also English they will have had a lot of people to see and there was a list in the front of the trip book of those with whom they had been able to establish contact before leaving – The Waghorns, the William Packs (son of Ezra), the Elizabeth Weeks', the Clark Weeks', the Eliza Whites, the Bessie Sandersons, the Annie Coggers, the Charlie Whites, William Bruce and Sarah and William Jumo and wife (the last 2 are probably her relatives, the others are his).

They arrived on June 29th 1926 in France. On July 5th they were in Paris and their daughters left for a tour of the continent while their parents set off in search of their ancestral roots. A few extracts give the flavour ... *"July 12 Egerton, had breakfast with the Sandersons, saw quite a few Packs, including Jeff Pack (who's he? – actually the writer's grandfather!), July 20 – 24 Edinburgh, July 26 waited for the girls to arrive from the continent, then did shopping at Herrods (sic) July 28 Charlie had taxi for the day, July 31 boarded ship for home.*

Charles H. Pack in youth and later in life, pictures courtesy of Elsie Hopton MacKethan.

119

Charles carried on his father's business as a building materials manufacturer after his father died. Much later, in 2002, granddaughter Elsie Hopton Mackethan and her husband visited his house. Elsie and Ed report that " *The driveway is paved with bricks imprinted "Pack", and the current owner gave Elsie an extra that he had"* (pictured below), and again that *"Charles had a cottage on at Tully Lake, north of Syracuse. Charles' daughter (and Elsie's mother), Phylis, went there during her youth but swore that she would never have one of her own because all she did was work!"*

Charles and Gertrude's children

Charles and Gertrude had 4 children; Elsie Frances Pack (1897 – 1991), Harold Charles Pack (1899 – 1953), Phylis Maude Pack (1902 – 1994) and Ralph William Pack (1909 – 1951). The 2 daughters were named after Charles' sister, Frances Maude Pack, who died aged 6 when Charles was 9.The stories of Charles and Gertrude's children are told below and another Egerton trip takes place.

1) Elsie Frances Pack (1897 – 1991)

Elsie married in 1936, aged 39, Charles Oliver Dewey (1896 – 1972) and they had no children. Charles was a distant relative of Thomas Dewcy, governor of New York state and unsuccessful Presidential candidate in 1944, and Admiral George Dewey of the Spanish-American War.

"On April 27th 1898, Dewey, a commodore at the time,sailed out from China with orders to attack the Spanish at Manila Bay. He stopped at the mouth of the Bay late on the night of April 30th and the following morning he gave the order to attack at first light, by saying the now famous words "You may fire when you are ready, Gridley". Within 6 hours, on May 1st, he had sunk or captured the entire Spanish Pacific fleet under Admiral Patricio Montojo y Pasaron and silenced the shore batteries at Manila, with the loss of only one life on the American side. News of the victory in the Battle of Manila Bay made Dewey a great hero in the United States, and he was promoted to Rear Admiral. Dewey's swift easy victory no doubt did much to encourage President McKinley's administration in its decision to place the Philippines under American control."

Elsie was a graduate of Syracuse University and was a librarian in Syracuse and Dayton, Ohio. She died in St Petersburg, Florida. In 1931, before she married, Elsie followed her parents with a trip, the third of the four referred to, back to England. In the following letter she writes to her sister, Phylis, from on board the S.S.LaFayette en route to the USA on 9th July 1931.

"I had a splendid visit at Egerton. I stayed with Hilda, Nora and Aunt Elizabeth [Pack Weeks (Mrs William)] We reached there Sat about 11.30 am and left Monday am about 11.45. We had some delightful rambles. We met Hilda's "young man" and he is very nice. Nora's swain was too shy to come in and meet us. We called at the schoolhouse and also

at Aunt Lizzie Waghorn's. At the latter place we met numerous other cousins & ramifications of the family. I am very fond of Hilda. We went to Tunbridge Wells for a day. We had lunch there at Marian Weeks'. She is Hilda's older sister and runs a huge boarding house where Queen Victoria once stayed when a girl. In the afternoon we were invited to "Frampton" (the Charlie White's) to tea. Stanley (a son) called for us and drove us there. He is a fine fellow and is engaged to be married but the girl is ill and in a nursing home. I met Leslie (another son) he is more reserved and a bit harder to get acquainted with but still delightful. John, their third son, was away teaching so I didn't meet him again. Cousin Charlie (White) and Cousin Bessie looked just about the same, whereas Stanley seemed to have aged about ten years. They are a fine family and made us feel at home"

Elsie and her sister Phylis corresponded into the 1980's with many Egerton residents including Hilda Weeks Botting and Nora Weeks Morris.

Note that this 1931 trip was just 2 years after the Wall street crash and world depression. Elsie must have been reasonably secure as a librarian to afford this. The roaring twenties were a time of prosperity and excess and the Dow Jones index of US Stock prices reached a peak of 381.17 on September 3rd 1929. The overheated markets then began to fall sharply to 198.6 on November 13th and then a steady slide down to 41.22 on July 8th 1931, the lowest the stock market had been since the 19th century. This caused record business closures and unemployment and led to the Great Depression in most industrialised countries. In Britain the effect of this was magnified by the fact that Sterling had been restored to the Gold Standard at too high a level. The Depression only ended with the start of World War 2 and the need for governments to take control of their economies and the perverse effects that war can have with unemployment falling as men are conscripted for the armed forces and the multiplier effect of large government orders for munitions and ships.

Elsie then made her 2nd trip, and the 4th overall, in 1977, when she would have been 80 years of age! Her trip took in Pluckley, near Egerton, Hitchin, Exeter, Bristol, Chester and Edinburgh. In a letter in 1979 Hilda Weeks Botting wrote that "Stella and I talk so much about the day we had you with us". Stella may have been Stella Pack, wife of Hubert, and godmother to the writer (see the previous chapter). Elsie lived until the age of 93 and her sister, Phylis, until age 92!

2) Harold Charles Pack (1899 – 1953)

Harold married Anne Christine Winchester (born 1900) in 1922 and they had 2 children; **Charles William** (1924 – 1995) he married Alice Mae Swift of Greenville, Ohio, in 1944 (giving Jonnel in 1945 and Charles William in 1950), then remarried Mildred Leona Mason (1924 – 1985) no children, and **George Winchester** (born 1926) of Syracuse, married Sally Slade in 1949 (leading to Valerie Ann Pack born 1951) then remarried and no children.

Harold Charles graduated from the University of Pennsylvania and then worked in his grandfather's building supplies company, George W. Pack & Son, following on from his father above. He died of a heart attack whilst on a flight from Phoenix Arizona only 9 years after his father.

3) Phylis Maude Pack (1902 – 1994)

Phylis graduated from Syracuse University in 1924 and before she was married taught school in Onandaga County, New York. She married Lester Charles Hopton (1902 – 1989) in 1928 and then moved from Syracuse to Pennsylvania and then to Plainfield, New Jersey where she lived for 40 years, and then to Boca Raton, Florida and finally to Grosse Pointe, Michigan. Lester Charles Hopton was President of Ingersoll Rand, based at 11 Broadway, New York. Your humble writer worked for Ingersoll Rand in the early 1980s, by which time it was headquartered at Woodcliff Lake, New Jersey but failed to meet the former President of the company or realise that he was a distant relation by marriage. Phylis Pack Hopton is buried in the Boca Raton cemetery.

Phylis and Lester had 2 children Lester Charles Hopton (born 1937) and Elsie Frances Hopton (born 1940).

Lester Charles Hopton married Patti Jane Dee (born 1938) in 1960 and they had 2 children; Walter Edwin Hopton (born 1961) who married in 1986 Dara Douglas Yates (born 1963) leading to Kelsey Pack Yates Hopton (born 1989) and Jeremiah Borton Hopton (born 1964) who married 1997 Karen J Gold leading to Daniel Gold-Hopton and Joseph Gold-Hopton

Elsie Frances Hopton married Edwin Robeson MacKethan (born 1939) in 1962 and they have 2 children; Edwin Robeson MacKethan (born 1963) he married in 1988 Amy Frances McDonnell (born 1963) leading to Tristan James (born 1995) Frances Reece (born 1998) and Christopher Dewar Heard (born 2001), and Philip Pack MacKethan (born 1967) who married Jennifer Burgoyne (born 1968) in 1990 and they have 2 children Alexander Jordan (born 1994) and Benjamin Lord (born 1996). Ed and Elsie MacKethan have helped considerably with aspects of this history.

4) Ralph William Pack (1909 – 1951)

Ralph lived in Syracuse until 1934 when he moved to Marion, Indiana to practise law in partnership with Donald D. Van Eseltine, and in the same year he married Sarah Douglas French (1910 – 1996) and they had 4 children.

Sarah Elizabeth Pack (born 1937). She married in1967 Maxwell Michio Urata (born 1933) and they had 2 children; John Maxwell Norio Urata (born 1968) he married in 2004 Caryn Alys Yamamoto (born 1969) and Anne Douglas Mika Urata (1970) she married in 1994 Nathan Wallace Moy (born 1969) and they had 2 children Kira Cooper Ruth Moy (2004) and Lukas Joshua Mansfield Moy (2004)

Ralph William Pack (born 1939) he married in 1963 Barbara Jean Williamson (born 1940) and they had 4 daughters; Elizabeth Ann (born 1964) she married in 1993 Brian Keith Knoderer (born 1965) leading to Nicholas Clay (born 2000) and Reese William (born 2004), Katherine Lynn Pack (born 1966) she married in 1999 Linc Patrick Mitchell (born 1966) no children, Marian Suzanne Pack (1971) she married 1996 John Michael Horazy (born 1971) no children, and Sarah Jane Pack (born 1972) she married 1996 David Bradley Grupe (born 1971) and they had 3 children Blake Robert (born 1998) Brett Austin (born 2001) and Lauren Ahley (born 2004).

Frances Gertrude Pack (born 1942) she married in 1974 Samuel E Etienne but divorced in 1977 and there were no children. Frances (Frannie) has also taken a great interest in the research of this book.

Charles Henry Pack (born 1945) he married in 1968 Dianne Louise Thorne (born 1947) and they had 3 children; Andrew Charles (born 1972) he married in 1996 Jennifer Jo Potter (born 1973) and they have 1 child Emily Jo (born 1999), Ralph Douglas (born 1975) he married in 2004 Julie Ann Newell (born 1972) and they have 2 children Joseph Andrew (born 2005) and Charles Robert (born 2007) and Melinda Dianne (born 1977) unmarried.

In addition to his law practice Ralph William (1909 – 1951) had a number of other business interests and especially enjoyed harness racing and may have owned a stock farm near La Fayette, New York (there is a written account of a stock farm but none of the family remember it). He was apparently active in politics and served as pauper attorney in Grant County which is a fascinating connection given George Pack's dependence on parish charity 150 years earlier in Egerton. He was only 42 when he died in Fairmont, Indiana, which must have been a tragedy for his family.

Is Syracuse "Egerton USA"?

As we have seen a lot of Packs and other Egerton families came to Syracuse and many are buried there in Oakwood Cemetery.

In Lot 55 Section 44 there is a central monument plus stones for each of George W. Pack (1840 – 1913), Ursula Pack (1848 – 1913), Charles H. Pack (1871 – 1944), H. Gertrude Pack (1874 – 1941), George J. Pack (1883 – 1901), Ralph William Pack (1909 – 1951, died in Fairmont Indiana) and Harold Charles Pack (1899 – 1953 died in Jamesville NY). These are pictured below.

Elsie Hopton MacKethan is featured inspecting the family monument.

In Lot 47 section 69 there are stones for Edward B Pack (1849 – 1926), Sarah B Pack (1854 – 1930), Sarah Pack (1882 – 1952) and Alice Pack (1889 – 1970 died in Pittsburgh Pa).

There are also a large number of Frost relatives of Gertrude, Charles Henry's wife, buried at Oakwood as well.

In Lot 72 section 6 there are the remains of a tall Monument to the Coppins family, pictured below, and there are 7 graves in the lot but only that of Charles Coppins is visible.

The graves are for George Coppins (1828 – 1867), younger brother of John Coppins? John G Pack (1868 – 1868), Charlotte Coppins (1870 – 1872), Sarah Coppins (1834 - 1885 died Dewitt NY), Charles Coppins (1844 – 1903), John Coppins (1816 – 1889 died Dewitt NY) and Frances Maude Pack (1874 -1880).

There are nearly as many Packs buried in Syracuse as there are in Egerton's 2 graveyards and there may well be other Egerton emigrants and their descendants since once one family had blazed a trail it was not uncommon for others to follow. There are several places that are central to the wider Pack story; Egerton obviously, Prestwold, Leicestershire where Sir Christopher Packe came from, Ballynakill, Kilkenny, where Sir Denis Pack came from, Streeter, West Virginia, where the first Packs congregated in the US, and now Syracuse, New York joins the list.

The parallels between Egerton and Syracuse are interesting. George Pack came first to Egerton in the late 18th century, started a family which multiplied, then most of them left for elsewhere (there are only 2 Packs now in Egerton) but many are still buried there. Nearly 100 years later another George Pack came to a new town, Syracuse USA, started a family, which multiplied, then most left but many, as we can see above, are buried there.

After a story of success and a happy and thriving family we now turn to George's younger brother, Charles, and an unhappy story.

Chapter 20 - Charles Pack and An Unhappy Story

Charles was born in 1845 and is shown in the 1881 census living in Pleasant Valley, 36 and a carpenter, married to Mary (nee Burton), 30, and employing an apprentice. They married on 11th November 1876, he was 31 and she was 26. He was buried 17th July 1900 aged 55. She was buried 16th December 1899, aged 49, from Mill cottage. They had 3 children **Alice,** baptised 8th July 1877, buried 24 May 1898, aged 21, **Maria,** born 17th November 1878, she married Albert Harris, 19, on 29th December 1898, and **Ethel** born 30th October 1880, possibly married in 1900 in Hollingbourne. Living with them for a time was Susanna Coppins, 77, grandmother (she must have been Mary's maternal grandmother) and George Coppins, 40, unmarried, an agricultural labourer and presumably Mary's uncle. By the 1891 census Mary, 40, was living at Burscombe as niece/housekeeper with George Coppins, 50, farm labourer, and her children, Alice, 13, Maria, 12, and Ethel, 10, described as great nieces to George Coppins. Charles Pack, 46, a carpenter, is registered living at Little houses (another name for Pleasant valley), married but on his own. It looks as if Charles and Mary split up.

Picture of Charles, courtesy of Elsie Hopton MacKethan, probably before his life started to get difficult although, with no Mary pictured, perhaps they had split up by then.

Until more recent times divorce has been a very difficult and expensive process generally to be avoided. Up to 1857 application had to be made to Church courts, which applied strict and unforgiving standards, and a private act of parliament was required. From 1857 the Court for Divorce and Matrimonial Causes took over responsibility but divorce could still only be obtained by men if they could prove adultery, and by women if they could prove cruelty or desertion. In most cases, and this presumably applied to Charles and Mary, they just lived separately but remained married.

Charles' burial record contains the words "From Union". This means that he died in a workhouse. The following is an account of the history of providing for the chronically poor and disabled. It was researched by George J.E. Pack from the record books of the parish overseers and written from his notes by Kath Hilder, and I am grateful for her permission to reproduce the account in full. This was the system in which Charles Pack lived almost certainly from 1891 until his death in 1900, aged only 55.

Before the Welfare State the poor in any village had to look to the Church, the only body with any system for getting things done. It administered the Elizabethan Poor Law Act of 1601, which was brought in to order the previous haphazard arrangements of public benefactors giving doles to the poor, and to set up a system of charging property owners according to their wealth and applying these taxes to the upkeep of the needy. Each parish appointed Overseers of the Poor, who had the thankless task of keeping people alive without outraging the local ratepayers. These men had to keep records (although often they could not read or write) and their books provide an intimate account of the lives of the poor.

Egerton records begin in 1676 although earlier ones must have existed. By 1680 plans were in hand for providing some sort of accommodation for paupers, situated "at the Church gates" and known as The Little Houses. What and where these were is impossible to say, but over the years regular payments were made for their upkeep, especially for thatching material. In 1780, apart from straw, thatching wood and wiffs cost 5/- and beer given to the carpenters, thatcher and masons came in at 1/4d. For years payments were made for "work done about the Parish House at the Church Gates" and finally, in 1688, Widow Miller, Widow Jones and Stephen Bennet moved in, the Parish paying their removal expenses of 5/- each. A few years later a glazier was paid 2/-. Was this the introduction of windows in the Little Houses? They may have been simple huts or hovels, but they needed an inordinate amount of thatching. They were obviously almshouses, but that term is used only once. Rent of 4d a year was paid for them to the Manor of Charing. Over the years the Parish bought bricks and tiles as well as loam, mortar and sand. Oddly enough, only the carriage of the bricks was paid for, so who paid the bill for them?

The Little Houses lasted for some time but were obviously fairly makeshift affairs and by 1708 the Vestry (the administrative body of the Church) had bought a property referred to as "Loadres House" for £15, taking up a bond for the purpose. This house, referred to as "the Workhouse" was situated in the Street, but its precise location is unknown, although 1, Stonecroft Cottage was certainly once a workhouse, and may well have been the one meant. Whereas the inhabitants of the Little Houses apparently fended for themselves, those in the workhouse or poorhouse had their wants provided for: a pair of sheets was made for sixpence, tubs and barrels, logwood, milk and yeast were among the purchases of 1765. Two men were shaved for 4/- seemingly a high price. In 1778, water is charged

for, for the first time. Occasional extravagancies creep in; a spinning wheel, a hoe and a hog can easily be justified, but writing paper at 1/- and, most amazingly, a sack of dates at 14/- must surely have raised a few eyebrows round the Vestry table.

By 1826 a warden was appointed to manage the workhouse. He agreed at one point to keep twenty-six people for five weeks at 2/10d per head. Inmates had to work on farms or on the roads; in 1827, for instance, some men pulled forty loads of turnips at 4d a load. Vestry meetings were now held in the poorhouse (for which the warden charged 9d for fire and candle) although in 1826 they had to adjourn to the George because of an infectious fever in the house. The old Egerton workhouse is pictured left, now converted to dwellings.

The Little Houses disappear from the records altogether after 1827. However George Pack, the historian, observes that the tithe map of 1843 shows some little houses at Pleasant Valley, an area known within living memory as "Little Houses", and speculates that these might have been those that once stood "at the Church Gates", removed and refurbished as buildings often were. These dwellings were demolished to make way for post war houses, and unfortunately there seems to be no record of them. The treatment of the poor at this time, which already seems harsh, was gradually hardening; the economy of the country was in dire straits after the Napoleonic Wars, which threw many ex-soldiers and sailors back jobless into their homes, and the price of bread was desperately high. Villages found it more and more difficult to support so many mouths; besides those in the workhouse, many men qualified for "outdoor relief", that is, a few shillings to keep their families alive. They regularly applied for small sums; enough to buy a horse or the tools of their trade; for instance George Pack, the ancestor of George mentioned above, once applied for a shilling or two for lodging money as he was "going wooding up the hill" i.e. woodcutting in some parish like Doddington, too far for a day's journey. With seven children and a wife to support he needed every penny. Kath Hilder's notes continue..

Travellers and vagrants were a constant problem, in case they "came on the parish". An Overseer in 1740 noted giving 1/- to "a vagrant woman who was big with child" to move on before her confinement. Parishes hotly disputed who was responsible for such liabilities. Paupers had to return to their home parish to get support, and usually got a dole from the parishes they passed through. The story of Fanny Robin in Hardy's "Far from the Madding Crowd" is a painful example of the suffering this caused.

Desperate though the position of these poor people was, it became infinitely worse after the new Poor Law of 1834 introduced Union Workhouses, institutions which became a byword for cruelty and harshness deliberately imposed. Oliver Twist's life was no mere fantasy of Charles Dickens.

Besides Charles Dickens, many other Victorian writers depicted the lives of desperately poor children; Charles Kingsley, for instance, portrayed the fate of children apprenticed to chimney sweeps. The practice of sending children out to whoever would give them work was common in Egerton as in other villages. If they were lucky, they might be farmed out locally; one such arrangement was the following; Mr Thomas Hopkins agreed to keep James White from Michaelmas (September 29th) to Ladiday (March 25th) for 2/- per week and the Parish to cloathe him and Mr Hopkins to make and mend for him for the said time. Another refers to the step son of the George Pack of that time, dated April 1817 : "That Mr Richard Jennings of the Red Lion, Charing Heath, has agreed to keep Peter Battlemore from the date hereof till Michaelmas next and to give the said Peter Battlemore at the expiration of the time agreed the sum of one pound eleven shillings and sixpence. The said Richard Jennings is to wash and mend for him and the Parish to clothe him. This boy was presumably old enough to be useful in a pub in return for his keep; later in the 1820's Mr and Mrs Missing paid the Parish £3 18/- for "the boy from the poorhouse for one year".

Clothes and shoes were often provided by the Parish to fit these boys out before they left home. Payments are recorded for the making on "a frock, britches, stockings and a coate" for each of two boys, and further items were a suit for 3/-, a Hatt and gloves, and also a comb costing 5d. One of them, the Jones boy, was then ready to be apprenticed, he was taken to Faversham and handed over to his new Master. The journey cost the Parish 1/6d, the writing of the indentures 3/- and the fee to the Justice's clerk another 1/-. Another parish boy went to Milton Fair to meet his new Master, Mr Bennet, who was paid £3- to take him on. We do not know what trades these boys were bound to, but the obligations of the authorities ended there. Two Egerton boys were put out as apprentices at Whitstable at £5 and £6 respectively, plus the legal expenses. The sums the Overseers had to spend amounted to a considerable burden on the ratepayers; the death of a pauper child, in contrast, cost relatively little. Sam Eliot's death was typical, including 6d for wool to bury

128

him in (a woollen shroud being a legal requirement, to support the wool trade); 2/- for reading the burial service; 3/- for laying the child out and making an affadavit. A coffin and digging the grave cost about 5/-. In the case of Sam Eliot, an inquest added 14/-, with 4/6 spent on the jury, presumably for refreshments.

The Enclosures Act of 1750 severely aggravated the lot of the rural poor, and fears of a working class insurrection among the well off percolated down to relatively minor property-owners like the ratepayers of Egerton. The Parish Officers were finding it more and more difficult to balance the books, and were having to borrow money for the upkeep of the poorhouse at heavy rates of interest. The inhabitants had their obligation to work brought home to them; for instance, those working on the roads (breaking and hauling stone) had a full 12 hour day. Other measures were resorted to, such as having single men billeted on ratepayers to work out the amount their temporary master was due for. The ten or eleven members of the Vestry who put their names to the documents in question were presumably personally responsible for the monies involved.

It was perhaps no wonder that in the nineteenth century the idea of emigration gained ground. America seemed to offer to penniless families the chance of a fresh start, and to the Parish the welcome prospect of getting rid of some of its worst burdens. In 1828, the Vestry offered three families a free passage, with £2 to be paid to each adult and £1 per child on landing (a stipulation made because many emigrants succumbed on the voyage). In March 1827 a document was drawn up and signed by 23 rate-payers (one of them only making his mark), borrowing £130 to send John Landen, William Turk and James Palmer and their respective families to America, and in the following year they set off.

Each family was given 25/- for their expenses to London and on to Liverpool. Sam Foster, the then Overseer, organised everything on behalf of the Parish; on March 19th he travelled to Liverpool by coach to make the arrangements, and the families joined him on 5th April. The whole lot were maintained while they awaited their ship, given their landing money, medicines for the voyage and fresh meat in addition to their passages. They then disappear from our view, but more followed the next year; three families and a single man and woman. This group were bought fresh meat for the voyage, a tin kettle and a frying pan. They could take little more than what they could carry and the tools of their trade, but Egerton paid to store their stuff in a warehouse and for boats to transport them out to the ship. The "hospital money" (some sort of insurance for the voyage?) for these eighteen people came to £3 16/6d. George Pack, the ancestor of George J.E. Pack who compiled these notes, once considered emigration, but apparently decided against it, as later he applied for 2/6 to repair his axe, and still later was paid 8/- for transporting someone else to the workhouse.

Even a brief survey of these records convinces the reader that the tasks undertaken by the Parish Overseers imposed a heavy and thankless load. Although they served only six months at a time, the work was time-consuming, and borrowing at high rates of interest must have been a constant source of anxiety. It is no wonder that by the 1830's there was little reluctance to hand over the whole business of supporting the poor to the Union Workhouses which were established by the 1834 Act. Egerton decided to sell the local poorhouse to reduce its massive debts, and local paupers were sent thereafter to the new workhouse at Hothfield.

The design of this workhouse was common throughout England. The sexes were strictly segregated, even husbands and wives being kept apart, and courtyards attached to the buildings to keep them so, outdoors as well as in. The basic philosophy was to make workhouse life so unpleasant that only the most desperate and helpless could stomach it. Work was obligatory for everyone, and the food was appalling.

The 1881 census offers a picture of the Hothfield establishment, which had then 132 inhabitants. There was a Master and a Matron; their daughter and their niece were also on the staff, as was a man of 81 from Pluckley listed as a pauper, and a schoolmistress of 20 who came from Nova Scotia. There was a porter-cum-taskmaster, aged 32. Of the 132 inmates, there were at this time four adults and three children from Egerton. The adults were mostly elderly men, formerly agricultural workers, and all unmarried or widowers; the children were aged eleven, twelve and nine, the latter apparently a brother and sister. These young people were all labelled "scholar", implying that they were receiving an education of sorts. Several inmates were baldly designated "imbecile". In 1865, it is recorded that the Parish paid the Union £210 for a half-year, but it is difficult to interpret this figure. Did it mean that was paid per head? Or did each Parish pay a set fee per year? If this was the limit of Egerton's liability, it was a great deal cheaper than running the village poorhouse or sending parcels of paupers to America.

The Hothfield Union continued as such until 1929, when it came under the aegis of the Kent Council and was given a milder name as a place of Public Assistance. Later it was used as a hospital, and at the time of Dunkirk was used as a treatment centre for soldiers evacuated from the beaches, who were encamped on the Common and went there for daily medical care. Then it became a geriatric hospital and was finally sold into private hands and transformed into the Lakeside Residential Home.

There were many other local Unions – West View, Tenterden, Willesborough and Coxheath also became hospitals for a time. West View, now an attractive convalescent centre, remains part of the NHS; the staff there no longer set out to make life as miserable as possible for their patients, as their Victorian predecessors did for our forefathers. Whoever says that those were the good old days should ponder the lives of the poor and helpless in those times.

Charles was living on his own in Little houses in 1891 and presumably had to enter the Union sometime after then and died in 1900. It is not known what circumstances forced him into the workhouse.

Now to a happier story, Eliza Pack White and another large family.

Chapter 21 - Eliza Pack and Another Huge Family

Eliza was born in 1847 and is shown in the 1851 census, aged 4, living at Pack cottages with her family. In the 1871 census there is an Eliza Pack who was a servant with Edward Bryant in Gravesend. Eliza married Henry (often Harry) White, a coachman, and they are both pictured below.

Pictures courtesy of Elsie Hopton MacKethan.

In 1891 they were living at Water villas in Egerton. In 1910 they met Mr and Mrs George Pack, visiting from the USA, George was Eliza's brother. This picture is also shown in George's chapter and they are standing outside Water villas.

Picture courtesy of Elsie Hopton MacKethan.

Eliza and Harry had 11 children as below.

James George White, later George White (born 19th July 1867) a carpenter, he married Lucy, and in 1891 they were living in Pleasant valley. He died in 1894 with Ezra, his uncle although Ezra was only six years older, at Egerton House, see later in Ezra's chapter. It appears James was born out of wedlock and adopted the surname White when his mother married. When he died he left a widow and two children Percy and Dorothy.

Charles E White (born 1869/70). By 1901 he was living in Dartford, Kent, a clothier outfitters assistant with Bessie, his wife from Gloster, Dinsley, age 26. In 1931 Elsie Pack visited from the USA and wrote a letter to her sister as follows:

"In the afternoon we were invited to "Frampton" (the Charlie White's) to tea. Stanley (a son) called for us and drove us there. He is a fine fellow and is engaged to be married but the girl is ill and in a nursing home. I met Leslie (another son) he is more reserved and a bit harder to get acquainted with but still delightful John, their third son, was away teaching so I didn't meet him again. Cousin Charlie (White) and Cousin Bessie looked just about the same, whereas Stanley seemed to have aged about ten years. They are a fine family and made us feel at home"

Charles White, Bessie, and their children Leslie, Stanley and Jack,
picture courtesy of Elsie Hopton Ed MacKethan.

William, a baler, later he had three children John, Leslie and Stanley

Frances (born 1871/2) nothing more known

Annie G (born 1874/5) – married William E Cogger from Maidstone, 4 years older than her. In 1901 they were living in Maidstone and were visited during the grand tour described in chapter 19.

William Peter, later Peter William (born 1876/7)

Mary M (born 1878/9)

Bessie (born 1881/2) – probably married Mr Sanderson – cited in the US trip record in chapter 19.

Belcher (born 1882/3) – not a common first name today! After the 1891 census there is no further trace of Belcher White, which makes it likely that he changed his name.

Mabel (born 1885/6)

Ethel (born 1888/9)

Tracing the White lineage from this point would be very time-consuming for such a common name but perhaps Whites around the world will be able to link up through the Pack web site.

In the next chapter we turn to Edward, James' 5th child, and another USA story.

Chapter 22 - Edward Pack - Another USA Story

Edward (born 24th October 1849) married Sarah Baker (born 1853/4), daughter of James Baker, innkeeper, on 20th December 1877. In 1881 Edward and family are living at Northend cottage and he is a stonemason/bricklayer employing 4 men and 1 boy and therefore presumably quite prosperous. But then sometime before 1891 they decided to emigrate to North America in an interesting way.

In the 1891 Canadian census Edward (41), Sarah (35) and their 3 children; Edward (12), Sarah (8) and Alice (1) were resident at York East, Ontario, Canada. But by 1900 Edward and Sarah were living at Onondaga County, NY State, USA and then in 1910 in Queens, New York and then in 1920 back to Onondaga.

Picture of Edward B. Pack (1849-1926), picture courtesy of Elsie Hopton MacKethan.

It is of course possible that they tried Canada and didn't like it and so moved south. Much more likely is that they got an assisted passage to Canada in order to get to North America and then slipped across the border to get to where they really wanted to be and where other family were. From the 1830s the English authorities did not sponsor emigration to the US any more; the system had been formalised and only emigration to the colonies was assisted. You could of course emigrate anywhere you liked but you would only get help if you were going to support the Empire. This may well be how Edward got, eventually, to Onandaga.

Edward and Sarah are both buried at Oakwood Cemetery, Syracuse, NY (pictured in an earlier chapter), he died 24th April 1926, she died 4th July 1930. They had 7 children of whom 4 were born in Egerton before they emigrated; **Edward** born 16th September 1878, **Sarah** born 2nd May 1882 died 24th November 1952, buried at Oakwood, **Frances Edith** born 23rd May 1884 and **Alice** born in 1889 just before they emigrated and died in Pittsburgh, Pennsylvania but is commemorated at Oakwood with her parents and sister Sarah. According to the US 1910 census Sarah had 7 children so 3 more were born in the US but their names are unknown.

In the next chapter we come to Robert Pack, my ancestor and a catalyst for this book.

Chapter 23 - Robert Pack - Another Catalyst for this Book

Robert Pack and Mary Anne (Annie) Stevens were married on December 28th 1873 at St John's Church, Tunbridge Wells. He was 22 (born 7th March 1852) and she was 20 and from Pluckley. They were both resident in Tunbridge Wells, not Egerton. Mary's father was Thomas Stevens, a farmer. Maria, Robert's younger sister, but only by 3 years, also married a Stevens, George, and as we shall see in the next chapter they emigrated to the USA. On Robert's birth certificate the informant is his mother and where a signature is required is noted "the mark of Frances Pack". Frances' residence is shown as Egerton so Robert was born in Egerton but moved away to Tunbridge Wells where he was married. What a strange time of year for Robert and Mary to get married, December 28th, presumably because it did not interfere with his building trade? Robert was interred at the Mount Zion Baptist chapel on December 24th 1935, aged 83 having died at Westwell house and Mary Anne was interred there on March 17th 1924 aged 68.

Many years later Robert's grandson Joe (chapter 33), my father, wrote the following;

"Robert was something of a tyrant to his family of five. Every night he would climb Egerton Hill to go to the George Inn, which he would leave only at closing time and return home, walking in the middle of the road. The local youths knew about this and would swerve to avoid him. The children were frightened of him when he returned each night. One dark night the inevitable happened and a cyclist knocked him into the ditch. He was helped home and still managed to make his usual visit to the George the following night; he was a tough old bird". Joe's sister Margaret (chapter 32) was even less flattering about Robert *"he was a nasty smelly old man!"*

Meg was 19 when Robert died in 1935 so she will have known him well.

Picture of Robert courtesy of Elsie Hopton MacKethan.

135

In the 1881 census are **Robert Pack**, 29, bricklayer, and **Anne Pack,** 26, and their family, Walter, 7, Arthur, 5, Victor, 3, and Jane Offens, 67 and a retired farmer, presumably a lodger. They were resident at Victor cottage. In the 1891 census they are resident at North End with Arthur, who must have passed away soon after, Victor, Maud, Martha and Jeffrey. They had 7 children.

- **Walter Caleb** was born in 1874, in Pluckley, mentally retarded, and spent his short life in an institution in Epsom; no date of death is known, it is said that his mother (Annie) had been knocked down the stairs when carrying Walter and that Robert drank a lot.
- **Arthur Thomas,** believed born 1876, in Maidstone, died March 25th 1897 of pneumonia and is interred at Mount Zion Baptist church.
- **Victor** was born on 28th July 1877 in Egerton
- **Maud Esther**, born 21st December 1881
- **Jeffrey**, born 5th October 1885
- **Martha Frances**, born 14th November 1888
- **Gladys** born 13th December 1893, died May 24th 1910, aged 17. She is interred at Mount Zion.

Their first 2 children were unfortunate as was their last; but in between they produced four healthy children. All 4 surviving children were registered in Egerton so Robert and Annie clearly had moved back from Tunbridge Wells.

Jeffrey (above) is the ancestor of my family and I knew nothing about his siblings until an event in 2004 obliged me to find out about them and this was one of the catalysts for writing this book.

In November 2004 my father received 2 letters from genealogy companies offering to act for him in the matter of Thomas Pack who had died intestate and without immediate surviving family. Because Thomas was a cousin of my father he might be entitled to a share of Thomas' estate. My father had never mentioned a Thomas Pack and I told him not to reply to the letters, the terms of which were not generous anyway, and that I would deal with it. My aunts, Meg and Audrey, also received such letters and I agreed the same with them.

Thomas Pack was the illegitimate son of Martha Pack (above); he was born on 13th November 1918 and died 5th March 2004. He married Dorothy in 1946 but they had no children and she predeceased him. Since he left no formal will or instructions his estate would become the property of the Treasury Solicitor who would make reasonable efforts by advertising in various journals to discover more distant family. It was these adverts that were seen by the genealogist firms, which led them to write to my father.

I made contact with the Treasury Solicitor and was told that my father could apply to administer the estate, which I did on his behalf, and administration was duly granted to him. Unfortunately my father died in August 2005 before anything could be done in administrating the estate. I then reapplied in my own name and administration was granted to me on 28th February 2006.

The task of the Administrator is to settle all the liabilities of the deceased and then share out the net proceeds according to probate law. Probate law requires that the estate passes up to the deceased's parents (only a mother, Martha, deceased) and then across to her siblings (all deceased) and then down their lines until living descendants are found, all in a pro rata allocation. Thus, Martha had 3 siblings (all deceased) and a third of the estate is allocated to each. That allocation then passes down to the next generation and is allocated equally to each of that generation. If one or more of that generation is deceased then their share passes to the next generation in their line in the same way. The administrator thus has to trace all the living descendants and this is what I had to do and what I found is shown later. It took a long time with many visits to the Family Records centre and backbreaking trawls through the enormous ledgers.

In this process I was told by the Treasury Solicitor that there was another claim on Thomas' estate by a Mrs "X" (name withheld for privacy). Martha, as an unmarried mother who had to work, eventually gave Thomas to an orphanage. From there he was unofficially "adopted" by the "Y" family and brought up by them. The procedures for the adoption of children were formalised in the Adoption of Children Act of 1926 and it would have been perfectly feasible for the family to have formally adopted Thomas and had they done so the eventual outcome would have been entirely different. Mrs "X", a descendant of the "Y" family, regarded Thomas as her uncle. It is probable that Thomas had intended his estate to pass to Mrs "X" and the Treasury Solicitor had indicated that she would exercise discretion in favour of Mrs "X" provided no direct family were discovered. The Treasury Solicitor then advertised for direct family and the rest is described above. Unfortunately as soon as the Treasury solicitor was aware that there were direct family (which happened when I wrote to her on behalf of my father, at which time I knew nothing of Mrs "X") then she could not exercise any discretion whether or not an application for administration was made. I therefore promised Mrs "X" that if she would write a letter explaining the circumstances I would send it to all the potential beneficiaries to give them the opportunity to exercise their own discretion in favour of Mrs "X" should they wish. The value of the estate was modest and Mrs "X" received about a third of it. In all of this process I had to discover the descendants of Victor, Maud and Martha; the descendants of Jeffrey being of course known to me and these are all described in later chapters once we have covered all of James' children.

The next chapter covers Maria, Robert's sister and James' 7th born child and another USA story.

Chapter 24 - Maria Pack - Another USA Story

Maria, sometimes Marie, was born in 1855 and married George Stevens, a farmer, on 28th October 1878 in Egerton; he was 28, i.e. born 1850, son of Thomas Stevens, farmer. George had emigrated to the US in 1870, aged 20, Maria was still resident in Egerton in the 1871 census, aged 16. So George came back to find an English bride to take back to the USA. In 1880 they are living in Tecumah, Shawnee, Kansas with Thomas and Frances Stevens, siblings of George? Then in 1900 they are in Missouri, and in 1910 and 1920 Oklahoma. Somewhere along the way they must also have lived in Syracuse because in 1913 George W. Pack's obituaries refer to a Mrs George Stevens, sister, "of this city". In 1930 George is back in Kansas living with his sister Frances and Maria must have passed away since George and Frances are both noted as widow (ers). George and Maria had 2 children Rose (born 1882) and Ezra (born 1884). Interestingly there is no reference to their children in any US census. The children were not born at the time of the 1880 census and the US 1890 census was lost and they must have left home by the time of the 1900 census when they would have been only 18 and 16.

Since they moved around so much between farming areas it is likely that they never owned a farm and George was just a hired hand although Maria looks prosperous in the pictures below.

A young Maria and a picture with her children.
Both pictures courtesy of Elsie Hopton MacKethan.

The Packs in the USA

As we have seen 4 Pack families emigrated to the USA from Egerton. They were all young and they all went out slightly differently. First was Edward in 1852 at the age of 21 (Chapter 15). He would return to Egerton to find a bride in 1857, then return to the US with his bride, then back to Egerton in 1860 where all but one of his children were born, and then back to the US in 1884. Next was George W. (Chapter 19) in 1866 at the age of 26; he married in the US, raised his family there and lived there all his life. Next was then Maria (above) in 1878 at the age of 23; she was married when she went out and her children were born in the US. And finally Edward the younger (Chapter 22), he would have been about 30 and married with a family when he went out via Canada sometime before 1891. They all appear to have prospered in the land of opportunity. They also appear to have all kept in touch. All the pictures shown so far from Elsie Hopton MacKethan's collection will have been handed down through George W.'s family indicating that he was in touch with them all. Also, of course, 3 of the 4 lived in or around Syracuse and are buried there. With the possible exception of Edward the younger none of the others were assisted in their emigrations; all will have paid their own passages. The reason this is certain is because assisted passages to the US stopped in about 1830; the British authorities would only assist passages to Empire countries from that date.

Emigrating to another country, especially one so far away, must have been an exceptionally worrying as well as exciting experience. The crossing to America took 30 to 40 days until, from the 1850s onwards steam ships took over, which made it much quicker. It was also hazardous, the main risks being infection and disease. It will have helped having fellow countrymen around and emigrants frequently followed other emigrant villagers or family to the same town.

There will be another Pack invasion in the 20th century when 2 Pack daughters, my aunts, arrived in California with their new husbands. There are also many other Packs who I have not been able to join up. Hopefully the web site will help to join up all these loose threads.

The next chapter is Elizabeth, James' 8th child and introducing a link to the Botting family.

Chapter 25 - Elizabeth Pack
A Connection with the Botting Family

Elizabeth was born in 1858 and in the 1871 census she was resident at Pleasant valley, aged 13 with her parents James, 52, and Frances, 51, and her siblings; James, 32, Charles, 26, Edward, 21, Robert, 19, Maria, 16, and Ezra, 10. By the 1881 census they are all still resident at Pleasant valley and Elizabeth, aged 23, is shown as a teacher. By 1891 she had married Edmund William Weeks, often William, a baker from Pluckley, and they are at North End and have 7 children. They had the shop now called Buckles in The Street in Egerton. Elizabeth is pictured below. According to Derek Weeks she lived to 94, and thus died in 1952; Edmund died aged 49 and thus predeceased his wife by nearly 50 years; they are both buried in St James' churchyard.

Elizabeth – picture courtesy of Elsie Hopton MacKethan.

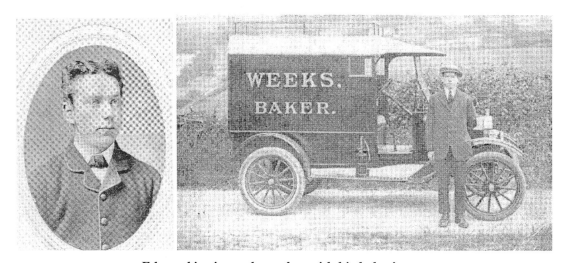

Edmund is pictured together with his baker's van.

They had seven children. All four sons followed in their father's footsteps and became master bakers owning their own businesses after serving their apprenticeships at the Egerton bakery.

- **Albert** (1884)
- **Marian** (1886) never married.

- **Clark** (1888) – had a daughter Ethel per H. Gertrude Pack's trip diary (chapter 19)
- **Louis** (1892) married Brown in Dover in 1915.
- **Hilda** (1893) – married Ernest Botting, a distinguished local name which we shall cover in a later chapter. Hilda had had a long-running courtship with "Spot" Botting, who had a shop and was a very successful photographer. They both had to care for elderly parents and consequently were unable to marry until they were in their sixties.
- **Oliver** (1897) married Russell in 1923.
- **Nora** (1902) married Charles Morris in 1946

Joe Pack, the authors father and described in more detail in a later chapter wrote:

*"I delivered the bread three times a week after school for Mr Botting, the baker, to local houses (*this would have been about 1930 or soon after*). Mr Botting's name had always intrigued me a little. I would collect the bread in a large basket with instructions on where to deliver it. On these days Mr Botting would come out to the front of his shop to watch me climb the hill with the bread, probably to see if I was playing about with any of the other kids. When I thought I was a safe distance away I would turn around and shout "goodbye Mr Bottom" and he would quickly go back into his shop. One day after I had shouted my usual taunt he ran up the hill after me, picked me up, turned me over and bit my bottom! When I arrived to do my bread round the following week he told me he had found a less cheeky boy to deliver his bread. When I told Mum what had happened she told me "it serves you right for being so cheeky."*

It would seem that Hilda and Ernest took over the business from Edmund Weeks. A teacher and a baker/grocer would have been a prosperous pairing.

Note how all the children's names are beginning to sound a bit more modern. We now abandon Elizabeth since she is a Weeks and no longer a Pack although, apart from Hilda and Earnest, it has proved very difficult to find out much about her family.

In 1931 Elsie Pack visited from the USA and in a letter to her sister she wrote:

"I had a splendid visit at Egerton. I stayed with Hilda, Nora and Aunt Elizabeth [Pack Weeks (Mrs William)] We reached there Sat about 11.30 am and left Monday am about 11.45. We had some delightful rambles. We met Hilda's "young man" and he is very nice. Nora's swain was too shy to come in and meet us. We called at the schoolhouse and also at Aunt Lizzie Waghorn's. At the latter place we met numerous other cousins & ramifications of the family. I am very fond of Hilda. We went to Tunbridge Wells for a day. We had lunch there at Marian Weeks'. She is Hilda's older sister and runs a huge boarding house where Queen Victoria once stayed when a girl"

Elsie Pack Dewey and Phylis Pack Hopton had a long correspondence until the 1980s with Hilda Weeks Botting and Nora Weeks Morris.

In the next chapter, James' last child is Ezra who, sadly, met with misfortune.

Chapter 26 - Ezra Pack - A Bitter/Sweet Story

Ezra was born on 1ˢᵗ September 1860. On 29ᵗʰ January 1885 he married Elizabeth Ann Buckman, daughter of William Buckman who was the coachman to Alfred Hickman at Court Lodge until he retired to keep the beer house "The Sportsman's Arms, now Oliver's Garage. In the 1891 census Ezra is aged 30, a carpenter, and living in Pleasant Valley with Elizabeth, 26, and daughters Gertrude and Daisy (there is no sign of their first born William James who would have been about 6 years old and was born about 6 months after they were married). The names Gert and Daisy may bring a wry smile of recognition to more mature British readers. Much later these were the pseudonyms for Elsie and Doris Waters in their popular 1940's and 1950's radio programme "Workers Playtime". Their brother was Horace Waters, better known as Dixon of Dock Green.

Ezra was baptised on October 9ᵗʰ 1886, the day before the baptism of his daughter Gertrude but a year after his son William. Was his wife tidying things up?

Ezra with his sisters Elizabeth and Marie,
picture courtesy of Elsie Hopton MacKethan.

Ezra died on December 7ᵗʰ 1894, aged 34, in a most unfortunate accident and was buried on 13th December 1894. Extracts from an account by Kath Hilder (which draw on the coroner's inquest as reported in the Kentish Express) are repeated below.

Ezra and his nephew (but only 7 years younger), George (Uriah) White, a son of Eliza, Ezra's sister, had been commissioned by a Mr Trimble to repair a pipe in the well at Egerton House which is pictured later.

They went down a ladder taking a light, a charcoal brazier and their soldering irons leaving John Coppins at the top of the ladder to fetch and carry things for them. It would seem that the fumes either from the brazier or from the solder in that confined space overcame Ezra and he started to slide down the ladder and George White, in trying to save his uncle, injured himself and they both drowned in the well. It is not known exactly how deep the well was (but see below, Jeffrey thought it was 60 feet deep) but it may have been sufficiently deep that the ladder did not rest on the bottom but was fixed at the top of the well. Thus when Ezra slid off the ladder, probably injuring himself in the process, there was no way back. Ezra.is buried in the churchyard at St. James' church in Egerton and his epitaph reads "Lord remember me" Luke XX 111 42.

In his diary my grandfather, Jeffrey, who would have been about 9 at the time, wrote:

"December 7th 1894. This day no doubt will be remembered by older people as a day of tragedy. At Egerton House two well-known parishioners lost their lives in the 60-foot well at the back of the house. One man was 34 years old the other 28. They went down the well to mend some pipes. I understand they burnt charcoal and as the well had not been opened before the men went down no doubt the air was very bad. The older person was the first to need help as the younger man called out "Help my master has fainted". There was a man who stood at the top of the ladders, which was their means of escape, but he was unable to do more than raise the alarm. I remember the day as we were out to play, being at school, and I saw my aunt and a Miss White go up the hill which runs close by the school. It was an afternoon of misty fine rain and I could hear the tolling of the church bell, which made it mournful indeed."

It is curious that Jeffrey refers to the 2 men as "parishioners" and doesn't name them despite Ezra being his uncle and George White being a cousin. Does this pick up themes from earlier chapters about 2 Pack families?

On November 1st 1899, about 5 years after Ezra died, Elizabeth remarried and in the 1901 census she is resident at Pleasant Valley, age 34, now Elizabeth Waghorn, with Henry Waghorn and their family. Local gossip said that Henry was so poor that Elizabeth had to buy him a suit to get married in, and he may well have been her employee. In a letter dated February 1917 to a cousin in Australia Elizabeth wrote "*Ezra had an accident down a well, two men were drowned at once, I pulled through and in 5 years I married again and have had two children*" She sounds like a very determined person and the driving force of the family. Their family in 1901 was William James Pack, 15, stepson (born 20th July 1885), he married Mary Graham, who was Scottish, and she was buried in St James' on 23rd September 1947. Gertrude Jane Pack, 14 (born 23rd July 1886), she would later marry John Walter Wooley in October 1907, they were both 21, Daisy Nellie Pack, 12 (born 26th August 1888) – she married James Henry Wickens, 24, on 25th October 1919, she is 31, and Ida Grace Pack, 8 (born 8th October 1891) – she married Alexander Graham, 31, on 20th August 1927, and Lily May Waghorn 9 months old, daughter, she would marry Tiley in 1924 and the local paper for November 1924 records that" *the bride wore grey Mirama, trimmed with pearls, and a veil to match which was surmounted with a charming pearl headdress. She carried a sheaf of lilies, the gift of the bridegroom. The service was fully choral and the reception was held in the Village Hall*". and Ivy Winifred Waghorn – the local paper records her marriage to Edward Wood of Ashford in 1927.

Henry Waghorn and his stepson, William, went into business as Pack and Waghorn, as may be seen from the picture below. They are noted as having been local builders, undertakers, hauliers and pig farmers. Besides the business they had a little land, some cattle and two horses and employed a bricklayer, a labourer and two carters. So a sad story for Ezra turned out to be a happy one for the rest of their family.

Pack and Waghorn when they were at Water Villas, Pleasant Valley

144

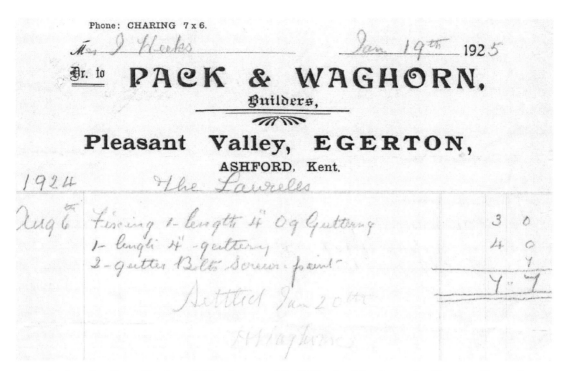

Phone: CHARING 7 x 6.

Mr J Weeks   *Jan 19th 1925*

Dr. to PACK & WAGHORN,

Builders,

Pleasant Valley, EGERTON,

ASHFORD, Kent.

1924   *The Laurels*

Aug 6th   Fixing 1 length 4" Og Guttering   3   0
1 length 4" guttering   4   0
2 gutter B&C Screw paint   7

Settled Jan 20th   7..7

H Waghorn

An invoice from Pack and Waghorn to Mr J Weeks, The Laurels, Egerton Forstal,

Henry Waghorn died on 24th July 1933, aged 62. Elizabeth lived on until October 10th 1953, aged 87.

Henry's funeral was reported in the Kentish Express under the heading "Undertakers Funeral" (which seems a little tasteless). "He had been a builder and undertaker for 35 years as well as church warden. There were many floral tributes"

Ezra was the last of James' children and we now turn to the descendants of Robert, my great grandfather.

Chapter 27 - Victor Pack - A Very Religious Man

Just to get our bearings we started the certain Pack history that leads to me with George Pack senior. He had 3 daughters and George junior. George junior had 13 children (11 surviving) and his first-born was James. James had 9 children and his 6th born was Robert. Robert had 7 children (4 surviving) and his first born surviving child was Victor and the other three children follow this chapter.

Victor Pack was born on 28th July 1877 and his birth was registered in Egerton by his mother. He died on the 11th November 1955 aged 78. The informant was Ruth Pack; his daughter aged 27 of the same address. Victor is described by Meg, his niece, my aunt, as "a dapper man with a moustache, very religious". His grandson, Robert, recalls that he was " a strict Baptist, weekends being spent going to church and hymn singing at home, no other entertainment was permitted". He had a drapers shop in Folkestone which he sold on retirement and moved to Rusthall, near Tunbridge Wells.

Victor made a will on 3rd September 1953 and in it he appointed Arthur Victor, his son, and Ivy Gladys, one of his daughters, to be his executors. He left quite a substantial portfolio of residential properties in Folkestone and Tunbridge Wells to his three children.

Victor married Louisa Clark on 7th September 1910. Victor's occupation was draper's assistant, resident at 45 Guildhall Street and Louisa was a domestic servant at (what appears to be) Faircrouch, Wadhurst. No other Packs witnessed the marriage. Victor witnessed Jeffrey (his brother) and Delia's marriage on 26th March 1913. Victor and Louisa's children were as follows;

Arthur Victor Pack was born 18th June 1911 and his birth was registered by his mother, resident at 12 Stuart Road Folkestone. Victor had wanted Arthur to continue his education and go into banking but Arthur was ready to leave home at 16 and took an apprenticeship in drapery at Chiesmans in Lewisham where he lived in initially and later lived in Forest Hill and then at 88 Earlshall Road SE9. He married Vera Elsie just before the war; she had worked in the accounts department at Chiesmans.

Arthur and Vera.

Arthur joined the navy as a signalman and served at the evacuation of Singapore, then had a long period in the Indian Ocean stationed at Addu Atoll, then in the Mediterranean and finally supporting the D-Day landings. He was mentioned in despatches for tipping off the Admiral about a surprise Churchill inspection. He was also reported missing presumed dead when his ship was sunk in the Mediterranean with considerable losses but he had been loaned to an American ship the day before his own ship sailed. Arthur and Vera had two children; **Robert Arthur Pack** (born 1945, he is a chartered civil engineer, married to a Portuguese, with 2 children, he has worked all over the world and is currently working in the UAE on marine projects) and **Alan Charles Pack** (born 1950). Arthur died 1st November 2001 and Vera Elsie died 19th July 2003.

Ivy Gladys Pack born 3rd June 1919, birth notified by her father resident at 26 Dover Road, Folkestone. Died 5th March 1994 after a stroke. Ruth's ashes were buried in Ivy's grave 8 years later. Ivy's occupation was typist and bookkeeper. Ivy did not marry and did not have children.

Ruth Pack. Born 25th February 1928 in Elham, Kent, she died 20th September 2002. Her occupation was Teachers Assistant. Ruth suffered a nervous breakdown in her 20s, possibly the result of losing her father when she was 27 and had difficulties thereafter. Ruth did not marry and did not have children. Ivy and Ruth worked together for some years until Ivy retired. They both "lived in" as helpers in a school in Lingfield for mentally disabled children.

Ivy and Ruth; Ruth is on the right and aged about 16.

We now turn to Maud, Robert's second surviving child.

Chapter 28 - Maud Esther Pack - A Disjointed Family

Maud Esther Pack was born on 21st December 1881 in Egerton and her birth was registered by her father. Maud had two illegitimate children and then married Herbert Albert Walter on 18th October 1919. He was apparently a rag and bone man in the East End of London, although he had been in service with the Royal Defence Corps between December 1915 and April 1918. He was born in Great Barton, Suffolk, in April 1874. They had one child. The births of both illegitimate children were registered in Egerton and thus Maud was presumably still in Kent at least until 1912, moving to London later and marrying in 1919. The marriage certificate is curious since it gives Maud's age as 36 when it should have been 38, gives her father's name as Albert Pack when it should have been Robert Pack and shows them both as resident at 64 Blomfield Road. It also records the witnesses as A.Amos and (what appears to be) M.F.Pack, presumably Martha Frances, her younger sister. I have no date of death for Maud although it may have been March 1927. When Maud married Herbert Walter in 1919 it appears, as we shall see below, that a condition was that the illegitimate children had to go. Maud's two illegitimate children were;

Frances Ida Pack born 20th August 1905. Maud's occupation on the birth cert is shown as Housemaid (domestic). No father is recorded. Frances married Percy Edward Thomas Pullee on April 11th 1936. An extract from a local paper recorded their marriage.

"At St Paul's Canterbury on Saturday the marriage took place between Percy Thomas Edward Pullee, only son of Mrs Abbott (no mention of a father and a different surname?) of Longport street Canterbury, and Frances Ida Pack, niece of Mr J Pack of Victor Villa Egerton. The bride was given away by Mr Standing (uncle of the bridegroom) and was gowned in ivory satin. She was attended by Miss E Chapman and Miss Doreen Chapman, who wore white and pink floral chiffon frocks. Mr E Lambert was best man. A reception was held at the Keir Hardie Hall and later the couple left for Ramsgate" [Extract courtesy of Renee Weeks.]

She was 30 he was 27 and a house decorator. They both registered the same address at 19 Longport Street, Canterbury. Oddly the father's name shown for Frances, who had no known father, was (what appears to be) Grace Stevens. Frances' grandmother was Annie Stevens (maiden name), otherwise it is impossible to know where this came from. Percy Pullee was born in 1909 in Canterbury and died 7th August 1963 aged 54. Talking to Patricia Stamp (Pullee), one of Frances's daughters, see later, she told me she believed her mother, Frances, had been brought up by her grandparents, James and Frances, since the age of 13, which is about when her mother married Herbert Walter. Frances died 27th April 1987 aged 82. Frances and Percy had 4 children.

- **Margaret Jean Pullee** born 2nd April 1937. Margaret married Peter John Anthony McQuaide, a council gardener, on 20th April 1957 and Percy Pullee was a witness. Peter was born 30th March 1937 and died Oct 2002, aged 65. Patricia told me that Margaret and Peter divorced and are now both passed away. They had 3 children Stephen McQuaide, Graham (passed away, did not marry and had no children) and Catherine Piggott .
- **Patricia Elaine Pullee** born 25th January 1940. She married a Mr Stamp who passed away in January 2004 and she has 2 children, a boy and a girl.

- **Audrey Elizabeth Pullee** born 7th August 1943, married Anthony John Mumford on March 27th 1965. Anthony's father is noted as Bernard Fletcher, which is puzzling, and his occupation is soldier. Audrey had an illegitimate child, John Anthony, on 8th March 1962 before her marriage, no father is recorded. The birth certificate records Audrey Elizabeth as mother but has a subsidiary note from the Superintendant Registrar "Adopted".

- **Edward Pullee** died aged 1 month on 21st December 1945 of pneumonia. Percy Pullee's occupation on the certificate is shown as gunner in the Royal Artillery and he even gives his serial number 1786356.

Leonard Albert Pack born 3rd March 1912 and his mother on the certificate is Maud Esther Pack, kitchen maid of West Ashford House, Westwell. No father is recorded. Leonard died on 27th May 1933 aged 21 at Archway hospital. His address is given as 26 Lonsdale Road, Paddington and he was an errand boy for a chemist and died of TB. The informant was M F Pack, aunt, of 3 Glenshaw Mansions, Priory Road, Hampstead. This is presumably Martha Frances. It would appear that Maud has lost contact with her son or did indeed die in 1927. Leonard did not marry. Note from the above that Leonard Albert Pack died at 26 Lonsdale Road W11 in 1933 and the address for Pauline's father on her birth certificate was the same address in 1950. This would seem to confirm Leonard for 1933 but raises other questions. Because Leonard died young and Frances only produced daughters the Pack name now dies out in this family. Maud's legitimate child with Herbert Albert Walter was;

Douglas Allen (sometimes Allan) Walter born 20th August 1920, the birth was registered by his mother in Egerton which is strange since she had only married a year or so earlier and was living at 64 Blomfield Road London. His father, Herbert Walter's, occupation on his son's birth certificate is shown as General Labourer, ex 9th Battalion, RO Corps. When Douglas Allen was born in 1920 Frances and Leonard would have been 15 and 8 and it is likely that it is then that they are obliged to move out to be brought up by their grandparents. The birth certificate for Douglas Allen Walter (junior), below, shows his father as Douglas Allen Walter and his mother as Winifred Lily Mary Harris, formerly Manser. Her previous marriage was dissolved and they married in Kensington Registry office on 10th August 1957. He is noted as a confectioner and they were both resident at 3 Victoria Mansions, Ladbroke Grove, London. Douglas Allen had 2 children with Winifred. He died 19th June 1986 and the informant was his son, also Douglas Allen Walter. The deceased's occupation is shown as Resident Porter (retired) of 18, Gladys Road. Douglas Allen's progeny were:

- **Douglas Allen Walter** (junior) born 7th September 1948 he married Ann Rose Bates in 1973 at Wembley Park. They have 3 sons, all living at home and none married, Alex Douglas (born 1981) a technician, Richard Allen (born 1983) also a technician, he has been helpful with parts of this chapter, and James Edward (born 1985) an electrical engineer. Douglas remembers very little of his early years only that they moved around a lot and lived with his maternal grandmother. He knows nothing about his father's family and does not know of Frances or Leonard He says his parents were together until his mother died. .

- **Pauline June Walter** born 6th June 1950 unmarried and no children. On her birth certificate her father's address is 26 Lonsdale Road, W11 (where Leonard Albert Pack died – see above and the property is pictured below) and her mothers address is 3 Victoria Mansions, Ladbroke Grove W10. It is not known why they were living in separate addresses when Douglas junior says they were together until the end. In a letter from Pauline she says that her father "and his wife" never talked about other relatives. Note the wording of "his wife" not "my mother".

26 Lonsdale Road

Lonsdale road today is substantially gentrified; 50 years ago the large houses in the Notting Hill area were mainly multi-occupancy and substantially run down.

Because the lives of Maud and Martha appear to be intertwined we now abandon chronology and go to Martha in the next chapter even though she was born after her brother, Jeffrey.

Chapter 29 - Martha Frances Pack - Housemaid of Hampstead and the Mayor of Harpenden

Martha Frances Pack was born on the 14th November 1888. Her birth was registered in Egerton by her father, Robert. Martha left home and followed the traditional route of domestic service but then she had an illegitimate son, Thomas, on 13th November 1918, when she was 30. Her occupation on the birth certificate was shown as 'Housemaid of Hampstead' (21 Broadhurst Gardens, Hampstead). No father is recorded. Thomas Pack told Mrs "X" (the probate story was told in chapter 23) that he was a dentist. At about the age of 7 Thomas was given up to eventually become part of the "Y" family as described in the earlier chapter. Presumably it was not possible for her to keep her son and fulfil her domestic duties or possibly as Thomas was growing up he would need more attention than his mother could give him.

21 Broadhurst Gardens today

By 1933 Martha had moved from Broadhurst Gardens into service at 3 Glenshaw Mansions, Priory Road, Hampstead, as this is the address given when she notified the death of Leonard Albert Pack, son of Maud. It is possible that she moved to this address in about 1925 when Thomas was 7 and this employment was conditional upon not keeping her son. According to Mrs "X" Martha did not keep in touch with Thomas and it was only later in life that Thomas sought out his mother and they were reunited. The parallels with Maud are striking. Both sisters had illegitimate children and were obliged to give them up, although for different reasons, and both abandoned them unconditionally, not expecting to see them again and not trying to keep in touch. Perversely Martha did keep in touch with Maud's illegitimate children. She notified Leonard Albert's death and corresponded with Frances' children. Perhaps they were her surrogate family?

Martha married David Henry Hoath on 18th January 1947. Their marriage was solemnised at the Zion Baptist Church Pembury Road Tonbridge, according to the rites and ceremonies of the strict Baptists by license. David Hoath was 64 years old, born in 1882 and living in Sevenoaks. He was a widower and a gardener (domestic) at Bough Beech Place Lodge, Edenbridge. Martha was 58 years old and her occupation was Companion Help of 48 Mereworth Road Tunbridge Wells. Witnesses at the wedding were G. Hoath, presumably one of David's children and Thomas Pack, her son, who had found his mother by then.

Martha and David.

David Hoath predeceased Martha since she is shown as the widow of David Hoath on her death certificate when she died on 30th July 1975 aged 87.

Martha's son, **Thomas**, was born on the 13th November 1918 and died 5th March 2004. He married Dorothy Atkinson in 1946. They had no children. Thomas had a varied career. He was a Methodist preacher, he worked for the National Children's home in Harpenden for the last 15 years of his life and before that he worked at youth hostels in Norfolk and Birmingham. He was a Harpenden councillor for 8 years and was Mayor of Harpenden in 1991/2. He was also a conscientious objector in the war.

The mysterious Mrs "X" described in chapter 23 claimed that Thomas used to say that the "Packs" ostracised him and his mother and that this troubled him all his life. If true this will not have been because he was illegitimate; as we have seen there have already been several illegitimate Packs. More likely is that he was very difficult to find, having been given into care and then rescued by the "Y" family whose details the orphanage may not have been prepared to divulge. In addition several strands of the Pack family, as we shall see, are about to venture overseas just like the ones nearly a hundred years before. Two of those are in Jeffrey's family, which now follows.

Chapter 30 - Jeffrey Pack - Getting Close to Home Now

Jeffrey was born on 5th October 1885 and baptised 2nd November 1902, aged 17. He married Edith Emma (always Delia, reasons unknown) Hopkins (born 1888). Dr Littledale, again for reasons unknown, advised Delia against the marriage. Was it because there had been many Pack/Hopkins marriages, as we shall see in a later chapter? They were married at St Mary's church High Halden on March 26th 1913. Victor Pack (Jeffrey's older brother) witnessed their marriage. A family story is that they married at High Halden because they didn't want the publicity that there might be marrying in Egerton. In fact Delia, on the wedding certificate is shown as being resident in High Halden. They hired a horse and trap for the journey and when they came back (presumably to Egerton) Jeffrey went off to work! He didn't quite go immediately because there was some sort of reception at Newland Green (the family home of the Hopkins's) as the following picture shows.

Jeffrey's father, Robert, is second from the left.

Jeffrey and Delia had 5 children, the first, a girl, died at birth, unnamed, and then Gladys, Margaret (always Meg), Joseph and Audrey. On the birth of Joseph, the author's father, in 1918, Jeffrey's occupation was shown as Ordinary Seaman Royal Navy (builder). Jeffrey's war story is told below and the catalyst for it was his box, which is pictured overleaf.

Jeffrey's Box

This was discovered in my father's effects when he died. Just about readable is J.Pack and a service number V 53945 and the date 1917. In addition he seems to have used the box as a notebook since there are several scribblings on it including interest payment dates, addresses and a note of 5 days leave on October 7th 1918.

At the start of the war in 1914 Jeffrey was 29 and married and an established builder. He would thus not have been one of the early conscripts. In fact the Navy, which would be his chosen service, at that time had too many sailors and the Royal Naval Division was formed, described as "Winston's little Army" (Churchill was First Lord of the Admiralty then), to serve within the Army. Jeffrey joined the Royal Naval Volunteer Reserve (which was allocated to the Royal Naval Division) probably in 1917, by which time the surplus of sailors was rapidly diminishing. His initial service number will have been as above, V 53945, and from the picture overleaf he appears to have spent some of his time in the Home Guard. He was based at Chatham and the box pictured below may well have contained tools for ship repairs. It is a small box, only 12 by 8 inches and 5 inches high so the tools probably were specialised ones. His initial naval duties appear to have been either maintenance ones at Chatham or Home Guard duties, probably near Egerton.

Jeffrey's Box.

But in 1918 he was called up for proper naval service. Accordingly his service number changed to J 85311. From his service record in the National Archives at Kew he was stationed from 19th February 1918 until 16th July 1918 at HMS Pembroke, then from 17th July 1918 until 30th September 1918 at HMS Fearless, then back to Pembroke from 1st October 1918 for 2 weeks and then from 14th October 1918 until 11th March 1919 (when he was demobilised) to HMS Columbine. HMS Pembroke was a land based training establishment at Chatham where Jeffrey undertook his training. Fearless was a Scout Cruiser and this was presumably part of the training as well. Columbine was a 1917 purpose built Torpedo Boat Destroyer based at Port Edgar, Queensferry, north of Edinburgh. Jeffrey was by now a fully trained ordinary seaman. With Columbine, as we shall see below, he participated in the surrender of the German fleet at Scapa Flow.

Jeffrey is in the back row on the left on Home Guard duties

In his diary Jeffrey writes:

"1914 – 1918 was the 1ˢᵗ World War. I joined up by going into the Navy. I saw all the German fleet surrender, small ships first, and so on to the big battle ships. It took an hour for them to pass by. Then we escorted them to Scapa Flow".

The Armistice ending the war was signed on the 11ᵗʰ November 1918. Under it's terms Germany's U boat fleet was surrendered unconditionally and without the possibility of return. Arrangements for the surface fleet, however, were more difficult to agree. There was argument between the Allied powers, each hoping to gain some of the ships, and there was a continuing problem of discipline in the German crews many of whom were close to mutiny. While these discussions were continuing the fleet of 74 ships was interned at Scapa Flow, near the Orkney Islands. But the mutinies proved impossible to contain and the Germans scuttled their ships in June 1919. 52 of the 74 ships were sunk. Jeffrey was involved in some of this process.

Delia also had a war role, but in the next World War. Tony Turner tells a story that early in World War 2, before there were air raid warning systems around the country, there would be local wardens who would warn of impending air strikes and Delia performed this service in Egerton cycling around the village ringing a bell. A proper system was eventually installed locally.

Jeffrey and Delia lived first at the Red House in Egerton (built by Jeffrey's father), at the top of Crocken Hill, then The Gables, a bungalow at Crocken Hill (also built by Robert) and then, when Jeffrey's mother, Annie, died they moved to Victor Villa to take over Robert's building business and to look after him. Jeffrey was a builder as his father and grandfather had been and in a later chapter we will find out how many of the buildings in Egerton were built by the Packs. In his diary Jeffrey talks about his building career.

"1899 I followed my father in the building trade and my grandfather was also a builder employing up to 30 men at times. From the age of 13/14 to 19 I was at home working for my father. Then an old bricklayer came to see my father to ask whether he would oblige him by doing a job at Headcorn as he could not go himself. My father said he would not go but I could, if I liked. So I went and it was just what I wanted to get on with other people and to gain experience. I walked from Egerton to Headcorn for 13 weeks before I bought a bicycle. I had almost 2 years working for a builder at Headcorn and one job I did for him was to build Barnland House. I gave a price for doing it. It was a 6 roomed house about a mile from Headcorn and close by the railway. I started it in March and finished it in June. I did not do the plastering or carpentry of course. During the time I left home my father let the business run down so I came home and started on my own. I was 21 then. My father said to me, as I was taking over the business, I should like you to have your chance, Jeff, and I replied I should like to have the chance that you had. When I built Barnland House my mate used to walk from Grafty Green 3 to 3 and a half miles away. Believe it or not we used to get to the house at 6am. He was a jolly good man in every way."

Jeffrey and Delia's 4 surviving children were; **Gladys** born 16th April 1915 baptised 23rd April 1915, **Margaret (always Meg)** born 12th September 1916, baptised 3rd September 1916, **Joseph Thomas** born 30th April 1918, baptised 26th May 1918 and **Audrey** born 23rd August 1923 baptised 27th August 1923. Their lives will be described in later chapters.

Jeffrey and Delia with their first two children, Gladys and Meg.

Picking up on earlier themes Meg and Audrey both emigrated with their husbands and families to North America in August 1955, as we shall see later in their chapters, and Jeffrey and Delia went several times to see them, once in August/September 1956 and then again the following year and then again in July 1967.

Having lived all their lives in Egerton Jeffrey and Delia then became unsettled late in life and moved in August 1950 to live with their son, Joe, in London, then in June 1951 they moved back to Detling in Kent, then in 1953 they moved to Iver to be near Joe and Gladys, then in August 1956 to Hemel Hempstead to be nearer to Gladys then in June 1959 back to son Joe.

Jeffrey died in 1971; aged 86 and Delia then went to live with Audrey and her family in Sussex. This chapter on Jeffrey is short because his main interests are described in other chapters. He was a builder and the properties built by him and other Packs in Egerton are listed later; he was a sportsman and sporting Egerton is covered separately and he was a bell ringer and chorister and this is described in his son Joe's chapter.

Jeffrey and Delia

In his diary Jeffrey wrote:

"A journey through life. Nothing has been written up to this present about the 26th March 1913, this was the great event of my life. Married at High Halden 8 miles from Egerton to a young lady whose home was at Newland Green farm in the same parish. From that day to this I have never regretted taking such a decision, my wife has been a true help and is still a wonderful person and I don't mind who knows it. We have 4 children, all grown up, 1 son and 3 daughters. 1 daughter is in Canada (in fact Meg was in California) *the other 3 are in England. We are living with our son and the daughters are all reasonably near. I daughter lost her husband when living in Canada. He was a test pilot and met with an accident. Our son during the 2nd World War was shot down in Belgium and taken prisoner but escaped and got down to Gibraltar and home by one of our ships. It was an anxious time for us. All the family go out of their way to help us and so do the grandchildren".*

Jeffrey and Delia's first surviving child was Gladys and she follows in the next chapter.

Chapter 31 - Gladys Pack - Keen Bellringer

Gladys was born 16th April 1915 and died in 2004. She married Neville Manchip in 1938.

Neville was born in Australia – his father owned plantations producing rubber and cotton in Malaya. He was sent to Stewarts College in Edinburgh when he was 12.

They had 4 children Sheila, John, Anne and Phyllis. Neville died in 1982, aged 80. Gladys spent her remaining years living happily on the Isle of Arran. Sheila was born in 1938 and married John Hardaker and they live in Wellingborough. Anne was born in 1940 and was married and divorced twice and lives in California. John was born in 1942, married Calan, and they had 2 children – Ivan and Tiffany. He married again but is separated. John lives in California. Ivan has 2 children. Phyllis was born in 1943 and married Tony Johnson who died in 1984. They had 3 children Petra (born 1965) living in California, Lorna (1967), married Peter Wilkinson, living in Dorset, and Lyndon (1974) who has 2 daughters with his partner Caitlin.

Like all her family Gladys was a bell ringer certainly when she was young and the picture below, which is in the bell tower at St James', records a notable peal with her mother in 1934 when she was 19.

Chapter 32 - Margaret Pack - The USA story continues

Margaret (always Meg) was born 12th August 1916 and married John Munton on 20th January 1943 and moved to California 19th September 1955. They have 1 daughter, Christine (born in 1945), with whom they now live in Oregon, USA. Christine married Robert Hile and they have 2 children, Victoria (now Hoffman) who lives with her family in New Market, Maryland and Robbie who lives in Crescent city California. The whole family are now US citizens.

The family picture below was taken just before Meg and John and Audrey and Jack (chapter 34) emigrated to the USA in 1955. Meg is middle row second from the right and John is back row second from the right. Audrey is back row second from the left and Jack is back row at the extreme right. Your humble author is seated bottom left.

Meg was my father, Joe's, favourite sister, and in **Love is in the air** he wrote about a money making exercise with Meg to try and raise enough money for a bicycle.

"It was a good year for acorns. They covered the ground under the oak trees like a carpet and I asked a farmer if he would like some acorns for his pigs and he said he would. Collecting acorns is a tedious business and I asked Meg, my middle sister, if she would help me. Meg was a tomboy. We were pals most of the time. She could climb trees, didn't mind worms, snakes or frogs although she didn't like horses or cows, I don't know why. She agreed to help me collect acorns into my trolley and the box was soon filled. The farmer was delighted and paid us well. We repeated this moneymaking exercise for two or three days until the farmer realised we were collecting the acorns from under his own trees. He refused any further payments and moved his pigs to the wood to feed themselves and save him money and that was the end of that."

"My trolley had many uses. If I saw a horse and cart passing the house I would follow it with my trolley. If the horse obliged, as it did frequently with it's exertions on the hill, I would scoop up the droppings from the road with my shovel and bring it home for Mum's vegetable garden, which would always make her smile. I always kept the box fairly clean, but Meg wouldn't always ride in it, she was always rather particular, being a girl."

"Conditions were now right for mushrooms. To be sure of a good basketful meant getting up early, long before the farmer was up. Meg agreed to help me, after a bit of haggling, and we decided to go the following morning. I was awake very early and woke Meg. We crept down and out the back door, which was never locked. We started off across the fields and were soon held up by a herd of bullocks which would not let us pass. We eventually chased them by running at them and waving our arms, they would turn and run away kicking up their hind legs in fun. Continuing our walk we eventually arrived at the field, just as it was getting light, and what a sight, mushrooms everywhere. We soon had our basket full to overflowing and were on our way home without seeing another person."

"There was not much to look forward to now, I was a long way from saving the £12 I needed for my bike, there was only school once again. The following day Dad asked me how much money Mum had saved for me. I told him and wondered why he asked. But the following day, surprise, surprise! An almost new second hand bike appeared in the shed. Dad had used my savings and added to it to buy the bike from someone he knew. When the bike was wheeled out of the shed it had no bar at the top – it was a girl's bike! At first I was very disappointed. Meg, my sister was highly delighted, she pointed out that the bike partly belonged to her, as I suppose it did. Neither of us had ridden a bike before, we quarrelled a bit as to who should ride it first, but in the main Meg was a good sport, for a girl!

Meg and her husband, John in California.

Chapter 33 - Joseph (always Joe) Pack, leading eventually to yours truly

Joe was born 30th April 1918. The story of his early years in Egerton and then his war story are fully told in another book by the author entitled **"Love is in the air"** and available from Woodfield Publishing. In summary he enlisted with the RAF in 1940, aged 22 and was trained as a Halifax bomber pilot. On the night of 7/8th June 1942, on his 18th mission, his plane was shot down on the Dutch/German border. His evasion and return to the UK involved a Dutch Inspector of ditches (who found Joe hiding in a ditch after his parachute jump), the famous Comet line (who hid him and got him to Brussels, then Paris and then St. Jean de Luz), a Basque smuggler (who escorted him and 3 others over the Pyrenees) and many other extraordinary people who put their own lives at risk to help stranded allied airmen evade capture. He arrived back in Egerton the day after his parents had received a telegram from the Air Ministry "Missing, believed killed on active service".

He was then reassigned to flying boats – first Sunderlands and then Catalinas – and while undergoing the extra training this required, his eye was caught by a certain Margaret Dillon, a WAAF Officer serving at RAF Oban, but before anything could develop she was posted to RAF Davidstow Moor in Cornwall and he was posted to 265 Squadron based in Madagascar.

They then corresponded by airmail letter for about 2 years before Joe came back in early April and they married on 2nd June 1945 barely a month after his return. Almost their entire courtship was conducted by airmail letter, hence the title of the book.

Pictured with them are Gladys, Joe's sister, and Frank, Margaret's brother.

After the war Joe did not return to Egerton or resume working in his father's building business, thus breaking a near 100-year tradition of the Packs being the main builders in the village. More of this in a later chapter. Joe and Neville Manchip, sister Gladys' husband, started a small company doing shop renovations and exhibition stands in London and this grew and prospered. Joe was a very enthusiastic bell ringer all his life, as were all his family, and fuller details of this are given in the chapter on recreational Egerton.

Along the way Joe and Margaret had two sons; Jeffrey married Jacqueline and they had Arabella and Joe junior; Robert married Stephane and they produced James and Christopher. We are all pictured overleaf about 20 years ago. Your humble author is at the back on the left.

After they retired Joe and Margaret spent a lot of time in Kent having bought and renovated an Oast house in Smarden, which is close to Egerton, and they are pictured there below, along with a cartoon of Joe drawn by a colleague in his RAF days.

They regularly had their grandchildren to stay every school holiday, which was a boon for their parents and a wonderful country experience for the children. Now we move on to Audrey, Jeffrey's last child.

"The last of the many"

Chapter 34 - Audrey Pack and Jack Lumsdaine

Audrey was born 5th August 1923, 5 years after Joe, and married Leon Sydney (always Jack) Lumsdaine on April 7th 1945 at St James' church in Egerton. He was 22; she was 21. Audrey and Jack's wedding is pictured below with Jack in service uniform.

Jack's father was Arthur Henry Vere Lumsdaine, an aircraft engineer. Jack's parents were in the China trade and Jack was educated in Shanghai and San Francisco and the first time he ever went to England was to enlist with the RAF. But he was more English than the English. His mother lived in San Francisco. Audrey and Jack emigrated in 1956 initially to San Francisco and then a year later to Cold Lake in Canada.

Jack joined the RAF in February 1942, aged 20. After training he was assigned to No. 30 Squadron in May 1943 flying Wellington and then Stirling bombers. He flew many missions over northern Europe including several special missions with targets not named in his logbook. He later converted to Mosquitos and flew over 1300 hours during the war. He was awarded the Distinguished Flying Cross. He continued after the war in the RAF until 1955 when he and Audrey were preparing to emigrate to Canada. There, Jack joined the RCAF Central Experimentation and Proving Establishment as a test pilot for new aircraft. He died on 29th March 1966 when a Tutor training aircraft rudder pedal jammed and he could not recover from a spin and ejected too late. He flew probably about 50 different aircraft types and completed nearly 7000 flying hours before his untimely death. 7000 flying hours over 24 years is 292 flying hours per annum or an hour's flight virtually every day of the year. His friend and flying colleague, John (Jack) Jackaman has written a full account of Jack's flying history, from which this is drawn, and it is reproduced in appendix 3.

Jack in flying gear.

After Jack's accident the family returned to England in August 1967 but daughter Delia and family returned to Chilliwack, British Columbia in 1998. Audrey and Jack had 3 children Diana, Bruce and Delia. Diana lives in Sussex and has 4 children; Melanie (1970), Leila (1972), Rebecca (1980) and Joy (1982) and 9 grandchildren at the time of writing but shortly to increase by two. Bruce married Tania and they live in Sussex with their 5 children; Mathew (1980), Hannah (1984), Naomi (1985), Leah (1990) and Jack (1982) and their 2 grandchildren. Delia married Howard and they returned to Canada in March 1998 with Audrey and their children; Nicola (1985) Andrew (1987) Caroline (1991) and Thomas (1994). Audrey died in Canada in 2007 having been widowed for 41 years.

The following is from the memorial sheet for Audrey; the service was held at St Thomas' Anglican Church in Chilliwack, BC.

A Celebration of Life

Audrey Lumsdaine

August 5, 1923 -
September 30, 2007

The address for Audrey was as follows;

Audrey was born in Egerton, Kent, England, the youngest of 4 children to parents Jeffrey and Delia Pack. She had a very happy childhood.

The very first May Festival minuet with (left to right) Jessie Cowdy, Audrey Pack, Beryl Homewood and Ruth Cowdy

This was not in the address but seems an appropriate place to put it

After leaving school she entered nursing training, but after 2 years decided to join the WRAF (Women's Royal Air Force) as WWII had begun. She met Jack, her future husband, when she, as fighter controller, was talking to him over the airwaves as his plane was coming back to base after a mission. They married in April 1945 and had three children; Diana, Bruce and Delia.

Jack was a great sportsman, competing for Britain in the Commonwealth Games and the Olympics in modern pentathlon. Audrey took great pleasure supporting Jack's sporting interests.

In 1955 the family emigrated from England to California along with Audrey's sister Meg and family. Audrey's family stayed 9 months in California before moving to Cold Lake, Alberta, where Jack could resume his love of flying in the RCAF. The family moved from Cold Lake to Hudson, Quebec in 1960, and Jack took up the position of chief air force test pilot testing the Starfighter (CF 104) with Canadair in Montreal. The family lived nearby in Hudson and several very happy years were spent there until Jack died in military service with the RCAF.

A year later in 1967 Audrey decided to move back to England to be nearer her family after the loss of her husband. However when Delia and Howard decided to move to Canada in 1998 with their family, Audrey, at the age of 75, and still with a sense of adventure moved with them to Chilliwack. Audrey very much enjoyed her years in Chilliwack, sharing many good times with friends and family.

The modern pentathlon in which Jack competed is an event comprising pistol shooting, epee fencing, freestyle swimming, show jumping and a 3 km run. It was introduced at the 1912 Olympics by Baron Pierre de Coubertin, founder of the modern Olympics and was intended to simulate the experience of a 19th century cavalry soldier.

For different reasons Audrey criss crossed the Atlantic several times just as her ancestor, Edward, had done about 100 years earlier. Audrey and Jack and their young family are pictured below when they were in Canada.

We started this book with sundry Packs that may or may not be related to my family – Sir Christopher, Sir Denis and so on – and now we finish it in similar fashion with some contemporaneous Packs that may or may not be related but certainly have interesting stories. Thus my Pack family is neatly sandwiched between sundry others. The 3 Packs that follow are Amy Elizabeth Thorpe Pack, K.H. (Madagascar) Pack and Howard Meade Pack. When we have looked at them we will return to Egerton.

Chapter 35 - Amy Elizabeth Pack 1910-1963
Wartime Mata Hari

She was neither born a Pack nor died a Pack but did carry the name during her incredible wartime exploits. She was born Amy Elizabeth Thorpe on November 22nd, 1910, in Minneapolis. Family and friends called her Betty. William Stephenson, who ran Great Britain's World War II intelligence activities in the Western Hemisphere, would one day give her a code name–'Cynthia.' She reputedly was one of the most successful spies in history.

Amy Thorpe's father was a U.S. Marine Corps officer, and the family travelled extensively. Her mother was the daughter of the State Senator for Minnesota and she came from a highly privileged background. By the age of 11, she had used postcards and guidebooks to provide the Neapolitan setting for a romantic novel she wrote, entitled *Fioretta*. A copy found its way to a young-at-heart naval attaché named Alberto Lais at the Italian Embassy in Washington, D.C.

Her father's resignation from the service to study law brought Amy Thorpe to the U.S. capital, where she met Commander Lais. The Italian officer's platonic relationship with the adolescent he called his 'golden girl' undoubtedly contributed to her appearance of maturity. By the time she made her debut in Washington society, 18-year-old Thorpe was beautiful, well bred and graceful, with green eyes and amber-coloured hair. She exuded a magnetism that drew men to her.

An affair with Arthur Pack, second secretary at the British Embassy in Washington and 19 years her senior, evolved into a mismatched marriage and gave her a second citizenship. Arthur was born in 1891 in Stepney, London (I can trace no link to my family, perhaps someone eventually will, the story is included mainly for interest). They married on April 29th 1930 in Washington when Betty was 4 months pregnant. She gave birth to a son, Anthony (always Tony), five months after the wedding, but for a variety of reasons, probably to do with Arthur's diplomatic career, they turned the infant over to foster parents in England. Betty then hardly saw her son for the rest of her life. Tony fought in Korea and was awarded the Military Cross for "conspicuous gallantry" but was killed in action on July 10th 1952 before he could receive it. A daughter, Denise, born in 1934, did nothing to help the eroding union but she did bring Denise up and didn't abandon her as they had Tony.

Arthur Pack was transferred to Madrid on the eve of the Spanish Civil War, where Amy Pack immersed herself in secret operations. She helped smuggle rebel Nationalists to safety, transported Red Cross supplies to Franco's forces, coordinated the destroyer evacuation of the British Embassy staff from northern Spain, and meddled in diplomatic affairs. Those activities ceased when she was denounced to her Nationalist friends as a Republican spy, apparently by a jealous woman.

In the autumn of 1937, accompanied by her young daughter and a nanny, Amy Pack boarded the Warsaw Express in Paris to, in her words, 'become a member of his Britannic Majesty's Secret Intelligence Service.' She was quickly 'adopted' by a group of young men working for the Polish foreign ministry, a situation facilitated by her husband. Arthur Pack, now an official at the embassy in Poland, had informed her he was in love with another woman. Shortly afterward, he suffered an attack of cerebral thrombosis that landed him in an English nursing home.

Amy Pack was recruited by British intelligence and allotted an entertainment allowance of 20 pounds sterling to cultivate her highly-placed Polish sources. Of her first official male conquest, she would later tell a biographer and future lover, 'Our meetings were very fruitful, and I let him make love to me as often as he wanted, since this guaranteed the smooth flow of political information I needed.' Pack met her next target at a dinner party hosted by the American ambassador. The handsome Pole seated next to her was a personal aide to foreign minister Jósef Beck. Although married, the aide was sufficiently impressed by his dinner companion to send her pink roses the next morning.

From him she learned that Polish experts were working on overcoming the threat posed by Germany's Enigma enciphering machine. The Enigma machine had started in the 1920s as a commercial "secret writing machine". The Germans recognised its military application and adopted a military variant. Encrypted messages were noticed by the Polish secret service in 1926 and they set about trying to crack the codes. SIS was aware of the work being done by the Poles but by 1938 there was concern in Britain that Poland would soon be overrun and the work done by the Poles would be lost.

The extent of her contribution to the 'Ultra secret', that gave the Allies a crucial edge over the Nazis, remains a matter of conjecture and it is quite likely she never knew the importance of what she obtained. In fact, however, Britain would owe its ability to decode so much of Germany's World War II radio traffic to the efforts of the Poles, who had cooperated with the French in working out the Enigma system.

In Prague, Pack obtained conclusive proof of Hitler's plans to dismember Czechoslovakia. For reasons that remain unclear, in the autumn of 1938 the ambassador ordered her to leave the country. The following April, having called a domestic truce, a recuperated Arthur Pack and his wife travelled to South America, where he took over his embassy's commercial section in Santiago, Chile.

When World War II started, Amy Pack offered her talents to the British intelligence service. She soon was writing political articles for Spanish and English language newspapers in Chile. Britain was then gearing up its intelligence and propaganda efforts in the hemisphere, placing them in the spring of 1940 under the British Security Coordination (BSC), headed by Canadian William Stephenson.

Amy Pack left her husband and sailed to New York, where she was given her code name, 'Cynthia,' and an assignment to set up shop in Washington, D.C. As her cover, she posed as a journalist. Her first major assignment was obtaining the Italian naval cryptosystem. Given her mission, it was only logical that Cynthia look up her old friend Alberto Lais, now an admiral and naval attaché at Italy's Washington embassy. Virtually all published accounts say that Cynthia prised from the 60-year-old admiral the Italian navy's code and cipher books, as well as plans to disable Italian ships in U.S. ports to prevent their seizure. The literary consensus is that Cynthia's amorous success contributed to British victories in the Mediterranean. The lady herself, who described her relationship with Lais as sentimental and even sensual rather than sexual,' said she received the ship sabotage information directly from the admiral and access to the sensitive books from his assistant with Lais' full cooperation.

Heirs of the admiral sued a British author in an Italian court for defamation in 1967, insisting Lais (who had died in 1951) had not betrayed military secrets, and won. In 1988, Lais' two sons protested publication of the seduction account in David Brinkley's best-selling *Washington Goes to War* and persuaded the Italian defence ministry to publish denial advertisements in three leading East Coast newspapers.

Cynthia's next assignment was one that assured her place in the intelligence hall of fame. The Vichy French government, established after France's collapse in 1940, was vehemently anti-British. Posing as an American journalist, Cynthia phoned the French Embassy in May 1941 and introduced herself to Charles Brousse, the press attaché. Right away, Brousse – 49 years old, several times married and anti-Nazi – was besotted with Cynthia.

The relationship began with elicited material and intelligence titbits. But by July, Cynthia felt confident enough to make a false flag recruitment, telling Brousse she worked for the Americans. The French official soon was offering his mistress embassy cables, letters, files and accounts of embassy activities and personalities. Before long, to foil FBI surveillance, she moved into the hotel where Brousse and his wife lived.

'London would like to have the Vichy French naval ciphers,' Cynthia was told in March 1942. Informed of her latest request, Brousse threw up his hands. Only the chief cipher officer and his assistant had access to the code room. The cipher books were in several volumes, locked in a safe. A dog-escorted watchman guarded the premises at night.

After a series of stymied efforts, Cynthia finally tried the direct approach – burglary. Tapping his friendship with William 'Wild Bill' Donovan, head of America's Office of Strategic Services (forerunner of the CIA), the BSC's Stephenson acquired the services of a thug nicknamed 'the Georgia Cracker.' Brousse was to tell the embassy night watchman that he needed a discreet place to conduct an affair and was prepared to pay him to look the other way. The couple would then visit the embassy for several nights to get the guard used to their presence. On the night of the burglary, they planned to slip the watchman a drugged glass of champagne. After that, they would admit the safecracker, go to the ground-floor code room, open the safe, pass the cipher books to a BSC man waiting on the tree-shaded lawn below and then wait for the volumes to be returned after they were photographed.

All seemed to go as planned. The pentobarbital knocked out the guard as well as his dog (whose food had been drugged). The Georgia Cracker coaxed open the old Mosler safe, but there was not enough time to remove and copy the books, and the intruders had to beat a hasty retreat. A second attempt, made without the Georgia Cracker, was foiled when Cynthia could not get the safe open, even with the combination.

Entering with Brousse's key for a final try, the couple had nervously positioned themselves on their usual sofa in the embassy when Cynthia's intuition told her something was wrong. Impulsively, she arose and removed her clothes. 'You haven't gone mad?' asked Brousse, looking at his lover, who was by then clad only in a necklace and high heels. She persuaded him to also start undressing. A door suddenly opened, and a flashlight beam stabbed the darkness. As it focused on her, Cynthia quickly placed her slip in front of her.

'I beg your pardon a thousand times,' said the watchman. He turned his flashlight aside and, suspicion allayed, returned to his basement room. Cynthia let in the safecracker. The rest was a milk run.

The Vichy ciphers, whether those obtained by Cynthia or from another source, were used to great effect when the Allies landed in French-held North Africa in November 1942. With the United States now in the war, Cynthia worked for the U.S. Office of Strategic Services as well as for the British. She considered herself a patriot. 'Ashamed? Not in the least,' she once said. 'My superiors told me that the results of my work saved thousands of British and American lives....It involved me in situations from which 'respectable' women draw back–but mine was total commitment. Wars are not won by respectable methods.'

The rest of Cynthia's story pales after her earlier adventures. Arthur Pack killed himself in 1945. Brousse and his wife divorced, and the modern Mata Hari married Brousse. In storybook fashion, they settled in a medieval castle on a mountain in France. The end of their story was tragic, however. On December 1, 1963, Amy Thorpe Brousse died of mouth cancer. Her daughter committed suicide just a few years after and her husband was electrocuted about 10 years later by his electric blanket. Part of their fairy tale castle was also consumed in the ensuing fire.

Betty's story is told in full in "Cast no Shadow, the life of the American spy who changed the course of World War II" by Mary Lovell.

Time Magazine on Brousse

A very resourceful man is Charles Emmanuel Brousse. Thrice turned down by the French Army in World War I because he was so woefully puny, he had his appendix removed, promptly filled out and with the help of his father, deputy from Perpignan, not only got in the Army but became commander of famed air bombing squadron Brequet 126.

After the war this hearty and charming southerner took a share of his family's publishing fortune (L'Indépendant of Perpignan) and proceeded to found an importing business in Indo-China which soon hit the jack pot, permitting him to amass one of the world's most important private collections of Napoleonana. As a press officer in the Air Ministry in World War II. "Chariot" Brousse acquired the reputation of being the most prodigious wangler in Paris and gained the gratitude of all U. S. newsmen for his many feats of bypassing departmental red tape in their behalf.

Even after the defeat, Captain Brousse was still operating in high gear, getting no less than 10,000 litres of gasoline for the U. S. Embassy in Vichy when there was no gasoline, fighting correspondents' battles against the military censorship, and arranging impossible interviews. He did not do so badly on his own behalf. Appointed press attaché to the French Embassy in Washington, he went from Vichy to Paris, outsmarted the Germans, returned with 23 truckloads of belongings, put them and his lovely Georgia-born wife in a car and trailer and drove all the way to Lisbon with a chauffeur who was under 40 and hence by terms of the armistice not supposed to be permitted outside France.

When the American Export Liner Exeter arrived in Bermuda for the now customary inspection of mail and passengers by the British, two customs officers took Captain Brousse to his cabin. They asked for his papers and were shown his diplomatic passport.

They then asked if he was carrying any letters. He showed them two sealed paquets de courrier from Foreign Minister Paul Baudouin to Ambassador Henry-Haye. To the Captain's astonishment the British demanded them.

Not until the Exeter's master could come and witness the surrender would Charles Brousse turn over the letters. The British said the letters would go to the British Embassy in Washington, then be sent to the French. As to the extraordinary practice of seizing the diplomatic correspondence of a nation with which diplomatic relations were still in effect, they had nothing to say. The positions of the two ex-allies with respect to each other had become even more bizarre.

This story of Cynthia, Arthur and Brousse is included simply because Cynthia was a Pack by marriage during her incredible exploits and is the first of three Pack accounts that may or may not be related to the Packs we have been following so far.

Chapter 36 - K.H. (Madagascar) Pack

My father, Joe Pack, was posted to Madagascar in December 1943 to fly Catalinas with 265 squadron. His story is told in full in "Love is in the air". Before the war Madagascar had been a French colony and then, with the fall of France, it fell into German hands. Diego Suarez, at the north of the island had a fine harbour and the island held a vital strategic position in the Indian Ocean and the Allies decided it was vital to take control and in May 1942 30,000 Royal Welsh Fusiliers took Diego Suarez and by September 1942 the whole island had been taken. In these circumstances my father would probably not have expected to find another Pack resident on the island.

Of course the Royal Welsh Fusiliers did not just march in and take the island overnight. The Special Operations Executive (SOE) spent a considerable time doing surveillance, generating intelligence and making contacts and plans beforehand. SOE preparations began towards the end of 1940. One contact that was made was a certain Mr K.H.Pack Managing Director of the Meat Canning Factory at Boanamary. He appears to have been helpful to SOE with his company's staff and assets such that the eventual invasion proceeded smoothly.

I have not been able to find out anything about K.H. Pack or where he fits in, or whether he is related in any way to me. Perhaps the web site might elicit some useful information. It is quite unlikely that my father actually met him.

Chapter 37 - Howard Meade Pack (1929-2009)
Shipping Magnate - the last Pack (in this book anyway)

The following was gleaned from an obituary. Howard Meade Pack was cofounder, in 1931, of Seatrain lines in the US, later Transeastern Associates, an early exploiter of containerised transport worldwide. By the early 1970s the company would have 4000 employees and turn over $250m annually. He was born in Manhattan and died there. His parents were Benjamin and Ida Winograd Pack and his father was a furrier.

Can anyone link him up with any other Packs in this book?

And now we return to Egerton for some general observations.

Chapter 38 - A history of Egerton

This is not a comprehensive history of Egerton but merely brings together a number of historical accounts and pictures that the author has come across in researching the Pack family.

Egerton is about 50 miles south east of Central London and 9 miles north west of Ashford and is almost dead centre in the County of Kent. The parishes of Smarden and Pluckley, which have featured in this story, adjoin Egerton, to the south and east respectively. Egerton is, in many ways, a curious village.

Firstly, it is very spread out. Charles Hooker, the traction engine driver who we met in an earlier chapter, wrote that Egerton was "roughly square, something less than 12 miles around, the distance from North to South, Water Mill to Lower Bedlam Lane, some three miles, and from East to West, Rose & Crown to Coldbridge Farm, again about three miles".

Charles Igglesden, in his book "A Saunter through Kent with pen and paper", published in 1919, describes Egerton as "A parish about 2 ½ miles each way and really a series of clusters of houses with winding roads and pastures in between." It could almost be thought of as a number of hamlets strung together.

Egerton has been populated for at least 1000 years and early names were Eardington (mentioned in the Domesday Monarchorum, about 1080), Egarditton (1202) and Edgarinton (1229). By 1610 the name had become "Egerton"; the meaning of this name, and presumably the earlier variations, is "the side of a hill". The reason for this name becomes apparent when we look at the topography of Egerton below.

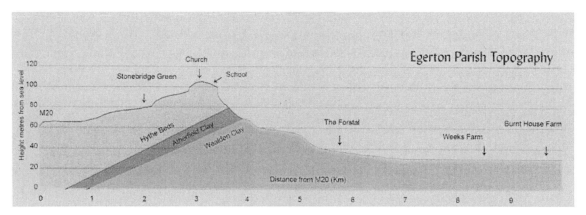

Geographically the village stands on a 350-foot ridge of greensand or ragstone with the village centre and the church at the top and hamlets scattered all around the ridge.

The present population of Egerton is just over 1000. In 1801 the population was 731 and it stayed more or less around this level for most of the next 150 years until the post war period when it increased to present levels. This is quite a small population for such a large area. Egerton is also curiously remote for a village so close to London. Quoting Charles Hooker again " Egerton is well away from the main roads and about 4 miles from the nearest railway stations at Lenham, Charing, Pluckley and Headcorn". As the author can attest, it is surprisingly easy to miss it.

Administratively Egerton is a parish and the Anglican parish church is St James' church pictured below.

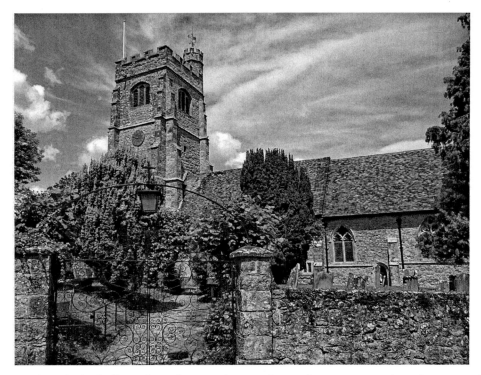

St James' church is believed to have taken a long time to complete because there is evidence in its features of work commenced in the 13th century, 14th century and 15th century. The Tower was built by Sir John Darell of Calehill in 1476, is 100 ft high and contains the clock, 2 bells dated 1602, 3 dated 1759 (from the Whitechapel Bell Foundry, courtesy of Thomas Pack) and 1 dated 1717. The church contains an enormous brass chandelier, reputed to be the oldest 36-branch chandelier in the world (made by Robert Rowland in 1699) and this is pictured below.

Charles Hooker wrote further about Egerton that " *not many villages have a green hill, a mount ephream and a Jacobs ladder, and this area was one of the beauty spots of which Egerton had many*".

A Jacobs ladder refers to a ladder to heaven, described in the book of Genesis, which Jacob envisions during his flight from his brother Esau, a meeting place between heaven and earth, which was often an actual architectural feature of a church and the one at St James' is pictured below.

Mount Ephraim is the historical name for a mountainous district of Israel once occupied by the tribe of Ephraim, densely wooded, well-watered and with fertile valleys and Charles Hooker was probably referring to an area between Stone Hill and Green Hill.

In addition to St James' Anglican church there is also a Baptist Chapel, pictured below, which is not quite as grand.

The Chapel was originally built about 1750 and burnt down in 1824 but was rebuilt the following year as a "strict" Baptist church. In 1974 it converted to a Free Church. Close to the Baptist Church was the Forstal Mission, which opened on November 1st 1888. This was an Anglican Church, which for a while was very popular but closed in 1966 and was demolished.

Today the matter of which Church one attends is of little interest to most people other than oneself. Back in the 19th century it was different. Until the late 19th Century the Anglican, or established, Church was very involved in civil administration through the Parish Overseers. They were in effect the local Council, the DHSS, the Police and the Inland Revenue all wrapped into one. Being an Anglican was akin to being establishment, being a Baptist was almost a declaration of unconventionality. The Church of England is often described as the Conservative party at prayer and St James' had the George and the large houses clustered round and this would be the Church of choice for the established class. The Baptist Chapel is at the bottom of the hill in the Forstal and near Pleasant Valley and this was where the workers lived. The Church was also one of the few meeting places other than public houses and so you would choose a Church where you would find like minds and thus to an extent your choice of Church will also be partially a class choice. In Egerton the Anglican Church is at the top of the hill close to Egerton House where the local dignitary lived. There are, of course, genuine religious differences between the two churches which may well have been important to some but for many the question of which congregation you felt most comfortable with was perhaps even more important.

The Packs in Egerton, as we have seen, were almost entirely Baptists until towards the end on the 19th century but then, from about 1884 onwards they become progressively more Anglican although the transition over the next 50 years is gradual. The trend to Anglicanism may have had an element of social climbing. Some of them are becoming successful and the Anglican Church would be attended by local dignitaries. Since they are almost all builders this might make good networking sense? There does appear to have been almost a rush of Pack baptisms from the mid 1880s including some adult baptisms (Ezra Pack and Elizabeth Pack).

Kath Hilder, long time resident of Egerton, and the granddaughter of Joseph Pack, has done a number of research projects on Egerton's history, and with her kind permission I reproduce them below.

Parish Council Snippets by Kath Hilder

In 1911 the Council adopted the Allotments Act, which meant that they had to meet parishioners' requests for plots of land to work. They were probably thrown by the first request, from a Mr G F Oliver for 5 acres. He was supported by the Board of Agriculture, however they finally compromised on three. A series of other requests followed and in 1912 the Council negotiated with the owners of Court Lodge Farm for the rental of part of Holy field at 30/- per acre per year. Holy field may have been named for the mysterious tumulus which now stands in the neighbouring orchard and here the allotments remained until demand for them fell off after world war 2. The number of requests for plots was so great that the Council was soon obliged to rent more ground, referred to as Dorson Meadow, but this I have not located. Plots in sizes from a quarter of an acre upwards were marked and stumped out by members of the Council and detailed records kept of rents paid by all tenants. Planting of fruit trees was not permitted but bush and soft fruit were grown even though there was no mains water supply.

By the time the allotments were up and running the Council were also looking for some land for a Parish recreation Ground. They tried for the George Field but without success. Elm Meadow, where Elm Close now stands, was often borrowed from the Cornwallis Estate for local celebrations and the Council decided to try to acquire it for the children at the school and parishioners in general. There was great rejoicing when Lord Cornwallis, who was disposing of his property in Egerton, gave 11 acres of land, including the present sports field and the Lower recreation ground, to the parish in 1920. The Cornwallis family remained the ground landlords of the old school and its garden and later sold it to the developer who built Old School Court. The grazing rights for the surplus grass on the Recreation Ground were let to local farmers. In 1921 the Council were in dispute with their former tenant, Mr H Millgate, who claimed that he had not received a notice to quit and their neglect had led to the loss of his mare, worth 30 guineas. The Council sent a furious reply stating that when Mr Millgate's mare was lost he was a trespasser and they absolutely rejected his claim. They counterclaimed for his rent of £13 which, after some huffing and puffing, Mr Millgate handed over.

Elm Meadow was the site of the local cesspit serving properties at the top of the hill. It frequently gave trouble and had to be cleaned out. In 1922 the local roadman, Mr J Pack, was contracted to take on the job of keeping it clear at 30 shillings a year (As Joseph Pack's granddaughter I feel sure he managed it very well). Sewer rents of £2 per annum were paid by the school and 2 nearby property owners. There was also a spring on Elm Meadow which supplied some houses in the Lower Street, so all these drains and sewers were running under the village playing fields. Thank goodness they were taken over by professionals in due course.

The first world war had little impact on the activities of the Parish Council. An appeal for support for prisoners of war in Germany led to a flag day. The only strong feeling recorded was an appeal from the village to the Food Controller in March 1918 to intervene to prevent the call-up of the village butcher, Norman Homewood, "on the grounds of the very great inconvenience that would be caused to the parish by his business being closed".

The early 1920's saw an outburst of activity in Egerton, notably with the acquisition of a Village Hall. The magnificent gift of the Cornwallis land gave a site and the sale of ex-Government buildings the opportunity, to buy a wooden building which was erected in 1920. The cost is not stated but it was insured for £250. It was officially opened by Colonel Cornwallis in August 1920 and the Council recorded a vote of thanks to Egerton's Women's Institute, then a very young organisation, for their splendid efforts in raising money for the hall under their President, Mrs Stisted of Egerton House. They also decorated the hall for the occasion and served the refreshments, another unchanging thread in the pattern of village life.

The builder of the village hall, as we will see again in the chapter on Pack properties, was Jeffrey Pack. The hall was replaced by a new millennium hall in 1999. This was the second case of Cornwallis munificence being replaced by the council since Cornwallis had also donated the village school and this was also later replaced.

The following picture of Egerton in 1930 is contemporaneous with Kath's notes above.

EGERTON 1930

More snippets from the Parish council by Kath Hilder

Life in the early 20thC was hard for poorer people in country districts, and various benefit societies, such as the Ancient Order of Buffaloes or the Oddfellows, existed to lighten the load for people who were ill or injured. One such, the Egerton Diamond Jubilee Benefit Society, held a club day in 1908, a convivial gathering held in a large booth in Elm meadow, where an "excellent dinner" was served by the landlord of the Sportsmans arms (where Oliver's garage now is). Seven toasts were proposed and drunk to individuals who were present. It was reported that £20 had been paid over the year in sick pay, with £5 for one death (at this time the old age pension was five shillings a week).

A press account of the Slate Club at the Queens Arms, paying out just before Christmas, states that 133 members each received twenty-three shillings and ninepence, and the evening concluded with songs and entertainment by members. The Rat and Sparrow Club held a dinner at the George in 1913, recording that during the year over 2000 sparrows and 3820 rats had been accounted for. J.Stewart killed 2272 of them but it is not recorded that there was any headage payment.

The payment of tithes by landowners was a frequent cause for complaint. The Parish Council supported a protest made against the "iniquitous charges" of the Ecclesiastical Tithe Act of 1920. When they took over the recreation ground gifted by Lord Cornwallis, the Council had to pay £3 2s 3d tithe on the ground annually, and the tax was still being paid as late as 1974.

In 1925 it was decided that a men's urinal should be provided on the Recreation ground. This idea was kicked around for some time, and attempts were made to find a suitable spot, but apparently without success, as in April 1925 the Parish hall committee was asked for a "portion of the woodshed adjoining the hall for a convenience for men". Perhaps this was an attempt to sanitise an already existing nuisances; but in any event no more was heard of it.

179

In the same year the Council had to consider the case of Mr B., whose name crops up frequently among allotment holders. When he applied for two acres of land the council felt obliged to consult the County Council about the legality of this, "he being a ticket-of-leave man". There could probably be no better occupation for a man on license from prison, but I suspect that the council were no admirers of Mr B. and would prefer not to do him any favours; but in any case the K.C.C. ruled for him and he got his plot. What his offence was we shall never know.

A few years later the West Ashford R.D.C called a conference at the George to sort out the strange anomaly of the parish boundaries in the Mundy Bois area, where for some historic reason there was a detached portion of the parish of Little Chart. Councillors from Egerton and Pluckley met under the chairmanship of Roy Wilthew of Court Lodge, a man who gave years of service to the village, and he put forward a scheme to divide the area between its two neighbours. This was agreed to the satisfaction of both, but the boundaries in that part of Egerton remain very odd; why did they put the Mundy Bois public house in Pluckley, but its car park on the west side in Egerton?

During its early years few women candidates stood for election in Egerton. The first was Mrs Sanguinetti of Verralls Oak, who was elected in 1920 but made little mark and served for only a few years. Since then there has never been more than two women Councillors at any one time, though there have been very able and hard working women in the village.

Electricity comes to Egerton

My father, Joe, wrote a piece in *Love is in the Air* recording the coming of electricity to Egerton in about 1929.

"But there was something of interest happening in the village – we were going to have electricity "laid on". We did not quite know what that meant but we were told that the houses in which it was installed could have light from a bulb at the flick of a switch. It was difficult to comprehend. Many of the villagers around where we lived thought this electricity quite unnecessary – what was wrong with the oil lamps we had always used in the living room and the candlesticks we lit when we went upstairs to bed. Yes, what was wrong with that? And how about the cost?

In spite of this feeling work went ahead. About half a mile below our house a trench was being dug at the side of the road along the grass verge by about 10 navvies. The huge foreman in charge of the labourers would space the men equally apart and when he blew his whistle they would start to dig and not stop until he blew his whistle again, when that length of trench had been dug. In no time at all, it seemed, they had dug the trench and passed our house on their way to the village street. After a few days an electrical cable had been laid in the trench and the trench filled in, it was months before our house was eventually wired for light, but what magic!"

Parish Council – The war and afterwards by Kath Hilder

Egerton met the approaching war in Europe with apparent calm. In response to a proposal by the West Ashford Rural District Council in May 1939 that the village should hold a parade on Empire Day to promote recruiting, the Parish Council rejected the suggestion, as the village was already completely organised. They similarly turned down a plan to establish an advisory committee to support increased food production, as it was

180

already good enough. They decided to make a schedule of all springs, wells and natural water resources for emergencies; however a suggestion that a deep shelter should be constructed for women and children "in one of the high banks nearby" fell down on the grounds of expense. The location of this scheme was not pinpointed, but it was probably on the Rec., where natural springs might have made it rather damp.

In Dec 1942 the Council petitioned the fuel overseer in Ashford about the shortage of paraffin used extensively by local people, who had no alternative, for cooking and lighting during the winter months. This was followed up by a petition organised by Mr Weeks, the proprietor of the stores at the Forstal, but the reply was unhelpful; the public would just have to put up with the cuts unless there was an influx of "billetees".

A proposed Flag Day for the relief of Air Raid Distress had to be called off owing to a hitch in the supply of flags.

As the war drew to a close the Council began to think about the provision of post-war housing and local landowners were asked to volunteer plots of land. The Crocken Hill houses were already built, and competition for the tenancies was keen. Finally it was agreed that more council houses should be built at Crocken Hill, but the major build should be at the George Field (the New Road houses) a convenient site for the necessary drainage. There were also plans to build at Brook Gates, where four cottages in a line with the airfield runway had been demolished, but for some reason this was not allowed, and the site developed into what is now the Brook Gates caravan park.

Celebrations for V.E. Day consisted of a children's tea, to be organised by Mrs Ray Gore of Island Farm and Mrs Gregson of Court Lodge, children's sports, to be organised by headmaster Mr Bowles, a bonfire, and a dance organised by Les Palmer of Kingsden. Total expenses for the day were less than 8 pounds. V.J. celebrations were similar but slightly more lavish; there were sports for adults (prizes cost thirty shillings) and an entertainment by an enterprise named Gun Law. The event was regarded as a great success.

Preparations were in hand for some time to welcome home local service personnel. From August 1945 money was raised by house-to-house collections, by dances, concerts and individual donations. The Parochial Church Council contributed half of the Victory Service collection; the W.I. gift sale raised £44; the Agricultural Workers' Union gave four pounds twelve shillings; Mr Rickson raffled one cwt of potatoes and raised two pounds eight shillings, and all this remarkable activity and more brought in £361 in total. It was distributed to the returning service people in specially inscribed wallets, and a plaque was made containing the signatures of those present at the presentation dinner in the village hall. This was last seen in a cupboard in the new hall, where it may still be. Surely there must also be somewhere one of the wallets ceremonially presented to all Egerton's servicemen and women in 1946?

War time Egerton

In his diary Jeffrey, my grandfather wrote: *"One Sunday morning in 1940 Mr Hitler sent his team over with a few bombs dropped at random. 2 incendiary bombs fell close to the church tower and I still have the metal head of 1 bomb. It was well made. The verger of the church had the other one. While the raid was on a corn stack was burnt out at Court Lodge farm, which was about 150 yards away. We had our share of bombs and so did the*

181

villages around us. One night we heard a bomb coming down but it did not explode. Next day I went and had a look down the big and deep hole it made. The following day it blew up. I said never again will I be so inquisitive. It was not more than 150 yards from Victor Villa". But, as we can see below, Egerton was prepared for Mr Hitler.

Charlie Pack and Bert Smith, special constables

Special Constables Appointed During the War

Back Row from left to right:
Selby Barton, Charlie Pack, Percy Hopkins, Frank Smith, Chris Pope, Les Palmer, E. Botting and Bert Smith
Seated: Walter Pearson, Dick Slaughter and Charlie Weeks

Buildings in Egerton

There are some fine buildings in Egerton.

We have already come across **Link House** in the Pack history. Charles Igglesden, in his book, writes *"the great feature is the doorway – cut solid out of a huge oaken trunk – 2 pieces of equal size that join in the centre over the door. They reach from the ground to the roof and are truly gothic. The centre of the house was a hall with a wing either side for the yeoman and his family on 1 side and the upper farm servants on the other (the labourers sleeping in the barns)"* Link House is reproduced again below.

Link House   **The Famous Oak Door**

"The style of this house is very common in Kent and Sussex and perhaps some adjoining counties, at the end of the 15th Century and during the first half of the 16th Century. The centre seems frequently to have been a hole open to the roof, which often has a thick coat of hardened wood soot on it, showing that the fire was below in the centre of the hole. In later times (James I) a floor was inserted, dividing the whole into two rooms, and a chimney built. In front of this house stands the stable, making a sort of road gate house through which is the road to the house."

Then there is **Egerton House,** home of Major Stisted and his wife for the first half of the 20th century and scene of the tragic accident to Ezra Pack in 1894.

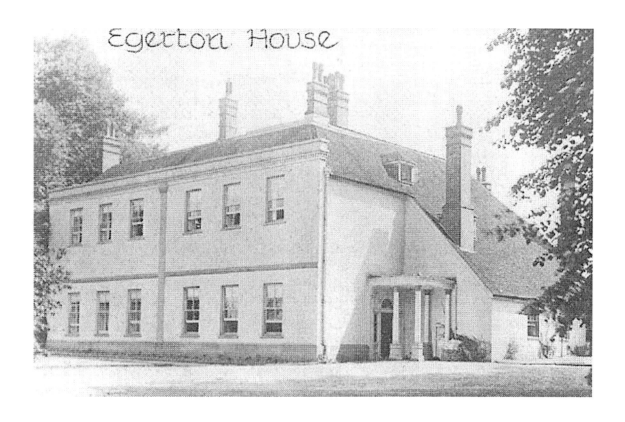

183

Another beautiful property is Malthouse Farm, pictured below in 1946.

1946

The Packs in Egerton

The Packs in Egerton seem to have gone through several waves. Up to about 1780 there were no Packs at all. Then George arrived and then his son, George, started breeding and by the time his wife, Keturah, died in 1876 there could have been upwards of a 100 Packs or Pack descendants. Of course some moved out and the females changed their names and in the 1901 census there were 27 Packs in Egerton, 15 were 0-21, 7 were 22-40 and 5 were 40+. At the same time there were 11 Hopkinses. By 1911 there were 47 Packs – in 1901 they were all young and just starting to breed. Today there is just 1 Pack in the village although probably up to a dozen Pack descendants.

There were several prominent families in Egerton – Packs, Hopkinses, Coppins', Turks, Missings and so on. But only 2 families are mentioned in the Book of Remembrance in St James' – Packs and Hopkins' - January - William James Pack, February - George William Pack, Dorothy Maud Pack, Henrietta Pack, Joseph Edward Pack, May - Frederick Alan Hopkins, June - Evelyn Annie Hopkins, August - Earnest Edward Hopkins, Sept - Trevor Hayden Hopkins.

Personalities in Egerton

In a separate chapter we will explore the stories of several prominent local personalities. But there were also some personalities, briefly in Egerton, who were prominent on the world stage. The local paper reported that in *November 1964 Mrs Pamela Milburne whose sister Benita Hume is married to George Sanders gave a Hallowe'en party at which Juliet Coleman (daughter of Ronald Coleman), Judy Garland, Vivien Leigh, Kim Novak, Richard Johnson, Terence Young and many others attended – at Weeks farm Egerton.*

Chapter 39 - Pack Properties in Egerton

There are a number of places integral to the Pack story; Prestwold was where one family of Packs started and has already been described, next was Ballinakill in Ireland, then Egerton, and then Syracuse and Streeter in the USA. Egerton will get special coverage for a number of reasons. Firstly it is where my family came from. It is also a relatively small village in which the Pack imprint at times was considerable. And finally there is more information about Egerton than about the other places. One reason for this is the research done by the Egerton historical group in their three books and I am indebted to them for permission to use their findings.

The Pack imprint on Egerton came both from where they lived as well from what they built since, as we have seen, three generations of Packs were builders in Egerton, James (1817 – 1890), Robert (1852 – 1935) and Jeffrey (1885 – 1971). Between them, and with the help of 1 or 2 other Packs they were responsible for most of the new building in the village, as well as repairs and renovations, for probably more than 100 years from about 1840 to about 1950. James was a substantial builder, as we saw in Jeffrey's diary, "*In 1899 I followed my father into the building trade and my grandfather was also a builder employing up to 30 men at times*". This would have made James one of the largest employers in the village. This building tradition, extending over 3 generations, must have made my father's decision not to continue it a difficult one. In **Love is in the air** he partially explains why he took this decision which will have had much to do with a feeling of release after the war and a desire to pursue new avenues.

There is more information about Egerton than the other places and one important reason for this is the research done by the Egerton historical group in their three books.

Places the Packs lived

In 1851 James was living at Pack cottages. This is believed to be the property to the left of Water Villa, pictured left.

The overall property today is split into four separate dwellings but appears to have been originally two houses built at different times. There are different roof heights and different windows at the back and it is likely that the left side of the terrace was built first, as Pack cottage(s?) and then Water Villa was added some 20 years later on the right hand side. The name Pack Cottage rather implies that James built it and probably added the extension as well.

By 1861 **James** and Frances were at Link house, as we have seen, with most of the rest of the family and later they are back at Pack cottages (which they may have owned to be able to go straight back?).

Robert lived in 1881 in Victor cottage; the location of this property is unknown but the name stuck because Robert would later build Victor Villa, which is pictured later and is now called Mathom House. Then by 1891 he is at Northend cottage, pictured below.

Northend cottage, on Rock Hill Road, and next to Mathom house, was built by one of the Packs, but it is not certain which, and it was later occupied by Edward Pack, brother of Hubert.

Jeffrey, after he married Delia lived first at the Red House (which had been built by his father, Robert) then at The Gables, also built by Robert; both are at Crocken Hill and pictured below. They are now known as Rydal House (first picture) and Cuillins (second picture). The reason for reasonable certainty that these are the houses is that these are the only 2 houses at Crocken Hill. I would assume that the Red House is now Cuillins and then as their family grew they moved next door into the Gables, now Rydal House, both built by his father.

Rydal House

186

Cuillins

When Annie died in 1924 Jeffrey and Delia moved into Victor Villa to look after Robert and run his business. Victor Villa had been built by Robert and is now called Mathom House and is pictured below. Jeffrey ran his building business from here with woodsheds and workshops at the back.

Victor Villa, now Mathom House

Places the Packs built or renovated

Some of the properties built by either James, Robert or Jeffrey are shown below. Most of them are Jeffrey's properties but this is only because these are most recently in memory and shows that there must have been many more Pack properties (especially by James, employing 30 men at times) than are listed here.

We have seen above that the Red House and the Gables, above, were built by Robert.

Beside Mathom House there is a lane leading to numbers 1 and 2 Homemeir, built by Jeffrey as 1 property, later converted into two. This is pictured below. Hubert Pack and Stella lived there.

Close to Homemeir is Oak Tree Villas, built by Jeffrey in the 1920s. Tony Turner and his family lived on the right hand side and the Turks lived on the left. Number 2 on the right was also occupied at one time by George and Pam Pack

Then there is Holly Tree bungalow, built by Jeffrey and pictured below.

Another property built by Jeffrey in the 1930s is Cedar Mount (pictured below).

The work was not all house building. One important piece of work was the Kentish rag stone retaining wall for the churchyard. Pictured below, this was done by Robert and is much larger than is shown.

And yet another piece of civil engineering was the bridge at Stonebridge Green. The bridge has "JP" inscribed on a centre stone, which identifies it to James. Tony Turner and the author had much fun up and down ladders photographing this.

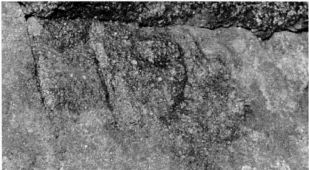

Believe me, the initials are "JP". Although not clear in the scan, it is clear close up

The fact that James left his initials suggests that his work was to build a new bridge not merely patch up an old bridge, and there is a lot of stone, presumably from the old bridge, in the fields nearby. If so, this will have been a major project involving diverting what is a strong current, while the work was done.

Jeffrey also worked on Link house. In his diary he wrote:

"A very heavy storm lasting 11/2 to 2 hours on Sunday morning in July 1914. Link House had its share of it. The people who lived there were terrified. It struck the roof at the back of the house about a 2ft width from top to bottom was stripped of tiles. No doubt the heavy rain prevented the place from catching alight. Inside the lightening came down the bedroom flue and the living room flue so the people went out into the scullery, which is built out beyond the main part of the house. A cat happened to be in the chimney so when the lightening came down the chimney it killed the cat, so the people after all were perhaps lucky.

In 1914 when this happened, the family of Jeffrey's uncle Charles will have only been moved out of Link House about 10 years or less. Jeffrey probably knew the property very well and this led him to build the model we have seen.

Another substantial project was repairs and maintenance to Malt House farm (which would be occupied later by Sandy Waddington), whose age is unknown but is apparently pre-Tudor. In this he worked with Alf Rickson and Bill Collins.

Malt House farm is pictured below.

Jeffrey's first project, as recorded in his diary, was to build *"Barnland House. I gave a price for doing it. It was a 6 roomed house about a mile from Headcorn and close by the railway."* Barnland House is pictured below.

Another project was at the Old Harrow Farm. Albie Pack from New Zealand happened to be passing there on a trip to Egerton and got talking to the then owner and was shown the tiles below.

"R. Pack" is clearly Robert and these seem to be roofing tiles with some decoration. Otherwise it is not known what work was done.

The Old Harrow Farm is pictured below.

The Old Harrow Farm

A very important commission for Jeffrey was to build the village hall donated by the Cornwallis family in 1920. The opening of the new hall by Lady Cornwallis is pictured below. Whilst Jeffrey is not visible he must have been somewhere nearby as the builder.

One of Jeffrey's invoices is shown below. What a pleasure to see the old pre-decimal currency as well as an invoice without Value added tax!

One of Jeffrey's last house building projects was South Broadham in 1947 for Alan Missing and this is pictured below.

And one final piece of work cropped up quite by accident. The author was chatting, with Tony Turner, to Tim and Danny Oliver at their garage and someone suggested having a look at something in the back garden and it is pictured below.

Jeffrey clearly did drainage as well as building, and monogrammed his work. He must have done quite a lot of such work for it to be worth getting his name put onto the covers by Mather and Platt of Ashford, the suppliers.

The source for most of the above information has been the three books published by the Egerton historical group who contacted many of the residents in the village. Whilst some clearly knew who the builder of their property was, there will have been many who didn't, especially when their house was built perhaps 100 years or more ago. Thus the 15 properties certainly built by James, Robert and Jeffrey could easily have been more like 50 and perhaps considerably more especially given that James employed up to 30 men at times. The population of Egerton over the years has averaged about 1000 implying about 200-250 properties. The properties built by these three Packs could thus equate to about a third or quite possibly even more of the housing stock in the village today. But to compound things James, Robert and Jeffrey were not the only Pack builders, as we will see below.

Other Pack builders

We have seen in the chapter on Ezra Pack that his son William, always Bill, went into business with his stepfather after his father's death and their business was called Pack and Waghorn.

Bramley Cottage and Bramley House, at Stonebridge Green, were built by Bill Pack for Stanley Homewood of Field farm. The two attached properties are shown below.

Bill Pack also built 3 bungalows in the 1960s; Sunnybank, Burnside (both pictured below) and Pagewood (no picture).

Sunnybank

Burnside

Bill Pack also built a new vicarage in 1899 called Egerton Grange (not pictured). Working for him at the time was Frank Pack who was called "Stump" because of an irregular gait. Frank was the son of Stephen Pack and grandson of Nathaniel and their family history is described in chapter 14.

Thus the Packs left a considerable imprint on a small village in Kent, but not only in a building sense, also on it's sporting fields as we see in the next chapter.

Chapter 40 - Recreational Egerton

Egerton was, and is, a sporting village. There is a football team and a cricket team and many other diversions and this has been so for many years and Packs have figured prominently in all these activities.

There have been some unusual activities. This one did not feature a Pack but in September 1869 the following challenge was issued in the local paper.

"J Russell of Smarden will run F Turk of Egerton one mile and give him 20 yards start, for £10 or £25 a side. To run in one month after signing. Or M Baker of Leeds can be on the same terms. Answer to this paper will be attended to". Then again *"March 1913 The annual dinner of the Sparrow and Rat club was held at the George Inn. During the year the club has accounted for 2090 sparrows and 3820 rats. Various prizes were given with the overall winner being Mr J. Stewart with 2272 victims".* And in the February 1924 Kentish Express *"In conjunction with the annual meeting of the Goal Running Club a sausage supper was held at the Queens Arms. 28 sat down to the capital spread. The rest of the evening was spent in harmony, songs being rendered by (among others) G Pack and J Pack."* And finally in 1931 – *the Queens Arms slate club held their annual share out when 113 members each received £1/3/9d. A very pleasant evening was spent with F Deveries at the piano and (amongst others) C Pack and Jeff Pack contributing.*

The more conventional sports were football and cricket. The 1920 village football team is shown below. Note that there are 4 Packs in the team and all have figured in this account; at other times there were even more. The team manager was Mr Waddington who we will cover later.

Egerton Football Club in 1920 with Mr. Waddington, Jeff Pack, Ted Pack, Stan Homewood, Jack Peach, Rowland Homewood, Arthur Roberts, Hubert Pack, Reg Cole, George Pack, Chas Weeks and Ted Munn

Jeff Pack, my grandfather is standing next to Mr Waddington. But Jeff's main sporting interest was cricket. He kept all his fixture cards and fortunately my father also kept them and some examples are shown below. Throughout the entire period of the cards, 1905 to 1937, 32 years, the club's President was Major Stisted who, again, we will describe later. Jeffrey had made entries in his cards up to 1934 so he was certainly still playing until he was 49.

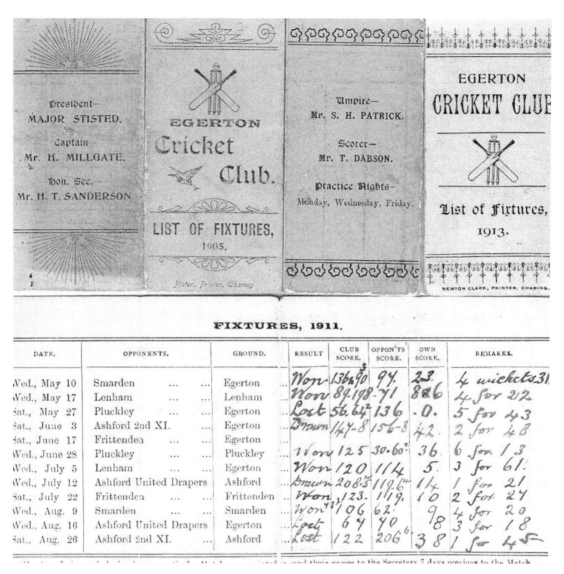

FIXTURES, 1911.

DATE.	OPPONENTS.	GROUND.	RESULT	CLUB SCORE.	OPPON'TS SCORE.	OWN SCORE.	REMARKS.
Wed., May 10	Smarden	Egerton	Won	136 & 90	94	23	4 wickets 31
Wed., May 17	Lenham	Lenham	Won	89.198-7	71	86	4 for 22
Sat., May 27	Pluckley	Egerton	Lost	56.64	136	0	5 for 43
Sat., June 3	Ashford 2nd XI.	Egerton	Drawn	147-8	156-3	42	2 for 48
Sat., June 17	Frittenden	Egerton					
Wed., June 28	Pluckley	Pluckley	Won	125	30.60	36	6 for 13
Wed., July 5	Lenham	Egerton	Won	120	114	5	3 for 61
Wed., July 12	Ashford United Drapers	Ashford	Drawn	208-5	119.6	14	1 for 21
Sat., July 22	Frittenden	Frittenden	Won	123	119	10	2 for 24
Wed., Aug. 9	Smarden	Smarden	Won	106	62	9	4 for 20
Wed., Aug. 16	Ashford United Drapers	Egerton	Lost	64	70	8	3 for 18
Sat., Aug. 26	Ashford 2nd XI.	Ashford	Lost	122	206	38	1 for 45

In Jeffrey's diary he wrote; *"1905 Was my first full year of cricket,* then *"1906 I believe Kent were first champions that year and I won the cricket cup the same year"* (the author still has his grandfather's cup which is pictured below).

The inscription on the cup reads *Presented by Major Stisted to Egerton C.C. Best Bowling average 1906 Won by Jeffrey Pack.* Jeffrey was 21 and clearly at the top of his form.

The 1910 village team is shown below with Jeffrey in the front row at the extreme left.

Egerton Cricket Club.   Season 1910

On his fixture cards Jeffrey kept a statistical record of his performances plus a few other notes. A summary of his notes from the cards and elsewhere is as follows, anyone who is not a cricket aficionado may find this difficult to follow;

- 1905 84 wickets and a note that in 1904 he had taken 33 wickets

- 1906 69 wickets and indecipherable calculations of his averages

- 1909 only half as many matches for some reason

- 1910 starting to score runs as well as take wickets. There is a note on the back of the fixtures card *May 11th to 18th matches abandoned because of death of King.* Edward 7th died on 6th May 1910.

- 1911 40 wickets

- 1912 23 wickets ay an average of 12.5

- 1913 Vice Captain J.Pack – lots of scribblings on the card

- 1914 618 runs, 22 innings, average 28, 47 wickets, average about 10, still vice captain, last match of season against Harrietsham "abandoned" – the war?

- 1921 The scorer was H.Pack

- 1922 The vice captain was G.Pack and the scorer still H.Pack

- 1923 211 runs 60 wickets

- 1924 Vice captain J.Pack

- 1925 Won 10, lost 6, 1 drawn

- Cricket averages for 1926 in the local paper G. Pack avg 22.18, H.Pack 10.07, J.Pack 10.06, E Pack 9.25 Bowling G Pack 14 wickets avg 4.44, H Pack 26 wickets for 5.88, J Pack 24 wickets for 10.33

- 1934 Vice Captain is G.Pack again. There is a match on September 22nd for Marrieds vs. Singles! Jeffrey would have been 49 or 50 in this year.
- 1934 averages G Pack 15 innings avg 22.9, E Pack 15 innings 16.9 H Pack 16 and 15.9 J Pack 7 and 10.4 Bowling E Pack 59 overs avg 6.7 H Pack 23 and 9.2
- 1937 G.Pack is now Vice Captain and Hon. Secretary and Treasurer, there are no scores entered on this card so it appears Jeffrey had stopped playing.

Jeffrey's son and my father, Joe, born in 1918, had time to join in some of the football and cricket matches before enlisting with the RAF because he wrote as follows in *Love Is In The Air*:

"To arrange a boys football match or cricket match with a local side – Ulcombe, Pluckley or Smarden, it would be necessary to cycle to the village, find out where the Captain lived, and arrange to meet for a match. It has always annoyed me that Mr Rushton, Headmaster of Smarden school, always turned up to watch the Smarden boy's matches – but we would have no such encouragement. For some years Smarden were not beaten by any other sides, junior or senior." He also wrote that *"there was a cricket team of Packs in the village".*

Although it is not strictly a sport, bell ringing or campanology, is certainly a recreation and it occupied most of the Pack family as Joe again writes in *Love Is In The Air*. Was there some genetic link back to Thomas of the Whitechapel bell foundry? This also marks the end of the Baptist tradition in this branch of the family as the Baptist church did not have bells and the Anglican church of St James was the only place for a campanologist to be.

Malt House was owned by Mr Waddington (known as "Boss"). He was an artist and a left arm spin bowler in the village cricket team. His son, Sandy (Alex) also played cricket and was the leading light of bell ringing. He taught many of us to ring. In our family my father, mother, three sisters and myself all rang. He would transport us on his motorbike to various ringing meetings.

On Saturday 5th December 1992 the Kent Association organised a 60th anniversary of Joe's first peal, he would have been 14. The peal was of 5040 Plain Bob Major tenor 23 cwt in D. He was 74 when he rang it.

The earliest recorded peal he rang was at St Paulinus Church, Crayford in Kent on Saturday 21st April 1934. The "band" was Percy Stone from Nuneaton, Arthur Jones from Croydon, Phyllis Tillett from Ipswich, Walter Dobbie from Sittingbourne, Margaret Pack (Joe's sister), aged 17 from Egerton, John Gilbert from Sheffield, Joe Pack, aged 15 and a half from Egerton and Edwin Barnett from Crayford. This was the youngest band ever to accomplish a true and complete peal on Church bells. It may have been put together by Sandy Waddington. The previous average age for an eight-bell peal was lowered by an average of three years and the record is believed to stand to this day. It was a Peal of Bob Major consisting of 5024 changes and achieved in 2 hours and 50 minutes. The average age was 15 years 2 weeks; the youngest ringer being 13 years 3 months, the oldest 17 years 8 months and the conductor was 15 and a half!

The Kentish Times featured a reunion of the band on April 24th 1959 when they rang the peal again. Joe's sister Margaret could not be present, having emigrated to California.

The picture is below and Joe is at the far right.

RINGING MEMORIES in Crayford Parish Church on Saturday were members of a band who created a record 25 years ago. It was in April, 1934, that eight young people rang a peal of bob major in the same church. They created a record which stands to this day because their ages averaged just over 15 years. In this photograph are (left to right): Mr. Percy Stone, Mrs. P. Marriott, Mr. Walter Dobbie, Mr. E. A. Barnett, Mr. John Gilbert and Mr. J. Pack. Mrs. Marriott the sister of one of the original record-breaking team who is now in America.—(K.T. Photo No. JM/2495.)

From notes Joe kept he rang at Shipbourne on April 16th 1932 with Glad and Meg, Charing on September 27th 1932 with Glad and Meg, December 26th 1932 at Linton with Glad, December 27th 1932 at Charing with Glad and Meg, April 17th 1933 at Charing with Meg and Glad, August 2nd at Charing with Glad, August 7th 1933 at Ulcombe with Glad, May 23rd 1934 at Charing with Glad, June 10th 1934 at Hothfield with Glad and Meg, September 13th at Little Chart, September 26th 1934 at St James' Egerton with Glad and Delia, October 12th 1957 at St Albans with Glad and on 18th April on the 25th anniversary of the youngest peal at Crayford with Glad.

In the 1990's he also rang regularly in Kentish churches and Ealing churches including a quarter peal of 1260 doubles rung at the Church of Christ the Saviour in Ealing on 4th June 1995 to celebrate his and Margaret's Golden Wedding Anniversary and the same peal rung on 6th May 1998 to celebrate Joe's 80th birthday. Naturally he participated in all of these.

There is another family who feature prominently in the history of Egerton and that is the Hopkins family and the next chapter is a brief one devoted to them.

Chapter 41 - The Hopkins Connection

There are many families with long histories in Egerton. The Turks, Hopkinses, Coppinses and Days go back much further than the Packs, who, as we have seen only started in Egerton with the arrival of George in the early 1780s. The reason for picking the Hopkins family for a special chapter is simple; Edith Emma (always Delia) Hopkins was my grandmother.

But Delia and Jeffrey were not the first Pack/Hopkins union. There have been at least 4 such unions. I say "at least" because I have not been able to account for all the Pack daughters throughout the story.

William Pack (1838 – 1915) married Susannah Charlotte Hopkins in 1861.

Charles Pack (1822 – 1897) married Sarah Hopkins in 1863.

Jeffrey Pack (1885 - 1971) married Edith Emma Hopkins in 1913

George William Pack (1891 – 1953) married Henrietta Hopkins in 1919.

William and Charles Pack were brothers and Susannah and Sarah were sisters. Jeffrey and George were second or third cousins and Edith and Henrietta (always Hettie) were sisters.

It is not altogether surprising that there have been so many unions of the 2 families; the Packs lived mostly in Pleasant valley and the base for the Hopkins family was Newland Green farm and these are close together in Egerton. Newland Green farm was part of the Cornwallis estate and Henry 8th is believed to have stayed there on a hunting trip. Newland Green House in 1990 is pictured below.

There has been a considerable amount of research on the Hopkins genealogy and I will only summarise it here. The earliest known Hopkins was Steven Hopkins (1603 – 69) and he married Catherine Scales in 1631 and they had 4 children. One of these was Thomas Hopkins (1639 – 1700) who had 8 children with Elizabeth. Their eldest son was Joseph and here begins a family tradition of giving that name to the eldest son that would continue for hundreds of years.

Skipping a number of intervening generations we come to Joseph James Hopkins (1847 – 1958, he lived to 111) who married Edith Emma (1852 – 1917) in 1878 and they are pictured below. They had 6 daughters (including Delia and Henrietta) and 1 son, Joseph James Hopkins (1898 – 1934), he was tragically killed in a car crash and had 1 son, Roland, the first son to not be Joseph for several hundreds of years.

Joseph and Emma Hopkins

Roland Hopkins (1930 – 1998) was a very larger than life character. As well as farming Newland Green he was also a talented jazz musician and at his funeral he was given a New Orleans type send off. I still remember Roland from when family holidays were spent camping at Newland Green Farm with our parents. Roland is pictured below in his early years and then in his mature years.

Finally in addition to the Packs and Hopkinses already mentioned there are four local Egerton personalities that deserve a special mention in the next chapter.

Chapter 42 - Local Personalities

There are, and have been, of course, many worthy residents of Egerton but the following four have been selected because they have been part of the Pack story.

The Stisteds

Charles Harcourt Stisted was born on 24th June 1857 in Madras, Bangalore. In 1871 he was living in Maidstone, aged 14, with his maternal grandmother Maria Stacey. It was clearly a wealthy family since it had a housemaid, cook/domestic, footman and Lady's maid, and probably was a military family with his parents perhaps stationed overseas. He joined the Royal Scots Guards. On the 7th August 1889 he married Cecilia Craighie Bell (born 7th December 1867) and in 1891 they were living at Mauricewood House, Glencorse, MidLothian, 7 miles west of Edinburgh and by now he is a Captain in the Royal Scots Guards. They were married in Roslin (sometimes Rosslyn) Chapel, now world famous from Dan Brown's book; the Da Vinci code.

Cecilia Craighie Bell was the daughter of Doctor Joseph Bell (1837-1911). Joe Bell was a very distinguished man. He was a Fellow of the Royal College of Surgeons of Edinburgh, a Justice of the Peace and a Deputy Lieutenant among many other honours. He served as personal surgeon to Queen Victoria whenever she visited Scotland. He knew and trained Florence Nightingale, he was involved personally in the hunt for Jack the Ripper and among his friends were Robert Louis Stevenson and Ellen Terry – he was a renaissance man – poet, surgeon, teacher, athlete, walker. He also lectured at the medical school of the University of Edinburgh where he emphasised the importance of close observation in making a diagnosis. He was a pioneer in forensic science. One of his students in Edinburgh was one Arthur Conan Doyle who studied under Bell and then worked with him until his literary career took off.

Arthur Conan Doyle (henceforth ACD) was distantly a Pack. ACD's parents were Charles Altamount Doyle (1832 - 1893) and Mary J E Foley (they married in1855).

Charles Altamount Doyle was the 7th child (5 boys 2 girls) of John Doyle (born in Dublin in 1797 he came to London in 1817 and lived there all his life) and Marianne Conan (which is where the Conan in Conan Doyle came from; none of his siblings used it).

Charles moved from London in 1849 to Edinburgh where he met Mary Foley whilst lodging with her mother, Catherine at 8 Scotland Street. He was not as successful an artist as he wished, and suffered from depression and alcoholism. His paintings, which were generally of fairies, such as 'A Dance Around The Moon' (see next page) or similar fantasy scenes, reflected this, becoming more macabre over time. In 1881 he was committed to a nursing home specialising in alcoholism. While there, his depression grew worse, and he began suffering epileptic seizures. Following a violent escape attempt he was sent to Sunnyside, Montrose Royal Lunatic Asylum, where he continued to paint. He died in Crighton Royal Institution in 1893. Charles and Mary had 10 children – 7 girls 2 boys and 1 unknown and their 3rd child was Arthur Conan Doyle, born at 11 Picardy Place, Edinburgh. Just before Charles died in 1893 he just had time to do illustrations for an edition of "A Study in Scarlet" by his son, ACD, published in 1888.

An example of Charles' work.

ACD's mother was Mary Josephine Elizabeth Foley (1837 – 1920) eldest daughter of William Foley (1807 – 1840) and Catherine Pack (1808 – 1862). Catherine was the daughter of William Percy Pack (Born 1760) and Catherine Scott. The Pack link is thus that Catherine Pack Foley was ACD's maternal grandmother, although this may not, of course, be my branch of the Packs. We have already seen in an earlier chapter ACD's mother Mary saying " *My mother, please observe, was born Catherine Pack. Her uncle was Major-General Sir Denis Pack, who led Pack's brigade at Waterloo. And the seventeenth-century Packs, as everyone knows or ought to know, were allied in marriage with Mary Percy of Balintemple, heir of the Irish branch of the Percy's of Northumberland. In that wooden chest are the papers of our descent for six hundred years; from the marriage of Henry Percy, sixth Baron, with Eleanor, niece of King Henry the Third*".

ACD is of course known the world over for his Sherlock Holmes books (there were members of ACD's extended family with surnames of Sherlock and Holmes which is where the hero's name comes from). But ACD first qualified as a doctor, having studied under Joe Bell, in 1881. Then he started a medical career as assistant to various doctors, including Joe Bell, and in 1891 he started an ophthalmic practice at 2 Upper Wimpole Street after having studied opthalmology in Vienna. It was when this failed that he started full time writing. In a letter dated 4th May 1892 he wrote to Joe Bell " It is most certainly to you that I owe Sherlock Holmes...I do not think his analytical work is in the least an exaggeration of what I have seen you produce in the outpatient ward... through deduction and influence and observation." ACD was of Pack descent and knew Joe Bell very well and Cecilia, wife of Major Stisted, was his daughter and they lived at Egerton House. Does this have any relevance to our story?

The Stisteds moved to Egerton in 1901 as tenants of Lord Cornwallis. Major Stisted had just retired from the Royal Scots. In 1914 he reregistered in the army and the family moved to Glencorse Barracks near Edinburgh where he was involved with training. After the war they returned to Egerton and bought Egerton house, probably in about 1920 when the Cornwallis estate was being broken up because of death duties. Major Stisted is pictured below.

Major Charles Harcourt Stisted

Many villages have their local squire and Major Stisted held that role in Egerton for many years (he died in 1946 so lived in Egerton, with a break for World War 1, for most of 40 years). He and his wife organised Christmas parties for the village children and he was President of the village cricket team for many years and highly involved in all aspects of village life. His contribution to the village was recognised in 1967 when a new cul-de-sac was being built and it was decided to name it Stisted Way. It is pictured below (and it is a pity that the badge has been removed from the sign).

Major Stisted also had contacts with local Packs since George Pack (father of another George Pack who will feature later in this chapter) started as a stable boy with him in 1905 and then enlisted in 1914 and was later wounded. After the war he became head gardener for Egerton House. Joe Bell was a frequent visitor to Egerton House to see his daughter and son-in-law and George Pack would be sent to Lenham Station to pick up the Doctor. At the end of his visit Dr Bell would always summon George to the front door and give him half a sovereign; this was equivalent to a month's wages.

Why then did the Stisteds choose Egerton for their country home? Both were of Scots descent and presumably wealthy enough to be able to choose anywhere for their retirement years. Was there some link that brought them to this small out-of-the-way village?

The Stisted's were visited regularly by Joe Bell and therefore presumably knew ACD as well. ACD lived for a while in Tenterden, which is close to Egerton and ACD was of Pack descent, as we have seen. Is it possible that the family links had been maintained and ACD then persuaded the Stisteds, descendants of his close friend and mentor, Joe Bell, to come to the area because of some Pack link? Naturally these questions cannot be answered but once again these are amazing coincidences to add to the others in the early chapters.

And yet another coincidence should be mentioned. Sir Denis Pack died on 24th July 1823 at Upper Wimpole Street, London at Lord Beresford's house. Number 2 Upper Wimpole Street is where ACD's short-lived ophthalmologic consulting room was located and is where the first Sherlock Holmes short stories were written 60 years or so after Sir Denis died. The house number of Lord Beresford's house is not known. Could these be the same house? Sir Denis' wife was a Beresford so the Packs and Beresfords will have known each other very well in Ireland. Is it possible the 2 families kept in contact for the next 60 years and the Beresfords helped ACD, a Pack relation, with accommodation early in his career?

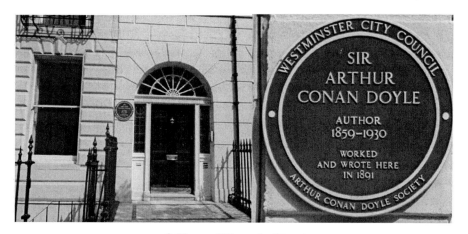

2 Upper Wimpole Street

Major Stisted's memorial at St James' church is shown below.

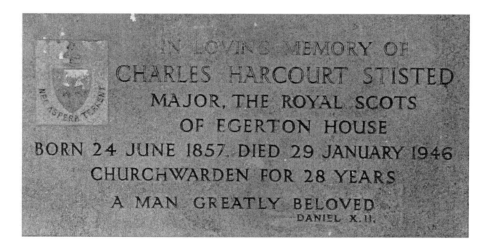

Ernest (Spot) Botting

In "**Love is in the air**" my father wrote the following about Spot Botting.

"I delivered the bread three times a week after school for Mr Botting, the baker, to local houses. Mr Botting's name had always intrigued me a little. I would collect the bread in a large basket with instructions on where to deliver it. On these days Mr Botting would come out to the front of his shop to watch me climb the hill with the bread, probably to see if I was playing about with any of the other kids. When I thought I was a safe distance away I would turn around and shout "goodbye Mr Bottom" and he would quickly go back into his shop. One day after I had shouted my usual taunt he ran up the hill after me, picked me up, turned me over and bit my bottom! When I arrived to do my bread round the following week he told me he had found a less cheeky boy to deliver his bread. When I told Mum what had happened she told me "it serves you right for being so cheeky" My source of income had stopped, my 2d a week pocket money was hardly worth saving."

In Chapter 25 on Elizabeth Pack we saw that she married Edmund William Weeks, often William, in 1891. He was a baker. They had 7 children and all the sons followed their father as master bakers. One of their daughters was Hilda (born 1893) and she married Spot Botting, himself a baker. They were both in their 60s when they married, on March 8th 1956, due to parental responsibilities.

Spot Botting's main claim to fame is that he was a very enthusiastic and early exponent of photography. The nickname "Spot" must have come from "Spot the Birdie", an earlier version of "Cheese" to focus the minds of people about to be snapped. He left a huge photographic library, some examples of which are shown later, and also experimented with animated video round about when Walt Disney was also starting. Each winter Spot would have a showing in the village hall of the films and photographs he had shot during the previous 12 months. The picture below shows Spot at work in 1967.

Spot Botting's collection of photographs and the more than 15 films he created (including "In Englands Garden", which is charming) are archived at the University of Brighton and may be seen and in some cases purchased online at www.brighton.ac.uk/screenarchive

In the 1974 *Kent Express* there was an article on Spot Botting, 84, of Hylmar, Egerton. It showed a number of hop picking pictures he had taken in the farmlands of Rock hill and Court Lodge, and some are shown below after another article on Spot by the Ashford paper in 1987 showing a picture he took in 1930, below.

MEMORIES

A look at the past — just by accident

CRASH, bang, wallop what a picture! This photograph of an early road accident was taken by well-known local snapper 'Spot' Botting.

The collision occurred on July 2, 1930, at the corner of the Egerton and Pluckley roads along Stone Hill.

Anyone who can remember the crash or can identify people in the photograph should contact Extra on Ashford 23232.

We'll be pleased to hear from you.

Unknown hop worker

Measuring the hops at Rock hill farm pre WW1

211

Tea break for a family of hop workers

Alexander (Sandy) Waddington (1882 – 1939) and his son, same name (1908 – 1984)

In "**Love is in the air**" My father wrote briefly about Sandy Waddington as follows;

"Malt House was owned by Mr Waddington (known as "Boss"). He was an artist and a left arm spin bowler in the village cricket team. His son, Sandy (Alex) also played cricket and was the leading light of bell ringing. He taught many of us to ring. In our family my father, mother, three sisters and myself all rang. He would transport us on his motorbike to various ringing meetings.

Sandy Waddington junior.

212

No church bells could be rung during the Second World War. When we returned to live in Smarden (in the 1980's) I found the local band, and on enquiring about Sandy Waddington, found they knew him, in fact they said that he collapsed while ringing at Smarden Church. I am wondering if Sandy's widow still lives at Malt House. At one time we collected our milk from Malt House Farm, in spite of a very savage dog they had named Tilly. Old man Waddington was an artist, he played cricket for the village and was a left arm spin bowler. His son Alec (Sandy) was also a fine cricketer".

Both father and son are buried at St James' church, Egerton, pictured below.

George Pack

Our final local personality is George Joseph Edward Pack (1926 – 1987). He was the son of George William Pack and Henrietta Hopkins. George William started work as a stable boy in 1905 (age 14), joined up in 1914 and was injured and after the war became head gardener and chauffeur at Egerton House working for Major Stisted and living in nearby Egerton cottage. George died suddenly while assisting a friend to feed stock at Greenhill Farm. He had been captain and secretary of the Cricket club and a playing member into his 62nd year. He was employed by the Stisteds for 48 years. He was a keen bell ringer, a member of the gardening society and served with the Buffs in the 1914/18 war (The Buffs were the Royal East Kent Regiment, one of the oldest regiments in the British Army dating back to 1572. They were called The Buffs because of their original buff coats). George William died 13th February 1953 aged 62 and Henrietta died 2nd February 1984, aged 98. Their tombstone, in St James' churchyard, is below.

George and Henrietta produced George Joseph Edward (born 18th July 1926), who married Pamela (Hargrove) in 1951 and they had 2 children Colin George and Julie. There is a memorial plaque in the choir at St James' to George J.E. Pack 1926-1987 Church Warden 1976-1987 a "respected and much loved servant of the parish". George Joseph Edward died 2nd.March.1986 aged 60 and is in the St James' churchyard records but as George Edward Joseph, not George Joseph Edward!

George served with the Buffs, like his father, in Palestine. He was also a keen gardener and a member of Egerton's gardening society and he served on the Egerton Parish Council and later became a Church Warden at St James' Church where he was a member of the choir. But, above all, he was a keen local historian and I have used, courtesy of his widow, Pam, his extensive papers in the early chapters of this book particularly in relation to the first 2 Georges and their use of Parish charity. He was also, like me, a product of the Pack and Hopkins families. With his close association with the Church and his Pack/Hopkins pedigree was George responsible for there being only 2 families mentioned in the Book of remembrance in St James' – Packs and Hopkins'? *January - William James Pack, February - George William Pack, Dorothy Maud Pack, Henrietta Pack, Joseph Edward Pack, May - Frederick Alan Hopkins, June - Evelyn Annie Hopkins, August - Ernest Edward Hopkins, September - Trevor Hayden Hopkins.*

George is pictured below.

Acknowledgements and Sources

The source material for this book came from the internet, parish records, books and people.

There is a wealth of material on the Internet. There are well-known fee-paying sites but also a number of free ones and family blogs and the Slee Booth web site was particularly useful, as was the CLDS web site. John Slee also helped me with a copy of privately published research on Arthur Conan Doyle.

For parish records there is no avoiding the drudge of ploughing through pages of microfiche until your eyes begin to cross. The Egerton records are held at the Ashford register office, Elwick House, Elwick road, Ashford, Kent.

There are a number of books that have been helpful. The 3 books published by the Egerton local history group; Egerton People Past and Present; A History of Egerton 1900-2000 and Pictorial Egerton were very helpful and are available from pat.parr@mypostoffice.co.uk The Dictionary of National Biography was also a good source for national figures. I have not read but have received extracts from "A memoir of Major general Sir Denis Pack KCB by his Grandson Denis R. Pack-Beresford" – the extracts were courtesy of Tom Packe. Charles Hookers book on traction engines is fascinating; "My Seventy Years With Traction Engines". Locomotion Papers number 67, published by Oakwood Press in 1973. Helen Allinson's book on assisted emigration from Kent, loaned to me by Kath Hilder, "Farewell to Kent" is also a fascinating read. Finally I will take this last opportunity to remind readers of my first book, chronicling the wartime history of my parents "Love is in the air" available from www.woodfieldpublishing.com.

But, of course, the most important source of material is the people one comes across. I am most grateful to Simon and Rita Packe-Drury-Lowe for a marvellous day visiting Prestwold and St Andrews Church and photographing all the Pack(e) memorials. Also to Tom Packe for the sheet of Simon Pack's music. Ed and Elsie MacKethan were the source of many of the 19th Century photographs of the Pack family and much family detail. Renee Weeks (sadly now departed) had a treasure trove of newspaper clippings and photos from years gone by. Tony Turner has been an enthusiastic supporter of the project and invaluable in identifying the Egerton properties and bridges. Kath Hilder, Sheila Palmer and Frannie Pack have also taken interest and given help in this project. And finally many members of my immediate family have helped looking through attics and bottom drawers for photos or scrapbooks. Albie Pack in New Zealand in particular has been tireless, and his relation, Hilary Burley has also been very helpful. Thanks also to John (Jack) Jackaman for his account of his friend and flying colleague Jack Lumsdaine's flying history in appendix 3. Peggy Dolan, an inveterate Pack hunter of her own family, has also been an invaluable sounding board for theories and a very honest commentator on loose thinking. Kathy and Christopher Turrall MCSD have also taken an interest in this book and kindly designed the exceptional covers.

Finally, and most importantly, I must thank all of my family, and especially Jacky, my wife, for their patient encouragement and their forbearance with the neglect of family duties which producing this book has entailed.

Whilst I am grateful to all the above the responsibility for the accuracy of the details in this book is mine and not theirs.

Appendix 1 - The Packs in Virginia
The Full Transcript of the Jake Hatcher Research

The Packs came from England where, for several centuries, they were a distinguished family. Alderman Pack, an ancestor, was a member of the Long Parliament during Cromwell's time. Another ancestor was General Pack, who served in the English Army under Lord Wellington.

From those Packs were descended three brothers whose given names are not known to this compiler. They came from England to this country in 1740. Two of them settled in South Carolina, while the third settled in Virginia. In 1763, Pack, Pittman, and Swope, were hunters along New River, in what then was a wilderness part of Virginia, and is now Monroe County, West Virginia. The first Mr. Pack had two sons, one of whom, Samuel, was born in 1760, in Augusta County, Virginia.

Samuel Pack married Mary Farley, a daughter of Captain Matthew Farley, and it was in the New River Valley that they settled. Samuel and Mary were among the most thrifty of the first settlers in that region. They owned all of the fertile bottom land along New River, from the mouth of Greenbrier River to Warford. The couple had seven sons and three daughters: John, Matthew, Samuel (2), Bartley, Lowe, William, Anderson, Betsey, Polly, and Jennie.

Samuel (2) settled on Glade Creek, now in Raleigh County; Bartlby settled at Pack's Ferry; Lowe lived in Monroe County; William went West; Betsey married Jackson Dickinson; Polly married Joe Lively; and Jennie became the wife of Jonah Morris.

John Pack, the oldest son of Samuel and Mary (Farley) Pack, married Jane Hutchinson. They settled on New River at Pack's Ferry, in what is now Summers County. He accumulated a large fortune and was a large land and slave owner. Of their six children, three were sons: Samuel, who married Harriet French; Archibald, who took Patsey Peck as a bride; and Rufus, who was wed to Catherine Peters. The three daughters were: Rebecca, who married Robert Dunlap; Polly, who was the wife of Dr. Richard Shanklin; and Julia, whose husband was Elliott Vawter.

Anderson Pack, the youngest son of Samuel and Mary (Farley) Pack, married Rebecca Peters, a daughter of Christian and Clara (Snidow) Peters. He settled on New River also, where he owned a large tract of fertile bottomland along that river in Summers County. He was a very wealthy and prominent man at the time of his death in 1858. They had nine children: Conrad B., Samuel D., and Allen C. settled in Kansas, while John A. and Charles H. made their homes in Oklahoma. Lowe L. lived and died at Ansted, West Virginia. Then there were the daughters: Virginia, who married Dr. John G. Manser; Clara B. who became the wife of E. B. Meador, and Elizabeth J., who married Captain Robert W. Saunders.

John A. Pack, a son of Anderson Pack was a captain in the Confederate Army during the Civil War in 1861-65. He was captured by Federal troops commanded by Colonel Hayes, who later was president of the United States. Hayes recognized Captain Pack as a relative and told him he had married a daughter of Jennie Pack Morris. He was kind and considerate to the young captain, and gave him the freedom of his camp.

MATTHEW PACK

Matthew (Matt) Pack, the son of Samuel and Mary (Farley) Pack, was married twice; first to Katherine Lilly, a daughter of Robert and Frances (Moody) Lilly. The marriage bond was dated September 5, 1806, and recorded in Monroe County, West Virginia. His second marriage was to Frances, a daughter of Edmund and Sarah Moody. Matthew settled on a farm on the west side of New River, at the mouth of Big Bluestone River. The Bluestone Dam is near the farm formerly owned by Matthew, which is now in Summers County, West Virginia. The children of Matthew and Katherine (Lilly) Pack were as follows: John, Robert, Frances, Samuel, Linda, Mary Polly, and James.

Frances married Dr. Bill Lilly -- for details, see the Lilly Family.

Samuel settled in Raleigh County, now West Virginia.

Mary Polly never married.

JOHN PACK

John Pack, the oldest son, was born June 1807, at the mouth of Big Bluestone River. John located on Little Bluestone River at Streeter, now Summers County, West Virginia. The deeds of John Pack and his wife, Elizabeth, show they were large landowners in that section.

John lived near Streeter for about thirty years then moved to Raleigh County, where he became a successful farmer and cattle dealer. John was married twice; first, to Elizabeth Harvey, and second, to Betsey Rollyson. The children by his first wife were:

1. Preston Pack married Amanda Cooper. They were the parents of three children: Belle, Clara M., and Alexander.
2. John Pack, Jr., married Eliza Basham, and they had several children. John was killed in the Civil War.
3. James M. Pack was married first to Jane Goodall, and second to Catherine Cooper. He was the father of five children: John A., Chris, William, Lee, and Grover.
4. William Pack's sons were: John, James M., and Lewis A.
5. Rachel Pack married Isaac Mann of Jumping Branch.
6. Nancy Pack was the first wife of Vandalia Harvey, and they had one daughter, Margaret, who married Preacher Jim (Bench) Lilly.
7. Jane Pack married Alex Basham, Sr., and they first settled on a farm near Streeter. Alex was later killed in the Civil War. They had one son, J. Wesley Basham, who married Lucy A. (Pack) Wills.
8. Samuel Pack, see biographical sketch.

The children of the second marriage were the following:

9. Albert Pack married Lithena Lilly and they settled on Big Bluestone River.
10. Tom Pack married Ruthie Ferguson and they lived near The Chimney Rocks.
11. Haley Pack never married.

SAMUEL PACK, SON OF JOHN

Samuel Pack was born at Streeter, West Virginia, October 19, 1845, a son of John and Elizabeth (Harvey) Pack. He married Rhoda Anne Elizabeth Cooper, and located at Streeter.

He was the owner of the historic "Pack's Mill" which was located at Streeter on Little Bluestone River. This old mill was run by waterpower and had served that community for almost one hundred years. It was built by Sam's father, John Pack, who was one of the pioneer settlers of Little Bluestone. Samuel and Rhoda Anne Pack were true Christians. One of the churches of Streeter was named in honor of Rhoda Anne. Samuel was an honest, loyal, and patriotic citizen. He died July 12, 1893, and his .death was a great loss to that community. Mrs. Pack departed this life April 11, 1937, at the age of eighty-six. The eleven children of Samuel and Rhoda Anne Pack were the following:

1. Lucy A. Pack was born December 7, 1870, at Streeter, West Virginia. She first married John Wills, who was a farmer, merchant, and postmaster at Streeter. They were the parents of one daughter, Stella Wills Harvey.Her second husband was J. Wesley Basham, who was a schoolteacher, farmer, merchant, and postmaster at Streeter. They were members of the Missionary Baptist Church at Streeter. Mrs. Basham died October 8, 1923. The children of J. Wesley and Lucy A. (Pack) Basham were: Earl, who married Lura Wood; Eula, who married Lester Hatcher; Oris, who married Hassie Hatcher; Guy, who married Macy Pack; and Finley, who married Patsy Meadows.

2. George W. Pack was born April 20, 1872, at Streeter, West Virginia. He married Louie B. Vest, September 6, 1891, and located on a farm near White Oak. George W. died April 16, 1962, four days before his ninetieth birthday. His wife, Louie B. celebrated her ninety-third birthday on December 30, 1965. They were members of the Streeter Missionary Baptist Church. Their children were: Oather, who first married Roxie Wills, second, Nellie Caudell; Herbert, who married Ethel Cooper; Jess, who first married Mae Adkins, second, Nallie Vest; Pearl, who married Ruby Cooper; Alfred, who married Ethel Adkins; Vada, who married Neubern Pack; Elsie, who married Arville Mann; Macy, who married Guy Basham; and Lillie May, who never married.

3. Andrew J. Pack was born August 7, 1873, at Streeter, West Virginia. He married Cleopatra B. Harvey of Streeter, and they lived in that community where he was actively engaged in farming. They were members of the Rhoda Ann Memorial Baptist Church. Mrs. Pack died October 7. 1913. Her husband, Andrew J. Pack, died March 2, 1956. Their children were: Annie, who married Fred Russell; Ralph, who married Lydia Johnson; John, who never married; Ester, who married Ora Cooper; Omer, who married Lorna Lilly; and Ethel, who never married.

4. William A. (Alex) Pack was born June 2, 1875, at Streeter, West Virginia. He married Lucinda 0. Johnson, and settled near Streeter, where he was a farmer, barber, and blacksmith. They were members of the Baptist Church. Mrs. Pack died December 3, 1926. William A. Pack died April 24, 1958. They had nine children: Laura, who never married; Emmett, who married Nellie Lilly; Wilson, who married Flora Meadows; Flossie, who married Kyle Bennett; Maggie, who married Alton Meadows; Noah, who never married; Eva, who first married Oran Young, second. Mr. Thompson; Lula, who married Oral Pack; and Alda, who married Ruth Bennett.

5. Alfred Berman Pack was born July 16, 1877, at Streeter, West Virginia. He was married first to Virginia A. Vest, who died during childbirth.

   His second marriage was to Mary M. Cooper, a daughter of Charles A. and Sarah A. Cooper. Mary M. was born March 3, 1909, near Streeter, where she was also reared and educated.

   Alfred B. was educated in the schools of Summers County, West Virginia. He started his career as a school teacher at the age of eighteen, and taught his first school at Fall Rock, West Virginia, in 1896. He held a first. class lifetime teacher's certificate, and taught for forty three years. He was one of the outstanding schoolteachers of Summers County.

   He was also a farmer, merchant, postmaster, notary public, and secretary of the Board of Education for a number of years From the lowest to the highest position, he always served with honor. He was a fine husband and father, and a faithful member of the Primtive Baptist Church. He was honest and dependable, and had the confidence of all who lived in that community.

   Alfred B. Pack died October 19, 1954, at the age of seventy-seven. The funeral services were conducted on the twenty first of October at the Little Bluestone Primitive Baptist Church. More than three hundred people attended this funeral. Burial followed in the Crews Cemetery at Nimitz, West Virginia.

   Alfred B. and Mary M. Pack were the parents of four children: Bonnie, who first married John Bower, second, Willis Cole; Anna Belle, who married Rexel Bennett; Pauline, who first married Roscoe Bennett, second, Otis Vest; and Bertha. who married Cecil Lilly.

6. Laura C. Pack was born July 19, 1879 at Streeter, West Virginia. She married John Lilly, a son of Frank and Virginia (Pack) Lilly. John was a schoolteacher and farmer, who lived on Little Bluestone River. They were members of the Streeter Missionary Baptist Church. Laura Lilly died February 26, 1960. Their children were: Blaine, who first married Mable Lilly, second, Laura Bennett; Frank. who first married L. Lilly, second, Ettie Harvey; Samuel, who married Willie Sevault; John R., who married Barbara Johnson; Clara, who married Cecil Breeding; Edith, who married Russell,Ballard Corbett, Carl (deceased), Donald (deceased), and Curtis (deceased).

7. Amanda C. Pack was born September 25, 1881, at Streeter, West Virginia. She married Grover C. Adkins, who was a farmer near Streeter. They were members of the Streeter Missionary Baptist Church. Amanda Adkins died in 1909. They had one daughter, Lula E., who married Nelson Bowling.

8. Samuel J. Tilden Pack was born December 27, 1883, at Streeter. West Virginia. He married Margaret E. Dunbar, and located near Streeter, where he was engaged in the timber business and farming. They were members of the Rhoda Ann Memorial Baptist Church at Streeter. Mrs. Pack died June 1, 1952. Samuel J. Tilden Pack died August 1, 1959. Their children were: Winnie, who married Jamie Lilly; Clara, who married Carl Hatcher; Audrey, who married Opal Pack; Bessie, who married Wade Harvey; Marie, who married Earl Lilly; Dewey who married Alma Jenkins; Tina, who marricd Mason Lilly, Mildred, who married Dolphus Hatcher; Bert, who married Helen Reed.

9. Jediah P. Pack was born April 9, 1886, at Streeter. West Virginia. He was a farmer on Little Bluestone River. He died October 15, 1934. He never married.

10. Cecil B. Pack was born September 23, 1888, at Streeter, West Virginia. She was married to Elder William E. Harvey, February 26. 1906. They live near Glen Morgan, West Virginia, where William E. was a carpenter, farmer, and a Primitive Baptist Preacher. Their children are Earnest, who died young; Ette, who married, first, L. Cuckler, second Frank Lilly; Dicie, who married Clowney Lilly; Lataska, who married Oris Bennett; Carrie, who married Basil Cochran; Hilda, who died young; Georgia, who married Everett Harvey; Carlos, who married Cloie Meadows; Cleo, who first married Alvin Harvey, second, Bob Peters; Eloway, who married Gene Davis; Wilma who married Clinton Moore; Wilda, who married Bill Martin; Margaret A., who died young.

11. Effie May Pack was born March 31, 1891, at Streeter, West Virginia, a daughter of Samuel and Rhoda Ann Pack. She died in 1896.

ROBERT PACK

Robert Pack was born in 1808, at the mouth of Big Bluestone River, a son of Matthew and Katherine (Lilly) Pack. He married Rhoda Basham, and they settled on Ellison Ridge near the Panther Knob. Robert was a noted hunter, having killed panthers, bears, and deer on Ellison Ridge when it was a wilderness. Robert and Rhoda (Basham) Pack became the parents of six children:

1. Rebecca Pack married Jessie Ferguson.

2. Isabelle Pack married John Basham, and they had one son, Alex, who married Lelia A. Hatcher. She was born March 20, 1863, and died February 11, 1889. They had one son, Sanford Basham, who lived at Mabscott, West Virginia.

3. Nancy Pack married Lee Wills, and their children were: Mary Jane, who married L. D. Ellison; Adeline, who married Frank Ellison; Robert E., who married Mary Farley; Henry L., who married Lottie Shrewsberry; Rhoda.V., who married Chris Pack; Louise, who married Mike Pack; Ellen, who married Rans Meadows; Eliza, who married Hut Meadows.

4. Amy Pack married Anderson Pack.

5. Malinda Pack became the second wife of Vandalia Harvey, and they had two children: Anna, and Prince.

6. Virginia Pack married John Wills, who was a merchant and postmaster, at Streeter, West Virginia.

LINDA PACK

Linda Pack, the daughter of Matthew and Katherine (Lilly) Pack, was born at the mouth of Big Bluestone River. She married Thomas Meador, and their children were: Samuel, Frances, Mathias, John, Mary, and Emily.

JAMES PACK

James Pack, the youngest son of Matthew and Katherine (Lilly) Pack, settled on Little Bluestone River. He married Molly Harvey, and they were the parents of six children:

1. Mike Pack married Louise Wills and they were the parents of two children: Henry, and Cora.

2. Harrison Pack married, and they lived in Blue Jay.

3. Anderson Pack married Amy Pack, and their children were: Malinda, Andrew. Gus, who married a Miss Russell; Richard, who also married a Miss Russell; Ollie, who married Aiden L. Basham and Emma, who married Sylvanus Eanon Basham.

4. Virginia Pack married Frank Lilly, and they were the parents of the following children: John, Ellen, Mary, Alfred, Luther, and Hamilton. Of this family, John and Luther Lilly were among the outstanding schoolteachers of Summers County.

5. Frances Pack, no data.

6. James Pack, no data.

Albert Pack was a son of John Pack and Betsey Rollyson Pack. He was born in 1867, in what is now Summers County, West Virginia. He attended a grade school. He was married September 1, 1887 to Lithena Lilly, a daughter of Robert W. Lilly and Mahala Farley Lilly. She was born in 1872, near Lilly Post Office, Summers County, West Virginia. She attended a grade school. Albert Pack had several occupations: farming, mercantile and miller. Albert Pack died in 1917, and his wife died in 1944.

Albert Pack and Linthene (Lilly) Pack were the parents of eleven children. They are listed as follows:

1. Adam Carl Pack, born in 1888, near Lilly Post Office on Bluestone River, Summers County. He attended grade school. He married Effie Farley, August 18, 1906. She was born in 1888 at Ellison, West Virginia and attended grade school. Adam Carl Pack was a farmer and timber man. He died in 1912. They were the parents of three children: Lessie, Fred, and Carl.

2. Elsie May_Pack, born in 1891, near Lilly Post Office in Summers County. She attended grade school. She was married June 24, 1907 to Elliott Cox, a son of Sanders Cox. Elliott Cox was in the timber business and farming. They were the parents of four children: Ibran, Clytie, Waldo, and Cassie Cox.

   Elsie May (Pack) Cox was married a second time to Willis Lilly in 1919, a son or Rev. James (Bench) Lilly. Willis Lilly was a schoolteacher and farmer. They were the parents of five children: Velmer, Hugh, Thena, Quinton and Russell.

3. Richard Lee Pack born in 1893 near Lilly Post Office, Summers County. He attended grade school and also other schools. He married Hettie Lilly December 24, 1913. She was born in 1898 at Ellison, West Virginia. He was a schoolteacher, post office clerk, and farmer. He died in 1974. They were the parents of eight children: Flossie, Mattie, Berniece, Ivory, Grace, Rosa Lee, Leroy and Anna Belle.

4. Winnie Grace Pack, born in 1896 near Lilly Post Office, Summers County. She attended grade school. She was married to Willie Lilly August 24, 1921. He was born in 1899, Dunns, Mercer County, West Virginia. He was a college graduate, and was a schoolteacher and farmer. He died in 1954. They were the parents of four children: Denver, Dewey, Ina and Herbert.

5. Margaret Pack, born in 1899 near Lilly Post Office, Summers County. She died in 1902 at the age of three.

6. Lottie Pearl Pack was born in 1902, near Lilly Post Office on Bluestone River, Summers County. She attended grade school. She was married May 23, 1917 to

Charles E. Whitlock. He was born in 1894 on Crumps Bottom, Summers County. He attended grade school. His occupation was farming. He died in 1950. They were the parents of eleven children: Myrtle, Madeline, Irene, Ira Lee, Albert, Evelyn, Charles, Janice, Betty, Billy and Peggy. .

Mrs. Pearl (Pack) Whitlock was married a second time to Clyde Dowdy on September 14, 1953. He was born in 1900 at Pickway, Monroe County and attended grade school. He was a stonemason and farmer. He died in 1975.

7. James Floyd Pack, born in 1904 at Lilly Post Office, Summers County, and died in 1906. He was only two years old.

8. Arbie Wayne Pack, born in 1907, near Lilly Post Office, Summers County. He attended grade school. He was married October 1927 to Florence Neely. She was born at Warford, Summers County in 1908. She attended grade school. Mr. Pack was a miner and farmer. He died in 1944. They were the parents of five children: Maxine, Harold, Mabel, Ronald, and Kenneth.

9. Emma Maude Pack, born in 1909, near Lilly Post Office, Summers County. She attended grade school. She was married to Oliver Lilly, November 1930. Mr. Lilly was born in Summers County. He attended grade school. He was a farmer and factory worker. They were the parents of six children: Archie, Jewel, Leta, Macie, Donald and Francis.

10. Howard Coleman Pack, born in 1911, near Lilly Post Office, Summers County. He attended grade school. He married Orene Nelly in October, 1933. She was born in 1913 at Warford, Summers County. She attended grade school. Mr. Pack was a farmer, miner and school bus driver. He died in 1972. They were the parents of six children: Edmond, Joyce, Betty, Brenda, Norman and Howard, Jr.

11. Emory Darrel Pack, born in 1914, near Lilly Post Office, Summers County. IIe attended grade school. He married Christine Pettry, Blue Jay, Raleigh County. She attended grade school. They were the parents of four children: Calvin, Roger, Roy, and Michael.

Appendix 2 - Jeffrey's Diary

My cousin, Delia, discovered a book in her mother's papers that our grandfather, Jeffrey, had maintained over many years. It is partly an account of business transactions, including tax returns, partly notes to himself and partly a diary. It was clearly not all written at the dated time (given the 2nd entry below). It is reproduced, in edited form, below.

The first entry is the address of his sister, Martha, Mrs Hoath, Invicta, 2 Catherine Road, Long Melford, Suffolk.

I was born 5th October 1885 at Victor Villa Egerton, Kent. 1887 was Queen Victoria's Jubilee year.

In 1888 the Vicarage at Egerton was built. The old Vicarage was opposite the school. From then on I began to remember things. I was being pushed in a pram when it came on to rain so instead of going to Pluckley to see friends we returned before getting very far. I was told this was in 1889. This is the first thing I remember after being born.

1891 The stable and cart house was built and you can see a stone built into the wall with R.P.1891. Robert Pack was my father and no doubt the stone is still there. It had a tiled roof but <u>very</u> thin walls necessitating a corrugated iron roof.

1893 Very dry summer in that part of Kent. I remember coming out of school and going across the road and on the grass verge I could put my arm down a large crack. Many buildings were damaged especially those with shallow foundations.

December 7th 1894. This day no doubt will be remembered by older people as a day of tragedy. At Egerton House two well-known parishioners lost their lives in the 60-foot well at the back of the house. One man was 34 years old the other 28. They went down the well to mend some pipes. I understand they burnt charcoal and as the well had not been opened before the men went down no doubt the air was very bad. The older person was the first to need help as the younger man called out "Help my master has fainted". There was a man who stood at the top of the ladders, which was their means of escape, but he was unable to do more than raise the alarm. I remember the day as we were out to play, being at school, and I saw my aunt and a Miss White go up the hill which runs close by the school. It was an afternoon of misty fine rain and I could hear the tolling of the church bell, which made it mournful indeed. This story is, of course, about Ezra Pack and George White as we have seen in chapter 26. It is curious that Jeffrey does not name the victims as Ezra was his uncle.

1895 A Miss Peterson and another Lady came to live opposite the shop in the lower Street. She practised revolver shooting at a tree at the back of Oliver's garage which was then called the Sportsmans Arms. You go up to the brow of the hill turn left up the old Holly steps to the wood which was about 150 yards from the trees. Miss Peterson did not stay long at Egerton, about a year or so I should guess. She went back to Biddenden where her father was the rector. She soon got to work on the idea she had in her mind. This was by asking a Mr Whibley to meet her one Sunday morning in the school to look out a picture and tell her what he thought of it. While he was looking at the picture she shot him with the revolver she practised with at Egerton. I do not know what happened after the event. Mr Whibley was a harness maker. [This was a Miss Bertha d'spaen Peterson, daughter of the Vicar of Biddenden who murdered John Whibley, a shoemaker from Biddenden in

1899. It was believed she was either very eccentric or mentally deranged as she used to wander through Biddenden in her dressing gown. She used her revolver in a small wood for target practice and then shot Mr Whibley on Sunday 5th February 1899. She was found guilty but insane and died in a mental hospital in the early 1950s.]

1896 My father and mother were like other parents and with seven children but only two alive now. (I think he must have meant only 2 at home now) *In my boyhood things were cheap. Bread 3d for a 1lb loaf, a packet of woodbines (5) for 2 pence, a pint of ale 3d, beer 2d a pint. Farm workers earned 13/6 to 15/- a week. In town rather more was paid.*

1899 I remember the schoolmaster saying you will soon see carriages going about without horses.

1899 I followed my father in the building trade and my grandfather was also a builder employing up to 30 men at times.

1899 Close to the entrance to Stonehill Farm is a rock retaining wall with a guard rail leading to a stile which takes you along the back of the farm buildings. I helped to "caddy" for the "bricky" who built the rock wall (he would have been 14 at the time). When you get to the barn you bear right which takes you along the top of the cliff to a large tree which has or did have quite a long seat where you could gaze over the Weald of Kent, a lovely view. Many initials were cut in the tree. If you follow the path towards Green Hill Farm you are now walking under the cliff, so to speak. I have more than once taken this walk as a boy with the purpose of seeing snakes there, there were hundreds of them.

1900 My father built the (writing unclear - Pig and Whistle?) *and it was my first chance to see a new house being built and help to do it, just the experience I wanted.*

The Boer war started Oct 8th 1899 and finished June 1902. When Mafeking was relieved we had a gala sports day. I played a lot of cricket.

1905 Was my first full year of cricket

1906 I believe Kent were first champions that year and I won the cricket cup the same year (the author still has his grandfather's cup).

1908 I believe King Edward died in May, my cricket fixtures would tell me as several matches were not played.

1914 – 1918 was the 1st World War. I joined up by going into the Navy. I saw all the German fleet surrender; small ships first, and so on to the big battle ships. It took an hour for them to pass by. Then we escorted them to Scapa Flow.

During my boyhood the sight of a team of horses pulling a wagon fascinated me. Why? Because each horse had 6 small bells which were fixed above the head of the horse on a kind of frame. The front horse had light bells and the next a little heavier and so on to the back horse, it really was something to remember and musical.

Chapel. My father and mother went to Chapel, my father used to play the flute. Of course I had to go, in fact I went each Sunday. But what I detested most was that I had to wear a sort of straw hat with a broad brim which had a band around it and what annoyed me was that there were two ribbons floating about at the back. When in Chapel the preacher took a long time over his sermon there was fidgeting because I thought he would never stop and I wanted my dinner badly.

August 19 1950 moved from Egerton to Newburgh Road, Acton

June 1ˢᵗ 1951 moved to Detling near Maidstone

Sep 9ᵗʰ 1953 moved to Iver near Uxbridge

Aug 8ᵗʰ 1956 to 22 Langley Avenue Hemel H

Aug 31ˢᵗ 1956 went to New York by ship, arrived Sep 6ᵗʰ, Sep 9ᵗʰ at Mill Valley

June 9 1957 went to Cold Lake. Sep 7ᵗʰ departed from Montreal Sep 14ᵗʰ arrived Southampton

July 28ᵗʰ 1959 to Newburgh Road

Jan 29ᵗʰ 1960 to 197 Gunnersbury Lane

Dec 7ᵗʰ 1962 to 31 Audley Road

June 30ᵗʰ 1967 went to Canada, back July 23ʳᵈ, by air both ways

Feb 14 1962 Audrey came over from Canada, went back Feb 24

June 1958 Neville took us to Scotland in his car, Sheila came too. We had a splendid trip

There used to be an old timbered house situated about 50 yards from the Good Intent. It had got some lovely old timbers. This house was bought by a Lady from Lenham who had it pulled down, all the timbers were marked for future identification, it was sent off to America to be erected there. Another bit of Old England gone.

One day I went across the meadows to Butcher farm. When I was about half way there I saw a large snake. No doubt I frightened it so it wriggled towards a fence made of spikes. Would you believe the snake could have got through the fence between the spikes but made to go through where 2 spikes at ground level happened to be very close. The snake tried but was unable to get through so it back-pedalled and tried another opening, this time it went through easily. The reason why it was unable to get through first time was that it had swallowed a frog, which snakes do. It was the second snake I had seen like this.

*The parish of Egerton where we lived for many years is about average size, about a quarter of it sits astride the South Downs, the remainder joining up with other portions of the Weald of Kent. The Church and Street are at the top of the South Downs and down below is the hamlet called the Forstal. The census which I last remembered was 698 population. Since then council houses have been built on 3 different sites and I would guess the population now is 900 to 950. Probably Egerton would have more people had there been a station. Pluckley is the nearest about 3-¼ miles away. Egerton has several licensed premises – the Good Intent and the George. Egerton has at least 4 outstanding old timbered houses. **Link House** – which is mentioned in Hasted's book on Kent **The Old Harrow**, which I am told, used to be a pub. At the top of the hill about 150 yards from*

Link house is **Bedewell** *nestling under the cliff, approached by a narrow road you "kind of run into it" and* **Elmhurst** *on the road from Egerton to Smarden or Headcorn not more than 2 miles from the village.*

School and School House. The House joins the Big Room, as it was always called. Like the Church it is built of stone and about half way down the hill at the Lower Street. During a storm the coping on the infants room wall was hit by lightening and you can see to this day what damage was done, but it was not serious. When the coping was struck a man was standing at the front gate of Jubilee villas, which was not more than 15 yards away. He wasn't hurt so perhaps he was lucky. The bell turret has been taken down. I have noticed many times on the south east side of the bell turret the date 1844. I remember the schoolmaster telling us we should soon see carriages going about without horses. The Big Room and School House were built first and the Infants class room added later. In my time the sanitary arrangements were very primitive, but since then things have been brought up to date both for School House and the School.

In 1947 I was unable to work from Jan 23 to March 10 due to snow and frost

From the age of 13/14 to 19 I was at home working for my father. Then an old bricklayer came to see my father to ask whether he would oblige him by doing a job at Headcorn as he could not go himself. My father said he would not go but I could, if I liked. So I went and it was just what I wanted to get on with other people and to gain experience. I walked from Egerton to Headcorn for 13 weeks before I bought a bicycle. I had almost 2 years working for a builder at Headcorn and one job I did for him was to build Barnland House. I gave a price for doing it. It was a 6 roomed house about a mile from Headcorn and close by the railway. I started it in March and finished it in June. I did not do the plastering or carpentry of course. During the time I left home my father let the business run down so I came home and started on my own. I was 21 then. My father said to me, as I was taking over the business, I should like you to have your chance, Jeff, and I replied I should like to have the chance that you had. When I built Barnland House my mate used to walk from Grafty Green 3 to 3 1/2 miles away. Believe it or not we used to get to the house at 6am. He was a jolly good man in every way.

The Church and Churchyard. The Church of St James is one end of the Village Street and is in a commanding position on top of the South Downs. From the top of the tower you get a magnificent view. The Tower and the rest of the Church are built of stone and look very solid indeed. The top of the weather vane is over 100 feet high. The tower has 6 bells and the ringing chamber is reasonably spacious. Above the ringing chamber is the Clock room. Above this the bells are situated. To go to the top of the tower you climb 100 steps, which are of stone. At one time the steps went up into the turret where the weather vane is fastened by being bolted on. It needs to be; you get some wind up there. It was bent 2 or 3 inches from the upright once so it was shortened about 2 feet, straightened and reerected. When on the lead flat at the top of the tower a 27-foot flagpole is fixed at an opposite angle to the turret. About half way to the ringing chamber there is a recess in the wall, which used to be the entrance to the gallery which is not there now. Inside, the Church has oak pews, aisle and nave and of course a chancel. I understand the organ was under the tower with the gallery. The organ is fairly powerful, about a dozen stops and foot pedals but only 1 keyboard.

As you enter the Church go towards the Choir stalls and you will see a small window about 2ft 3in high with 2 lights on the right. This window with its 2 panels was put there in memory of Lt Phillips killed in the Boer war on Christmas day 1901. His parents lived at the Old Vicarage. Lt Phillips played for Egerton cricket team and he and I travelled to the match with Frittenden together.

A very heavy storm lasting 11/2 to 2 hours on Sunday morning in July 1914. Link House had its share of it. The people who lived there were terrified. It struck the roof at the back of the house about a 2ft width from top to bottom was stripped of tiles. No doubt the heavy rain prevented the place from catching alight. Inside the lightening came down the bedroom flue and the living room flue so the people went out into the scullery, which is built out beyond the main part of the house. A cat happened to be in the chimney so when the lightening came down the chimney it killed the cat, so the people after all were perhaps lucky.

One Sunday morning in 1940 Mr Hitler sent his team over with a few bombs dropped at random. 2 incendiary bombs fell close to the church tower and I still have the metal head of 1 bomb. It was well made. The verger of the church had the other one. While the raid was on a corn stack was burnt out at Court Lodge farm, which was about 150 yards away. We had our share of bombs and so did the villages around us. One night we heard a bomb coming down but it did not explode. Next day I went and had a look down the big and deep hole it made. The following day it blew up. I said never again will I be so inquisitive. It was not more than 150 yards from Victor Villa.

True snake story. A farmer's daughter went to feed the hens and being a very hot day she rested under a tree, put the pail down and fell asleep. When she awoke she found a snake curled up at the bottom of the pail. Of course it could not get out. I wonder how it got in.

I was cycling home one day and had just got to the top of the hill leading towards Court Lodge when I met a man and he stopped and had this to say. "You know Mr Pack another pub should be built between the Good Intent and the George Inn." The distance between the 2 pubs would be about 400 yards at the most. The man lived at Southfield Farm. He practically drank himself to death.

A journey through life. Nothing has been written up to this present about the 26th March 1913; this was the great event of my life. Married at High Halden 8 miles from Egerton to a young lady whose home was at Newland Green farm in the same parish. From that day to this I have never regretted taking such a decision, my wife has been a true help and is still a wonderful person and I don't mind who knows it. We have 4 children, all grown up, 1 son and 3 daughters. 1 daughter is in Canada (he must mean California) *the other 3 are in England. We are living with our son and the daughters are all reasonably near. I daughter lost her husband when living in Canada. He was a test pilot and met with an accident. Our son during the 2nd World War was shot down in Belgium and taken prisoner but escaped and got down to Gibraltar and home by one of our ships. It was an anxious time for us. All the family go out of their way to help us and so do the grandchildren.*

Appendix 3 - Flying Experiences of Jack Lumsdaine

Wartime (1942-45) and Peacetime (1945-66) – written by John Jackaman

Jack made his first flight in a Tiger Moth on 23rd February 1942 at RAF Booker, Marlow. He flew 8 hours dual at this unit and that, I suspect, proved he had the capability for further training.

On the 5th June made his first flight in a PT17 aircraft, another bi-plane, but bigger and with a more powerful radial engine. He had been posted to Lakeland School of Aeronautics, Florida, USA. At the end of this training he had completed some 60 hours.

In August 1942 he was posted to the US Army Basic Flying School (Gunter Field) Alabama, USA and commenced flying on the BT 13 Vultee Valiant. It was a similar aircraft to the Harvard and the first monoplane that Jack flew. By the time he graduated from this flying course he had flown some 138 hours.

In October he was posted to Advanced Flying Training School, Turner Field, Albany, Georgia USA and was trained on the Curtis AT 9 Jeep and the Cessna AT 17 Bobcat. These were twin-engined aircraft with retractable undercarriage used to bridge the gap between small training aircraft and the modern multi engined bomber.

By December he graduated from the advanced flying school with an above average rating and had flow 212 hours.

In March 1943 he was posted to PAFU Long Newton where he flew the Airspeed Oxford and his total flying time reached 244 hours.

In April 1943 he completed Standard Beam Approach Training at the Beam Approach Squadron at Cranage and his total flying hours reached 300. He was also introduced to the Anson aircraft during this training

In May 1943 he was posted to No 30 Operational Training Unit at Hixon, Staffs and commenced flying on the Wellington Mk11 bomber. At the end of this course he had completed 382 hours.

In August he was posted to 1651 Heavy Conversion Unit, Waterbeach and commenced flying on the Stirling Bomber. At the end of this course he had flown 425 hours.

In August Jack commenced flying with 199 Squadron in Stirling aircraft. His logbook shows he completed mine laying in the Friesians, bombing raids on Hanover and Mannheim dropping High Explosives and incendiaries. On October 3rd he flew to Kassle but lost his starboard outer engine with the inner one very shaky. He force landed at home base with no casualties. Later he mined the Kattegat and bombed Bremen. In

November he made missions to Mannheim, Berlin and many special missions, targets not named. He also mined Kiel Bay, the Baltic, Heligoland and bombed Laon and Aulnoye. He also completed a number of special operations with flights lasting up to nine hours in March 1944

In April 1944 he was still flying the Stirling as well as various flights in the Tiger Moth. His bomber flights were made in support of bombing raids and indicate he dropped lots of window to confuse German Radar. These flights took him well over enemy territory.

At the end of August he had completed 792 flying hours and was posted to 1692 Bomber Support Unit, Great Massingham, flying the Mosquito Mark 11. By September he had had flown 846 hours and was posted to 169 Squadron, Great Massingham. Jack's logbook indicates that he flew a number of intruder missions where he destroyed trains. He also escorted bomber missions to Frankfort and Mannheim. He was a target marker for some of these missions. He flew a variety of marques of Mosquitoes including the Mark XIX with Air Interception Radar. By the end of March 1945 he was operating out of advanced bases such as one at Juvincourt. He was also flying to Le Bourget Paris and Brussels.

There is no mention in his logbooks but he was awarded the Distinguished Flying Cross at the end of his operational flying.

In April after completing some 1150 hours of flying he was posted to 1692 Bomber Support Training Unit to train new bomber pilots and their crews. During this period he flew a broad variety of aircraft including the Tiger Moth, Wellington, Halifax, Martinet, Flying Fortress, Mosquito, Oxford, and Anson.

In June 1945 he was posted to No 6 Lancaster Finishing School in Ossington and after a few hours on this aircraft was seconded to BOAC at Hurn to fly the Lancastrian, a Lancaster converted to an airliner that interestingly enough was developed in Canada that was to become Jack's home. He was awarded a commercial flying license to fly civil aircraft. His logbook indicates that from March to July 1945 he flew numerous trips to Palestine and to India.

In August 1945 he was posted to No1 Ferry Unit Pershore in Worcestershire where he flew most of the aircraft that he had qualified with over the years plus the Proctor.

The war was now over so he then was posted to C.S.E Shepherd's Grove where he again flew many of the aircraft that he had qualified with over the years. By now he had flown some 1,655 hours.

In 1947 he was posted to 85 Squadron on Mosquitoes stationed at Tangmere before going to the Empire Test Pilot's School where he added more aircraft to his inventory of types flown. They included the Lincoln, Seafire, Firefly, Tempest and the first jets the Vampire and Meteor. He also flew the Auster, Dominie and Harvard.

In January 1948 he was posted to MAEE (Marine Aircraft Experimental Establishment) Felixstowe where he flew the Sea Otter on floats. By April he was posted to A&AEE Boscombe Down for further test flying duties. Once again he added numerous aircraft types to his long list of qualifications. They included the Brigand, Anson, York, Tipsy, Valetta, Hornet, Dakota, Auster, Tudor, Athena, Hastings, Devon, Shackleton, Wyvern, Beaufighter and the German ME108. By now he had accrued 2336 flying hours.

In 1953 he was posted to 87 Squadron and then to 68 Squadron flying Meteor XI followed by a posting to the Central Flying School South Cerney followed by a tour at the Central Flying School (Advanced) at Little Rissington on Meteor VIIs. He was sent to Cranwell ME108 as an instructor on the Chipmunk and Provost.

In 1955 He left the RAF and subsequently joined the Royal Canadian Air Force to fly with the Central Experimental and Proving Establishment (CEPE) and flew out of Ottawa and the CEPE detachments at AVROE in Malton and Cold Lake. Once again he became qualified on a number of other aircraft types including the T33 Silver Star, F86 Sabre, Canuck(CF100) Expeditor, B25 Mitchell, Dakota, Argus, and renewed his qualifications on the Lancaster, Otter, Piper Vampire, and Cessna 140 on CP 109 Yukon, Argus, CC109 Cosmopolitan, Tutor, and CF 104. He first flew the CF 104 in 1961 and completed some 827 hours of test flying in this twice-the-speed-of-sound-in-level-flight aircraft.

*A gaggle of Tutors and Starfighters all of which Jack will have
actually flown during acceptance checks at Canadair*

Jack finally died in a test flying accident in the Tutor Training aircraft after flying close to 7,000 hours in a multitude of aircraft including operational wartime bombing raids and thousands of hours test flying.

His final flight consisted of test spinning the Tutor to discover what was causing the aircraft to enter a tumble rather than a normal spin. He was unable to recover from a spin due to a metal plate coming lose in the rudder pedal channel that jammed the rudder in full deflection preventing him from applying the necessary opposite rudder. Jack ejected but left it just too late and he hit the ground before his chute fully deployed.

It was some time before the problem with the panel in the rudder channel was found. A student had the same problem that Jack experienced and bailed out. The aircraft went into a flat spin and was relatively intact on hitting the ground. It was then that they found the problem.

The accident investigators then went back to look at Jack's flying boots and saw a deep impression on the instep of his boot where he tried to force the rudder into the opposite direction. Jack had successfully ejected from a Starfighter a few years before.

Jack is buried on the banks of the Ottawa River at Hudson Heights Village.

Jack's Medals.

Love Is in the Air

*The wartime letters & memories of
Joe Pack and Margaret Dillon*

edited by **Jeff Pack**

ISBN 1-84683-046-X | 280 pages | softback | 140 x 205 mm | £9.95

This enjoyable book is compiled from two main sources ~ the wartime memoir of Joe Pack, an RAF pilot and the many letters he exchanged with his wife-to-be whilst serving overseas during World War 2.

Joe saw plenty of action, both in the air and on the ground, firstly in Europe and later in Africa and the Indian Ocean. Born in 1918 and raised in the village of Egerton in rural Kent, Joe volunteered for the RAF in 1940 and was rapidly trained as a pilot. Just over a year later he was posted to an operational heavy bomber squadron (No.35) based at Linton-on-Ouse in Yorkshire. He flew a Halifax bomber on operations over enemy territory between January and June 1942 until the night of 7/8 June when, on his 18th 'Op', his aircraft was shot down over the Dutch/German border.

His evasion and return to the UK involved the famous Comète line ~ plus the efforts of a Dutch Inspector of ditches, a Basque smuggler and many other extraordinary people who put their own lives at risk to help stranded allied airmen evade capture.

On his return he was reassigned to flying boats ~ first Sunderlands and then Catalinas ~ and while undergoing the extra training this required, his eye was caught by a certain Margaret Dillon, a WAAF Officer serving at RAF Oban. His amorous advances were rejected, however, and she was subsequently posted to RAF Davidstow Moor in Cornwall, whilst he was destined to join 265 Squadron on patrol in the Indian Ocean.

Romance seemed well-and-truly off the menu, but at some point ~ and it is not clear exactly when or why ~ they began corresponding. The many airmail letters they subsequently exchanged, charmingly document their developing courtship and reveal many fascinating details about the wartime lives of two young people separated by extraordinary events.

You can purchase this book direct from Woodfield Publishing in a variety of ways:

By post: enclosing payment by cheque (payable to 'Woodfield Publishing Ltd')
send to: Orders Dept, Woodfield Publishing Ltd, Bognor Regis PO21 5EL
postage & packing (per copy) UK £1.50 | EC £2.70 | RoW £4.50

By phone: call 01243 821234 (9–5 GMT) *Please be ready to give card details*

Or visit **www.woodfieldpublishing.com** for 24-hour secure online purchasing